DISCOVERING GREAT PLAYS

As Literature and as Philosophy

AynRand.org

CONTENTS

AUTHOR'S PREFACE

People have often asked for a written version of my oral lecture courses, on the premise—with which I agree—that written lectures are much more accessible to the student. Writing, however, is in this context virtually a different language from speaking; a raw transcript of an extemporaneous speech, however excellent, is almost always filled with defects and confusions of one sort or another—and so is frequently boring as well. To turn a lecture course into an accurate, clear, and valuable book, a huge amount of time-consuming editing is required, a task which can be performed only by an individual with the necessary motivation, knowledge of the subject, and editorial skills. My own age and priorities make it impossible for me to undertake such a task.

I have therefore decided to authorize several individuals who possess the necessary qualifications to edit and bring out in book form certain of my courses, and to do so entirely without my participation. Although I have confidence in these editors to the extent that I know them, I have had no part in their work at any stage—no guiding discussions, no reading of transcripts, not even a glance at early drafts or final copy. Even a glance might reveal errors, and I could not then evade the need to read more, and so forth, which is precisely what is out of the question.

In my opinion, the lecture course presented in this book is of real value to those interested in the subject. But when you read it, please bear two things in mind: Marlene Trollope is an experienced editor and teacher—and I have no idea what she has done in this book.

P.S. If you happen to spot and wish to point out seeming errors in the text, please email Marlene Trollope at the Ayn Rand Institute c/o mail@aynrand.org. If you like this book, I may add, do not give me too much of the credit. My course provided, let us say, the spirit, but Marlene Trollope gave it the flesh required to live.

Leonard Peikoff
October 15, 2015

FOREWORD

Leonard Peikoff is well known as Ayn Rand's best student, her chosen heir and the foremost authority on her philosophy, Objectivism. He has a distinguished, life-long career as a philosopher and educator, teaching and applying the tenets of Objectivism to worldwide audiences through his lectures, books and internet presence.

Forty years of living and breathing philosophy culminated in 1991 with the publication of his definitive statement, *Objectivism: The Philosophy of Ayn Rand*. After this demanding accomplishment, he felt the need for a break from pure philosophy and turned his attention to a different subject, a restorative pursuit that he described as "pure pleasure." And that was the arts; specifically, an investigation of drama from a literary and a philosophic perspective.

In 1993, he delivered the course he had developed, "Seven Great Plays as Literature and as Philosophy," to an Objectivist audience. In 1994, he followed with his analysis of *Cyrano de Bergerac*, a personal favorite of his. He had eliminated this play from the original course on the grounds that it was too well-known by Objectivists, and would contravene his objective of introducing less accessible plays to participants. After persistent requests, he finally relented. That lecture is included here as Chapter Nine and stands as a tribute to the value placed on his teaching, whether the material is new or familiar.

Aside from his own passion for drama, Dr. Peikoff was motivated by the desire to share the values he derives from it, particularly from the classics outside the modern canon. Many of these great works are moldering unread, unstaged and unappreciated in today's culture—and are in danger of being lost to a reading audience, never mind the theater.

In preparing this course, Dr. Peikoff had assumed a basic knowledge of philosophy and of Objectivism in particular, as well as some familiarity with Ayn Rand's fiction, especially *The Fountainhead*. He does, however, provide considerable context to enhance the understanding and enjoyment of these dramatic works by any motivated reader. He offers a logically structured way to approach unfamiliar plays with confidence and the opportunity to revisit known ones with increased vigor.

In his oral presentation, he embodies all the enthusiasm and skills of the exceptional teacher, reveling in transmitting a beloved subject with wit and acumen. You marvel with him at the brilliance of the perfectly phrased line, at the skill with which the playwright constructs the most complex situations. Dr. Peikoff illuminates the art of the well-drawn character, the intricacies of the well-crafted play, the power of the unforgettable climax—all achieved in barest essentials; that is, strictly through dialogue. You share in his admiration of the genius that achieved these remarkable feats.

A word is necessary regarding one aspect of translating oral discourse to written text, particularly when quotations from the plays are frequently cited. As a consummate communicator, Dr. Peikoff often, and appropriately, paraphrases and adlibs parts of the characters' dialogue. This is an exceptionally helpful technique on at least two counts. One, a rephrasing clarifies meaning and two, it offers the opportunity for making the language and style of translated or older works more accessible to a modern, English-speaking audience. In a live presentation, it is relatively easy for the audience to recognize this restatement through the speaker's tone, body language and facial expressions.

In this written transcription, however, only direct quotations from the original source are punctuated in the usual manner. To mark the distinction between dialogue quoted from the play and Dr. Peikoff's paraphrasing, I have indicated his paraphrase by preceding it with a colon (:) and setting it in italics. It is necessary to bear in mind that only one of these plays (*Saint Joan*) is written in modern English, while *Othello* is in Elizabethan English with an overwhelming number of footnotes. The remainder are in translation and are often plagued with a crowd of translators of varying ability. Dr. Peikoff's rewording is especially welcome when deciphering some of these passages.

Another consideration was my sincere desire to reflect a similar balance between scholarly discussion and the conversational style and flow that characterized Dr. Peikoff's oral presentation. To that end, I have retained many of the conventions common to teaching situations, such as contractions, colloquialisms and idioms. I hope their inclusion helps to convey something of the atmosphere of the live course.

The esthetic evaluation questionnaire (Chapter Eight) requires participants to assess the dramatic elements of the plays and then determine which plays are objectively the best when considering only aesthetics and only philosophy. Finally, the evaluation seeks to discover which play combines these two aspects in the most masterful way. Dr. Peikoff's guidance through this process helps lead the reader to invaluable insights and strategies which can be used to improve the ability to objectively evaluate in other fields and in his own life, tools to assist in judging people and situations encountered on a daily basis.

I was privileged to attend the original lecture course and the subsequent presentation of *Cyrano de Bergerac*. I was then fortunate enough to edit the recordings for a commercial audio lecture course. What a rare opportunity to come full circle and preserve it in a permanent, written text. Dr. Peikoff's insights are always stimulating and motivating. You could have no more enthusiastic and knowledgeable a mentor to guide you. I hope you will be inspired to reach for works once dismissed as too difficult or archaic—and immerse yourself in the values that great drama holds. Further, your enjoyment and understanding of live performances will be multiplied with this arsenal you can bring to the theater.

Dr. Peikoff's ability to clarify and integrate the most baffling and complex philosophic principles is well documented. With *Discovering Great Plays*, he delivers once again with candor, rigor and humor. This course is a sparkling source of inspiration, pleasure and knowledge to students, literary buffs, drama mavens and, yes, even philosophers.

Marlene Trollope
October 2015

RECOMMENDED EDITIONS

Several of the listed editions are no longer in print, but may be located through used-book services. As Dr. Peikoff advised, in the absence of the recommended text, find one with which you are most confident and comfortable.

Antigone	Sophocles: *The Oedipus Cycle: An English Version* Translation by Dudley Fitts and Robert Fitzgerald Harcourt Brace
Othello	*The New Penguin Shakespeare* Edited by Kenneth Muir Penguin USA
Le Cid	*Le Cid* by Pierre Corneille *Seventeenth-Century French Drama* Translation by Kenneth Muir McGraw Hill
Don Carlos	*Friedrich Schiller: Plays* The German Library Volume 15 Translation by A. Leslie and Jeanne Willson Continuum
An Enemy of the People	*Eight Plays* by Henrik Ibsen Translation by Eva Le Gallienne McGraw Hill
Saint Joan	*Saint Joan: A Chronicle Play in Six Scenes and an Epilogue* by George Bernard Shaw Penguin USA
Monna Vanna	*Monna Vanna* by Maurice Maeterlinck Translation by Alexis Irénée Du Pont Coleman Ayn Rand Bookstore

RECOMMENDED EDITIONS (continued)

Cyrano de Bergerac *Cyrano de Bergerac* by Edmond Rostand
Translation by Brian Hooker
Bantam Doubleday Dell

DISCOVERING GREAT PLAYS

As Literature and as Philosophy

INTRODUCTION

After forty years of pure philosophy, I finally understand why Ayn Rand needed to express her ideas in the form of art; to make them concrete and applicable to life. I am, in effect, reversing Ayn Rand's lifetime progression. She started with fiction and ended by writing pure philosophy. I worked for decades trying to get her philosophy clear, and now I feel a very strong need to turn to art; not necessarily to create it, but to immerse myself in it. My favorite art form among the tremendous options is drama—the theater and plays. Literature is the easiest art to talk about because it involves concepts. And plays, because they are usually shorter than novels and epic poems, are relatively simpler to discuss in practical terms.

I love the theater. A play is at once to me the most abstract and the most vivid form of literature; abstract because the author gives you only dialogue. All the interior life of the characters, their introspection, and most of the narrative and visual detail you supply in your imagination, or at least the actors do. The author gives you only the bare essence in drama, just some key conversations. You have to imagine and provide the rest. For me this makes it an extremely intense art form, more so than a novel or even a movie, precisely because it is so bare and essentialized. Drama is stark and stylized.

I remind you in advance that plays are written to be acted. To merely read the play is the equivalent of reading a musical score, which is not the intention of the composer. You have to read a play imagining it perfectly realized on stage—brilliantly set, costumed, staged, lighted, acted and directed. But that is not going to be our concern here. Our concern is: great plays as literature (that is; focused on plot and character) and as philosophy.

My opening remarks are not to be construed to mean that I am now indifferent to philosophy. I still need—as every human being needs—and want philosophy; that is, an abstract view of life.

I have chosen plays that I call great by a two-fold definition of the term. They are great as *art* in terms of esthetic execution, brilliant plots, heroic characters, etc. And they are great because they include—at least implicitly—a total *philosophy*. They are not plays narrowly devoted to one theme. There are many magnificent plays, which are one-themed or narrower plays, such as *The Miracle Worker* or many of the plays by Terence Rattigan. I have not included these plays because in this course I am requiring a whole view of life—including metaphysics, epistemology and ethics—to be implicit in the play.

This combination of a total philosophy and an esthetic execution of genius is so rare that only a handful of plays, to my knowledge, are extant in the entire Western canon. You will see that there are no pure comedies in this course. I don't know of any comedies that fulfill these criteria. They are not all heavy tragedies, although they incline that way.

The kind of play I am going to focus on adds to the very quality of your life, in my opinion. First, quality in the sense of scale of vision as opposed to the trivial and boring routines and repetitions of daily life. And secondly, quality in the sense of uplift and exhilaration, which is possible even in the case of such an awful tragedy as *Othello*. In this case the uplift comes not from the sense of life—not all of these authors are consistent in that regard—but from the sense of admiration you experience at the brilliance of the author's esthetics and of the scope of his vision.

Scope does not necessarily mean *truth*. It means the grand-scale survey of the total universe. I draw in my mind a very firm line between casual amusement and a great play. The former can be fun: it kills time, it relaxes you, it can be like having a Long Island Iced Tea. But the latter is a metaphysical experience, deeply moving and profound. Subjectively and emotionally, my test here was: is my life better for having experienced this play? I would not say "yes" about most of the movies and plays I see, even those I like. But I would definitely say "yes" about all these plays, even the ones I violently disagree with. I would not have wanted to have lived and died, and not have had the experience of confronting and reading these plays.

All of these plays have a philosophical meaning, in effect a whole system of philosophy implicit in them. But they are not only philosophy. Do not read them like ideological policemen, looking for their messages. Read them first as plays: as art. Respond emotionally to the characters, the dialogue, the drama, the music of the words, the events, the universe. The crucial thing they offer is the concretization of reality. The Objectivist definition of art is: the re-creation of reality according to an artist's metaphysical value-judgments. Art is the creation of a world. To get what a play has to offer you, you have to enter and live in that world. And you do it at first without being able to consciously identify what kind of world it is. First you have to see it. Only then can you define it.

In your first reading, you have to just let yourself go. Let the story take you over. Submit to it, as to a lover that you are going to judge later. But now you want to experience the quality of the foreplay—or the climax. Let yourself be led by it or raped by it, if necessary. Do not let yourself say, "Aha, this character just uttered the primacy of consciousness; that one is a total altruist, etc." These are not a set of ideological cues, and you are not engaged in a mindless, stimulus-response reaction either. After you have experienced and know the essence of the story and the characters, you'll see how easy it is to come back and evaluate the theme and the overall philosophy—which will not necessarily be what struck you on the first reading.

The first things you must get are the events and the characters, not the message or the meaning. The meaning is the last thing because it emerges from the rest.

So we have three purposes. Number one, and above all, *pleasure*; the sheer pleasure of exciting art, both in its means and its scale. Second, *philosophic detection*; finding the philosophy in the art. And last, *objective judgment*; an exercise in the objective evaluation of art— can you or can you not prove your analyses of these plays?

I will be trying to make real and accessible to you what your schooling has probably killed forever. My mission is to rescue the inspiring and magnificent classics of the past, which are now languishing generally unread and unintelligible. I must tell you at this point that translation is everything, since only Shaw is in easily understandable English originally. Bad translation, which is ninety-eight percent of all translation, destroys the greatest works. What would you think of a novel whose opening line was: "What personage is signified or otherwise denoted by the appellation of Johannes Galtium?" That's "Who is John Galt?"

Every play has fifteen versions written like that. I've chosen translations carefully to try to minimize these problems. But I don't have perfect translations. So as a general warning, never start a play until you thumb through it and see that the language is easily accessible to you. I like the language to be great, to be beautiful, to be exalted—but at the same time I want it to be colloquial and easily understood. If you find that there are too many *thee*s and *wouldst*s and *canst*s, etc., throw it out and find one that is written more on a comic strip level.

If you don't get the meaning clearly, all the rest of the artistic and philosophic considerations just disappear. You should be able to read it as easily as you watch TV or a movie. If you can't, even with the best translation, then read it through slowly once and figure out what it means. Put your own translations in the margins and then read it again. Until you get that problem out of the way, you can't turn to the play.

We are going to discuss each play under six headings, in the same order for each play.

1. Introduction—A brief orientation to the playwright, the period and the background.
2. Plot-theme—The essence of the action expressed in one sentence.
3. Plot Development—The *rise in the action* to the *climax*, the point in a story where you grasp what is going to happen ultimately; who will win and who will lose, followed by the *resolution*.
4. Characterization—The identification of the main characters and their motivations.
5. Theme—The abstract message of the play's events, usually a single principle of philosophy.
6. Philosophy—The deepest meaning of the play; the final explanation of the play derived from the events and any explicit, integrated philosophical statements by the playwright.

CHAPTER ONE

ANTIGONE

Sophocles

1. Introduction

Theater started, as did so much else that was great, in Greece. It began as religious rites honoring the god Dionysus. At first it was singing and dancing performed by a chorus, in which everyone participated.

The first big innovation was the development of what is called the "separation of the spectator." Another way of putting it is "esthetic distance"; that is, someone contemplating the spectacle rather than participating in it. It was discovered that a spectator could get a special and unique kind of pleasure from observing and immersing his mind and senses in what was happening. That was the birth of performance art. It was not yet theater because it was basically a concert.

At some point, it occurred to someone to introduce the element of a narrative, or story or plot-line. These were taken usually from Homer, Hesiod and Greek mythology, and were almost always well-known to the audience. So for the first time we had a fusion of music and narrative being contemplated by a body of spectators; singing and story as a spectacle contemplated for its own sake; poetry and plot enacted on a stage. And that was the birth of drama, something utterly new and wonderful in the world.

Since drama evolved from the worship of the god Dionysus, the religious features of Greek plays should not puzzle or bother you. Every once in a while there are various hymns to the gods, and that's simply a survival of the earlier versions. The chorus itself is a survival of the period when it was primarily a singing art. In the actual Greek plays, the actors spoke but the chorus sang. At first there were only one or two actors but gradually, as more actors were added, the chorus began to shrink.

Don't be put off by the chorus. The chorus has functions which all modern art forms have, although not so obvious a device as a group of people commenting from the sidelines. The chorus is valuable for exposition; it tells you things that happened before the play or offstage. It is a great vehicle for community reaction. If you remember the cocktail party in *The Fountainhead* movie: they want to know what people think of the Enright Building and they zip from one couple to another at the cocktail party listening in on the conversations. The chorus basically fulfills that function. It's a taste of what the community thinks about the latest development. In *Antigone* the chorus is a particularly undistinguished group of fence-sitting pragmatists, who are afraid of Creon. The chorus can function as a single actor in the story. It might but it doesn't have to be, the expression of the author's view. It can be a tool of special emphasis. As a rule, take the chorus as a single person, as a character. Don't let it throw you.

The big three serious dramatists of Greece were Aeschylus, Sophocles and Euripides. I made my choice of Sophocles on this basis: Aeschylus is too religious for me while Euripides is too journalistic and socio-political. Sophocles is just right: he is profound and also worldly enough to be here on this earth. Aristotle, who deeply admired Sophocles, believed his greatest play was *Oedipus*. There is no doubt that if you are going by plot alone, *Oedipus* is the greatest play ever. Just think of the plot situation: the man searching for a murderer, discovering that it is himself that committed the crime. Despite that fabulous plot, the play is just too fatalistic for me. It is so thoroughly governed by divine curses and men as puppets pulled by the strings of the gods, that it can be difficult to relate to.

Antigone, on the other hand, is a heroine who truly has free will and free choice. She is the one unequivocal case in all Greek drama of a thoroughly free-will character, with no gods pulling the strings. That's why I picked Sophocles' *Antigone* for this course.

Sophocles is 497 BC to 406 BC, a contemporary of Socrates and the Sophists. He wrote a hundred and twenty-five plays, seven of which have survived, including *Antigone*. In my opinion, it is the most pro-man play in all Sophocles. It was produced in 442 BC, when Sophocles was about fifty-five. So he was still that intense an idealist when he was getting on in life.

2. Plot-theme

The first crucial thing to grasp in every play is the plot-theme; not the plot, but the plot-theme. Plot-theme is the term that Ayn Rand coined and used in literary analysis. The plot-theme is the essence of the action situation stated in a sentence. You must be able to send it in an inexpensive telegram.

Just for an example, here is a rough statement of the plot of *Atlas Shrugged:* the producers of the world go on strike against their exploiters. Contrast this with two other elements. At one extreme would be the abstract theme. The other would be a synopsis of the story. Neither of those is the plot-theme.

For instance, in *Atlas Shrugged* I could say the abstract theme is: reason as man's means of survival, and altruism as its destroyer. That does not tell you the plot. It does not tell you the essence of the action situation. It is not a statement of the situation with characters, events, and so on. It doesn't say "somebody does something," which is required for a plot-theme.

Nor would it be a plot-theme to say: In *Atlas Shrugged*, the producers discover that the most important issue in life is reason versus mysticism. That is purely cognitive. That is philosophy, not a story. A story cannot be simply "somebody learns something important."

If one mistake in identifying the plot-theme is to equate it with philosophy, the other mistake is to equate it with the synopsis of the events. For instance, what is *Atlas Shrugged* about? You could say: Dagny comes into the railroad office one day and sees that her brother James is wrecking the Mexican line. So she goes to Rearden to get some metal, but he is having trouble with Lillian, etc. You could go on like that for an utterly useless hundred pages. That is a synopsis, a blow-by-blow, scene-by-scene summary. It is a value only to someone who hasn't read the play. It is like a substitute for reading the play. Otherwise it's a waste of time, and you learn nothing from it.

We want a formulation for each play—the essential action situation. Not the theory (the philosophy) and not the blow-by-blow. We want a one-sentence key to unlock the whole thing, which will give us implicitly the major event, the ruling conflict, the main characters, the entrée into the total work. After we know this, it will be easy enough to grasp the abstract theme and the philosophic meaning.

This is a matter of logic. The only way to prove what the abstract or philosophic theme is, is to show that it is inherent in the characters and the action. But the only way to know what is inherent in the characters and the action is to know the essence of the action. That is what determines the details of the plot, the nature of the characters—and thus the message and meaning of the play. Therefore that is what must come first. To understand any play, to grasp why it develops as it does, why it has the characters it does, what it means, you have to always start with the plot-theme—the condensed essence of the action.

So what is the plot-theme of *Antigone*? In other words, what is the central action situation in one (hopefully short) sentence? In some of these plays the plot-theme sentences have many clauses but the goal is: the shorter, the better.

My method of defining the plot-theme is just to plunge in with a crude statement about the action, blurt out something and then refine it gradually until I end up with the essence. With all of these plays, I am going to give you my mental process as I actually went through it. You can't look up the plot-theme. Because the plot-theme requires thought, it is unavailable. All you get from the commentators is the philosophic theme or a synopsis.

I start with: one person defies another. Now obviously that's too vague and generalized. I don't know what kind of people, what the context is, and have no idea what kind of defiance. So I don't have an actual story or situation yet. All I have is an empty relationship; one person says no to another. Is it Roark defying Francon? Is it Keating defying Roark? Is it my daughter defying me as to her bedtime? The plot-theme has to be concrete enough to depict specific characters and a specific situation.

Once you see that the theme is too vague, you want to push towards concretization. Don't then go to the other extreme and fall into a synopsis or summary. We have to find the essence, which is not just one person defies another, but it's not a blow-by-blow either. I'll give my answer and then defend it. I have chosen every word deliberately. I have to defend why each word is in it and why I left out what I left out. So plot-themes are highly calculated.

This is my definition of the plot-theme of *Antigone*: *A young princess defies a powerful king over a moral issue.*

This gives us a specific and real situation, and yet it's not a concrete-bound synopsis. It gives the essence of the action. Let me defend it in steps:

- Young princess—the defier has to have some identity. "Princess" conveys sex and also stature. She is somebody highborn, and that suggests potentially strong-willed, independent and proud as opposed to a young scullery maid who you would expect to be more withdrawn. "Young" suggests her age, her inexperience, potentially her vulnerability and perhaps her youthful idealism. So "young princess" gives you something to work with; it suggests a real character and real situations.

- Defies a powerful king—the person she defies must be someone who has the authority and superiority to do something in the face of her defiance.
- Moral issue—this is the most crucial. Is her defiance over a whim or a triviality? No, it's over a serious question of right and wrong, a moral issue.

Notice that the specific serious moral issue is not included in the plot-theme. That is a detail. The burial of her brother, in another variant of the same play, could have been birth control, euthanasia, turning her parents over to the secret police, etc. There are a hundred different moral issues that would make the same essential plot-theme and the same essential play with the same conflict and meaning. What counts is it is a moral issue. It is not a financial one, she's not in need of money. It is not a romantic issue because the play does not revolve around whether she and Haimon get together. Nor is it just a desire to assert herself. She has a solemn moral issue that she is bound by. And that defines the level of engagement and the type of conflict.

Sophocles' plot-theme is relatively easy because plots were not very complex at this stage. So we get: *a young princess defies a powerful king over a moral issue.*

As soon as we know the plot-theme, we must state the defining conflict of the play. Every great play depicts conflict. One character pursues a value. Another opposes it or pursues the opposite. And they clash head on. That is the heart of a play and that is why we call it drama. Then, of course, comes the resolution; one wins or maybe they both lose. But if there is no conflict, there is no story, no values, no play.

To grasp the nature of a play, therefore, right after we identify the plot-theme, we state the essential conflict. We state it in terms of action, not in philosophical terms yet. We are not on the level of abstractions. Here, the essential conflict is between the young princess and the powerful king; between Antigone and Creon.

The conflict in action terms is: Antigone wants to bury her brother. Creon forbids it and intends to stop her and punish her. That's it; that is the central action conflict of the play.

There are many other conflicts, especially in a great play. But in a great play all other conflicts revolve around, and are derivative from, the basic one. For instance, Haimon versus Creon—he is fighting his father because he is on Antigone's side in the main conflict. Antigone versus Ismene—she loves her sister and doesn't want her to get involved in this struggle to the death. Eurydice versus Creon—she is enraged about what happened to her son as a result of Creon's opposition to Antigone. Teiresias versus Creon—he tells him what the gods think of him. So *Antigone* is jam-packed with conflicts, which is an essential of a great play.

But they are not just a series of "I hate you, you hate him, she hates her." They all flow from and are integrated to a central conflict. To understand them, you must know *that* from the outset. If you state your plot-theme correctly, the central conflict should leap right out at you. In fact, the plot-theme is nothing but a statement of the central conflict in action terms.

3. Plot Development

Every plot-theme is developed. In other words, the author, having conceived the plot-theme, has to concretize it, dramatize it, figure out a certain order of events and then tell it as a step-by-step story. Once we have the general plot-theme, the next step is to translate it into a story with what Aristotle called a beginning, a middle and an end, which are the three crucial parts of any play—if it's worth seeing or reading or talking about.

I want to re-create what I think would have been the type of process Sophocles went through to get from the plot-theme to the actual story. He had to choose the particular moral issue he was going to dramatize. He picked a very common Greek principle: the importance of respect for the dead and giving proper burial to the corpse. This principle was clear to his audience; it was accepted by all as an obvious moral necessity.

This idea—the need of respect for the dead and proper burial of the corpse—is just as valid and relevant today as it was then. If any of you have the misbegotten, wrong-headed and utterly false idea that "well, I'm a modern man, there's no afterlife, I don't care what happens to a corpse, so this play leaves me cold," you are dead wrong. And there's no option about that. Because if you have any values at all, you do care what happens to a corpse, at least certain corpses. Imagine, for example, that your wife died and the President makes a public declaration that his wife never liked your wife. Therefore he proposes to have your beloved's corpse thrown into the gutter for the rats to eat. You would be outraged. And, undoubtedly, if you had any moral fiber at all, you would just disobey him flat out. And that would be exactly like Antigone. The deeper philosophic principle here would be that man is an integrated union of mind and body. The body by itself, therefore, is not meaningless even to an atheist, let alone a believer. The body is the last vestige of the great value that once was and, as such, demands respect. And you can see our attitude today—a valid attitude—even in regard to transplanting organs of dead bodies; the legitimate agony and conflict that families go through in regard to mutilating the corpse of the beloved.

I've had a form of this problem. I had to write a living will and it was a ghoulish thing. At a certain point they itemize all your main organs, and then you have to match up which donors will receive them. At a certain point I said absolutely I'm not giving my kidney to that place. So it made a difference to me. Now you say, "You're going to die so what do you care?" But I cared, in the sense that it was me, and insofar as I can dispose of it, I want to treat it properly. It comes back to the reason why there are burial ceremonies still to this day. Because the body remains a symbolic value even after death.

Antigone's burial of her brother is a concretization of her reverence for her values, her reverence for her brother's person. Remember her speech about how irreplaceable her brother was to her. We moderns should absolutely be able to sympathize and care about her plight.

After choosing the moral issue, Sophocles must devise what we call the backstory. In other words, the preceding events which form the context for the present. Characters don't act in a vacuum. They need a situation that has already taken place as the framework. Every play has that kind of framework, what happened before the story started. Here he takes the story straight from Greek mythology. He doesn't bother telling you in the play, because he assumed his audience knew this material inside out. In later centuries and today, it becomes a feat of genius to sneak this backstory in without boring the audience, so that you find out all the things you need to know. But Sophocles took it for granted.

This is the backstory that he took from Greek mythology. Two brothers fall out over who is to be the heir to the throne when their father dies. Their father was Oedipus and their uncle Creon was put temporarily in charge. The two brothers fight each other and they both get killed. One was defending Creon, the other attacking him. So Creon naturally regards the attacker as an enemy, as a traitor.

We are given very little information about these two brothers and what they stood for. All we are given is generalized sympathy for Antigone, and thus for her brother, Polyneices, who she wants to bury. We are not told about either brother's politics. We have no idea which of them, if either, is for freedom; which of them, if either, is for tyranny. There is no way to judge from the information presented in the play whether Polyneices was really a virtuous man or not. We're merely given a clash, which we must take at face value: a rebel is killed in battle; the king he fought is outraged; the sister who loves him is adamant. I think you can, on that level, sympathize to an extent with both without having to know the political credentials of the various characters.

We are still working out the plot development. We have a concrete issue and a backstory context. We need to milk it. There is no good drama that doesn't squeeze you, and then squeeze you more, and then squeeze you even more, and hit you in the face with the conflicts. The dramatist has to make the basic conflict ever more exciting, ever more fraught with implications and suspense. I call that milking.

Remember it all has to go back to the plot-theme, the core situation. This is not Hollywood we are talking about. Sophocles can't take off in a spaceship war and suddenly have dinosaurs running across the screen. It has to be logically implicit in the plot-theme, not in special effects. And this is where the real genius of the playwright comes in.

The first thing he must have thought was: there has to be a penalty for Antigone. It's a useless play if she says I'm going to defy Creon and he says no, and she says I'm going to anyway, and he says okay. Something must hang on this conflict. And of course in real drama it is always the supreme penalty, which it is here.

That is not enough, though. Let's make it worse. Suppose she has a lover, and suppose the lover is Creon's son. The son's fate also hangs in the balance. Creon really loves the son so he is terribly torn. At the same time, this gives Antigone a further reason to want to give in but she can't give in. So it's worse for everybody. What about if we throw in a sister of Antigone's? She is a nice girl, but she's not as decisive as Antigone. She tries to stop Antigone, but she's torn. Maybe Antigone's right, and she should take her side. Antigone will have to deal with that, too. What about if we throw in a mother of the lover? You see how you can go on? You create a whole nest of characters that are at each other's throats, all stemming from and expressing this one fundamental conflict.

With a really great dramatist this goes down to every detail. Every detail milks the conflict. So, for instance, you do not see what you see on TV. You do not have the messenger coming in and saying, "Hey, king, they tried to bury him." No, that would be awful. We need a buildup even for that little piece of information. Creon is raging. The messenger is terrified. He has to speak, but he's afraid to speak. Even he is in conflict. So the note is struck before the action even begins: to do it or not to do it; to defy him or not. He finally summons his courage and speaks.

You see, it's just a detail. But it is all a way of milking the core situation. And when you finally finish it, if you are a genius, you get a story structure or plot development with a beginning, a middle and an end. These are the three parts of all good plays. In our time it is called the well-made play, and it applies to all of our plays. Believe me, I would never pick as a great play, a non-well-made play.

Here are the three parts for *Antigone*:

A. The Beginning
The basic conflict has to come into existence in the early part of the play. Here the chorus gives you the backstory. Antigone comes on and we see what type she is—she wants to bury her brother. Creon comes on and we see what type he is and the issue of the death penalty. At that point we know the basic story. That, in a way, is the hardest to write, because you have to hook your reader and get him involved with characters he doesn't know and a story he hasn't read. But if the dramatist does that well and grips you, you go on from there.

B. Rise to the Climax
The juiciest and most enjoyable element of drama is the milking. That is the buildup to a climax. You take that basic story and you intensify the conflict, you make it stronger, you make it worse and more ramified. In this story that is: Antigone actually buries her brother; Creon says find the villain; Antigone confesses proudly; and Creon says it is death for you. Now is the play over? No, because either Creon or Antigone may still relent when the chips are down. So we still haven't reached the top of the rise here. We have to find out what's going to happen when each of them is pushed to the limit.

First we see Creon. Haimon and Creon fight it out. Creon is adamant. He will not relent, even under a tremendous barrage of logical argument from Haimon. That is wonderful argumentation and brilliant poetry. It is the kind of thing to read aloud. But Creon won't give in.

The only chance of averting the head-on collision is if Antigone gives in. So we reach the scene where she is shown in a moment of softness, which is very true to character. She bewails her unmarried state; she regrets that she is going to lose her life before she has a husband and children. You sense a moment of hesitation on her part. Our hearts are in our mouths; we still don't know what she is going to do. (This is still rising action.) And then she makes her decision, which was never really in doubt. For the first time we see that she is going to go all the way. And that is her last speech to Creon and to the city around her. She says, "You see me now, the last unhappy daughter of a line of kings, your kings, *led away* to death. You will remember what things I suffer, and at what men's hands because I would not transgress the laws of heaven." Then she turns to the guards and says, "Come, let us wait no longer." They do not need to drag her away. She stands by her code and says, okay, let's get it over with.

That is the climax of this story. The climax is the point in a story where you grasp what is going to happen ultimately; which side in the conflict will win, which will lose. At this point, you know that Antigone is going to be crushed. It's irrevocable, because she is inflexible and a powerful king is committed.

C. The Resolution

In a great play the resolution should be fraught with suspense. Even though the climax has told us what to expect, we don't know how it is going to happen. How will she die? Who will go with her? What will happen to Creon? So the resolution should also be a tumult of suspense, even though in a well-constructed play you know what is going to happen. But in a really great play you hope against hope that the inevitable will not happen.

Here the resolution starts with the prediction of doom to the city by Teiresias, the blind seer. (Seers are always blind because they are not distracted by this world; they are in touch with another one.) He is an entirely sympathetic character, as drawn by Sophocles. He confronts Creon, terrifies him with the information that the gods are angry because they had said that corpses should be buried properly, and Creon had arrogated to himself the cancellation of their decree. Creon rushes to atone, to bury Polyneices and save Antigone.

And so we have this exquisite scene:

We saw her lying. She had made a noose of her fine linen veil and hanged herself. Haimon lay beside her, his arms about her waist, lamenting her, his love lost under ground, crying out that his father had stolen her away from him. When Creon saw him the tears rushed to his eyes and he called to him: "What have you done, child? Speak to me. What are you thinking that makes your eyes so strange? Oh, my son, my son, I come to you on my knees!" But Haimon spat in his face. He said not a word, staring—and suddenly drew his sword and lunged. Creon shrank back, the blade missed; and the boy [this translation says "desperate against himself." A better translation says], torn between grief, rage, and penitence drove it half its length into his own side, and fell. And as he died he gathered Antigone close in his arms again, choking, his blood bright red on her white cheek. And now he lies dead with the dead, and she is his at last, his bride in the houses of the dead.

I can't even read that passage without tears in my eyes. That is what you call a great tragedy. Just one scene like that is all you need for a great play.

4. Characterization

We now have to identify the main characters. Plot-theme gives us the main event and characterization gives us the main characters, including their motivations. We should be able to read them off from the plot-theme because those characters are required to enact the plot.

Characterization is really a further concretizing on the author's part. It tells you more about the universe or the reality being created. Who are the indispensable characters? In this play it's self-evident. There are only two, Antigone and Creon. All the others are variants, go-betweens, foils, messengers, etc.

We have to look at the motivation and the essential attributes of each. We are going to start with Antigone, the title character. She is the protagonist, the character whose decisions move the story, the decisive moving force, the source of the momentum of the play. (The title usually reveals the protagonist.) In this play, she defies Creon and he simply reacts to her defiance. So she is the emotional focus of the story.

If the play is to be a success, the central characters must have strong and opposite motivations that are convincing to you. That way, there will be a battle of values throughout the play. The more that the life and future of a character hinges on the depth of his passion for something, the more our excitement and involvement. So the characters have to be passionate. But, of course, they have to also be convincing. Not just empty, floating abstractions but real, possible, alive. Greek drama has the real blessing that the protagonists are always alive with passion for something. And *Antigone* is a wonderful example. The depth of characters that Sophocles could bring off with just a few scenes and a handful of lines of dialogue is amazing. That itself is a feat of characterization that entitles him to the reverence of the ages as an artistic genius.

We know that Antigone loves her brother and, at the risk to her life, she is dedicated to giving him the burial rites that he deserves. But more broadly she is an idealist. To her, the morally right comes above everything else. She will even risk her life for it. She is clear-sighted; she has no inner doubts about what is the good or the right; she is not a modern, bent on saying "who can know?" She has that rare attribute for a person or a character: moral passion. Not just personal passion for the man that she loves, but passion for the good and the right, the passion of a moralist. She determines the good independently of her society and of the government's decree. She is willing to stand alone against the world. She has, as one person put it, the strength of a man (she is even stronger than a man as the Greeks understood those things) combined with the nature and desires of a woman, who can lament that she has to die before she has known the bridal bed and the nurturing of children.

Here is her final, unrepentant, unyielding statement:

"I have done no wrong. I have not sinned before God. Or if I have, I shall know the truth in death." [That is obviously a technicality she is putting in just to cover the record. She doesn't believe it for a minute.] "But if the guilt lies upon Creon who judged me, then, I pray, may his punishment equal my own."

That is a true, strong Greek sentiment. Her last thought is that he should get what's coming to him for treating her this way. In short, she is utterly strong, admirable, great and womanly.

You might think that commentators would strive to outdo each other in singing her praises. You would be wrong. Here is just a brief sample of standard interpretations taught regularly to college students from coast to coast. "Antigone represents the emotional resistance of the female to the orderly male reason of the state." In other words, Creon is law and order and rationality, and Antigone is female rebellion and unpredictability.

Another very common interpretation is that since life requires compromise and she refuses to, Antigone is obviously a death-worshipper with a martyr complex. She is a neurotic perfectionist. The Freudians make it very easy: she is in love with her dead brother sexually and that's the whole motive of the play. She wants to go back to his arms in the underworld and that's it.

The pragmatists today are the worst of all, I think. Their attitude is that she is a senseless troublemaker. Why is she so polarizing and rigid? We know there are no absolutes, so why all this fuss for nothing?

In other words, it may seem self-evident to you what the stature of Antigone is, but today you have to be an unusual person to respond to her. I'm very proud to say that I think she is fabulous: perfect, purely good. Judged by Objectivism, she is the top heroine possible.

Does Sophocles agree with me? The answer, unfortunately, is yes and no. Obviously, he approves of her. He certainly comes down hard enough on Creon. He never says one negative thing about Antigone. But how does he interpret her? You have to notice that he makes her religious. She regularly invokes the gods as a source of morality; she states her motivation as respect for the divine injunctions. To the Greeks of this period, there was little knowledge that moral laws could be other than religious. The idea of a morality that was not based on religion did not exist. The dichotomy in the fifth century BC was between the Sophists and the religionists. The Sophists were the ones praising man: "man is the measure of all things." But they took that to mean relativism, skepticism, subjectivism, amoralism. Values were all relative, and might made right. Conversely, the religionists praised God, and *that* was the basis of all moral absolutes.

In that context, Sophocles was torn. He wanted a heroine who was a strong-willed, self-assertive moralist. And yet to him, this intellectually required a religious woman; a pious, observant believer. The question is: would a pious woman act like Antigone or does she have hubris? Hubris is often translated as "pride," but the Greeks admired what we call pride. Hubris in this context means improper arrogance, i.e., a self-opinion that is unwarranted by facts. The Greeks considered this a major sin.

So the question is, does Antigone have hubris? On the face of it, it doesn't look like she does: she says she is just doing her religious duty; she is upholding the laws of the gods; and she is being an obedient servant of Zeus. But on the other hand, she is like no servant ever. The Greeks and Sophocles expected a servant of God to be a servant of a higher power. All recognized that servants of God at this time, and even more so since, are supposed to be modest. They have an element of: "I'm just the messenger, who am I to know, I just take orders." They are moderate. They don't go to extremes because they know they have these frailties. They are willing to listen to advice and are prepared to correct their ways when friends intervene. They know, in effect, "I'm only human," and they watch their step in the scheme of things.

Certainly Antigone is the opposite of all this. She knows what's right and to hell with everybody else, whether it's Creon or her sister—it couldn't matter less to her. She is ruthless about her beliefs in a way that a modest, moderate, self-doubting religionist would never dream of being.

So what does Sophocles make of her? He created her and he obviously loved her. I think the final answer has to be that it is unclear from the play whether or not she does or doesn't have the sin of hubris (or at least we're going to have to wait a bit to find out). As an Objectivist, I can say she is pure and proud. But to discover what Sophocles' exact opinion is, we have to get more evidence.

Notice that Antigone is widely disliked by commentators on the grounds that she is "a cold egotist," which she certainly is. Christian commentators in particular like to point out Antigone's harsh rejection of her sister's belated support. Ismene says that she wants to die with her and Antigone brushes her aside. It is obvious that she feels that Ismene does not understand her battle, does not hold values on the level that she does, and she doesn't want the useless sacrifice of her sister. To Christians this is a monstrous and unfeeling thing to do; she ought to nourish her sister and allow her to die with her. As you can see, your philosophy is essential in interpreting and evaluating these characters.

One commentator utters a truly wonderful sentence in defining the character of Antigone. I studied eight to ten volumes of commentary and analysis for each of these plays. And this is the best sentence I ever found for capturing a character briefly. He says, "She is in love with the impossible and has a fury in her heart." If, by the impossible, he meant justice and morality, it's a wonderful characterization of Antigone—and, I have to add, of Ayn Rand as well. That sentence exactly captures her, and Antigone is the closest character in literature to Ayn Rand as she actually was in person. I am prepared to testify to that on the basis of thirty years of knowing her. She was in love with the impossible, what she would call justice, and she certainly had a fury in her heart.

I love Antigone and Sophocles for the genius of being able to imagine and bring alive so fantastically unique a character an entire century before Aristotle. For this alone he belongs in the pantheon.

The other main character, Antigone's uncle Creon, is a statist and a totalitarian. In several places it reads as though Sophocles read *Atlas Shrugged* and took Creon out of it. Creon makes extreme collectivist statements that are just too purposeful and stylized to be accidental. For instance, he rejects private friendship in favor of the purely communal life. He denounces money as corrupting. He demands blind obedience to his decrees whether they are just or unjust. He is the classic collectivist dictator; authoritarian, tyrannical, opposed to egoism and actually highly conventional for the period. He spouts all the platitudes of unthinking people in fifth century BC: military virtues are supreme virtues, women are inferiors, sons must unquestioningly obey their fathers, etc. He is a walking vessel of platitudes.

He is not strong like Antigone, but he is stubborn and bull-headed. He just digs his heels in and refuses to listen to reason. This is most clearly dramatized in his intellectual helplessness in the face of his son's display of rational argument. He has no answers for Haimon, only bromides. And you can see his self-doubt and insecurities come out in remarks such as, "I'm not going to be beaten by a woman." So, in a word, he is weak. As someone put it, "If Antigone is more than a woman, Creon is less than a man."

But he is not depicted as purely evil. He has an element of stature and dignity. He is articulate—we should all be able to speak like Creon. He is poised. Above all, of course, the main event that does something for his character is he atones and changes. And he suffers when he finally realizes the error of his ways, too late.

Does he atone out of a better element of his nature which asserts itself, such as some recognition of morality? Or does he atone simply out of fear of divine retribution? I don't think the play is entirely clear, but to me he atones out of fear more than anything else because his atonement is very rapid. He doesn't go through any process of reintegrating and analysis. He blunders along and then when the gods don't like it, he changes too fast to convince us that there is some profoundly better quality that is emerging.

Nevertheless, it is obvious that Sophocles expects us to sympathize with Creon at the end and to feel moved by his fate, as against feeling "great, another rat bites the dust." His lesson is moving, not just a slap down at wickedness for its own sake.

5. Theme

A theme is the abstract meaning or message of a play's events. Abstract does not necessarily mean philosophical. There are non-philosophical themes abundant in detective stories, for instance. But all of our plays are highly philosophical, so all the themes will be, too.

By *theme* we do not mean the same thing as the total philosophy of the work. Usually the theme is a single principle of a philosophy, the one issue dramatized by the play. Of course, the theme rests in an author's mind based on an overall philosophy, implicit or explicit. And in great playwrights like ours, you can find this philosophy in the play also but only at the end of your analysis. First you find the theme. And then you try to identify the broader philosophy, which is the context that makes this theme possible.

We are moving on a rising level of abstraction. First, from the events and the characters on to "what does that mean?" and finally on to the whole synoptic vision of the whole implied universe.

A typical theme is easy to state because plays are a conflict between A and B. One wins and one loses. One has the author's sympathy, and the other the author hates. Typically the theme would be something like "the superiority of A's values over B's" or "the primacy of A over B." That formula applies, of course, to *Antigone*. There are three common variants in this play which express the theme of the play. We should be able to read these three off easily now, given our knowledge of the plot and the characters. In no particular order, they are:

a) The primacy of morality over politics or society. Put another way: moral principles are absolutes and come above any government decrees. If there is ever a clash between them, do what is right, not what the government or society expects.

b) The primacy of religious law over political law. This theme is also expressed as the primacy of God's law over man's law. For Sophocles, remember, moral law is divine law. You hear this formulation today from conservatives attacking the government: we are to follow God's law, not man's law. This is obviously one of the themes of *Antigone*. This formulation is dangerously close to the idea of the power of God's will over man, and therefore the relative helplessness of man. If Sophocles pushed this formulation, we would end up in a much more religious play than this is. Nevertheless, this theme is there in the play and we have to acknowledge it.

c) The primacy of the individual over the state. This play is one of the earliest credos ever of individualism. That has something to do with why I picked it. Sophocles is not championing the rights of the individual because there was no idea of individual rights yet. It is much too early for that. What he is championing is the individual's independent judgment as against obedience. He is saying, in effect, "You, the individual, must follow your own conclusions no matter what the authorities tell you." So it is a moral issue, not a political issue.

All three of these variations of the theme are tantamount to the same thing in the context. You can see that these are remarkable messages for the fifth century BC, prior to the discovery of secular morality or logic or science. I hope you are as impressed as I am that Sophocles could write such themes at such an early time.

6. Philosophy

What is the deepest, widest meaning of this play? What is Sophocles telling us beyond the obvious theme? There are only two ways to find out what the broader philosophy is. First, from the events, including the characters and their fate—who wins, who loses, and why—and from explicit philosophical statements, if there are any. Only those statements that are endorsed by the author and integrated to the rest of the play should be considered. If they are just thrown in, then you can ignore them.

The overall philosophy of a play is its final explanation. But you can reach it only at the end of your study. And until you know it, you do not fully understand the play, if it is a philosophical play. It is probable that the great majority of you do not understand why Antigone has to die. That is why grasping the philosophy will finally make every event in the play transparent. At the same time, every event will finally integrate to the philosophy and will make the philosophy crystal clear by concretization. Until you know that this is the question about *Antigone*, you haven't penetrated to its total meaning.

Why does Antigone have to die in this play? Let's get rid of some wrong answers: "It's sheer chance." No, that only happens in Hollywood. This is much too purposeful a play. Everything in it is deliberate, stylized and selected. An event of that kind happening by whim would be simply unheard of in Greece. At least it wouldn't get on the stage and survive for thousands of years.

"It's a political statement." After all, Kira dies at the end of *We the Living* and the message there is the necessity of a society that respects the individual and the inability of the unusual individual to survive in a dictatorship. If that were the theme of *Antigone*, then we could understand her death on the model of Kira's death. But that is obviously *not* the answer. It is not a political play. It makes no reference to what a proper society would be like. It makes no suggestion of a different kind of government. The Greeks had no idea of individual rights yet. In fact, if you know Sophocles, he wouldn't believe an ideal society would be possible to man anyway, even if we could figure out what it was. We will see why soon. So this play has nothing to do with Creon's evil in not recognizing rights. Sophocles didn't recognize rights, either, so that is not the issue.

So why does Antigone, with morality on her side, suffer and die? Why isn't she triumphant? Why doesn't it end on a note of ecstasy, that she asserts herself and upholds the right? You have to remember that art is metaphysical, as is this play. It expresses a vision of man, life and the universe. It is what Ayn Rand called metaphysical value-judgments. Now what are Sophocles' metaphysical value-judgments, as expressed in this play?

As a clue—not yet the answer, but as a clue—we will refer to the four great Odes in the play. Each is a short song, integrated to the action, summarizing the meaning of what we have seen. We have to decide what they all add up to and, in conjunction with the events, how they explain the play.

These four Odes have a definite logical structure. They are arranged in a definite order, based on specific events that have to occur in a certain order. Each of these Odes modifies the previous. Together they give you the overall philosophy. I want to stress that they are not merely appended to the action. It is not as though somebody said to Sophocles, "Give it a little depth here and throw in a song." They are integrated; and they flow out of and comment directly on what we have seen. What we have seen itself is a logical progression, with a beginning, middle and end. So these Odes are an integral part of the play. You should have no trouble reading them, except for the fact that it is a chorus instead of one person. You should be able to abstract from that.

Ode I, to the power of man, is the most famous. It comes right after we have seen a man; in other words, Antigone. We are now ready to appreciate her. Creon has just decreed her death and the messenger is sent to find the offender. And that is a time to ask: what kind of a power is this being he has sentenced?

There are no words to describe the eloquence of this Ode: the concretization of man's power over nature. It is full of brilliant metaphors. For example, "the birds and the fish tamed in the net of man's mind." In the opening line—"Numberless are the world's wonders, but none more wonderful than man"—the word "wonderful" means awesome or almost terrible, in the sense of striking fear in us to think of a being of this stature.

This is one of the earliest pro-man statements in Western civilization. And it's not a surprise, therefore, that it comes in one of the most individualistic plays ever written. What is amazing philosophically is that it precedes both Plato and Aristotle. It gives you an example of how virtuous the pagan Greeks were, no matter how religious they later became. Their religiosity was picked up by the Christians and run into the ground—or run into heaven. But the content of this Ode is distinctively Greek, and that is what you never find again after the triumph of Christianity. So treasure it while you have it.

Where is this Ode going to lead? You can observe its ending. After all these lines on how great man is, his problem remains that he can't withstand death; he is mortal. He is also capable of being both good and evil, and that means, of breaking the law. And when he does, he suffers accordingly.

The big question here: who does the Ode refer to at this point? Antigone is going to break Creon's law, but Creon is going to break God's law. Are we talking about both of them here, when we talk about the danger of breaking the law? That's what you call a hook. It is a question that's thrown out, it's suggested by the action and we will have to consider it as the play continues. If Sophocles put an aside in here and said, "No, I don't mean Antigone," he would kill the suspense. We are still trying to find out: Is Antigone right or is she wrong? All he is telling us here is that man is great, but he must obey the law. We have to wait and see which law he had in mind.

Ode II occurs immediately after Creon has decided that he is going to take vengeance on Antigone. The theme of this Ode is not the power of man, but the power of God over man. Creon has captured Antigone, and here we talk about the power of God's vengeance. There is a reference here to the curse on her father Oedipus, the implication being that she is still suffering for the curse on her family. If we follow that line, we render the play nonsense because it would make the whole thing devoid of free will. So just ignore that. But that remnant is there.

But notice, even if we put that aside, all the formulations that are tremendously anti-man and pro-God in this Ode, such as "the dreams of men bring them ghosts of joy." Or "man's little pleasure is the spring of sorrow." Or "no great things come to mortals without a curse." So it is the idea of the illusory nature of human achievement, the sin of hubris; man is nothing in relation to God.

What does this do to Ode I? What does it do to our interpretation of Antigone? Is she suffering the sin of hubris? Creon obviously is. But is Antigone being cursed by the gods for being too great, too assertive? Is she suffering sorrow because she asserted her own pleasures and her own judgment?

Ode III is devoted not to man nor to God, but to something which we are told is higher than either. That is going to give us a real clue. It occurs right after Haimon breaks with Creon. What did he break with him over? Haimon is in love with Antigone. Antigone is in the situation she is because she loves Polyneices. Antigone also loves Haimon and he also loves his father. So we probe down to the bottom of these characters. In one form or another, what is it that motivates them? Love. So it is certainly appropriate at this point to have an ode to the power of love.

So you see these things are growing out of the play. This comes out of and has been directed and integrated out of what we have seen.

Observe the line that love is the most unconquerable power of all. Even the pure immortals, the gods, cannot escape love. Even the most just of men will be brought to ruin by love. Love can turn a just man off his natural course, make him unjust and leave him ruined. So even though, in a sense, love here is the goddess Aphrodite, it is conceived as a passion even higher than the gods—a kind of unconquerable passion that plays havoc with the lives of men and gods alike.

Remember that Greek gods were not all-powerful. They played tricks, they got jealous, they engaged in childish vengeance, they did all kinds of mischievous things. In this Ode is Sophocles saying that there seems to be no moral order in the universe? Above both man and God there comes this inexplicable passion, which seems to move them both. That would suggest that life is essentially unpredictable and that virtue is not necessarily rewarded, because the universe has a certain caprice at its heart. In this connection observe the messenger's speech about the whims of fate, including the line, "fate cast down the happy and unhappy alike," as though it just doesn't care if you are good or bad. If your number is up, that's it. So it is starting to look different from what it looked like in Ode I.

Now we get to Ode IV, the last one. This takes place immediately after Antigone is sentenced and leaves the stage to suffer forever. This final Ode tells us just what we would expect, given the first three. It reminds us of the great mythological victims of the past. To the Greeks, myths were like an extended family. They knew them all. You don't have to bother looking them up, just take it for granted that these are people you have lived with all your life and you know them all thoroughly. They are simply reminding you that the gods or passion or fate or whatever you want to call it, have a history of visiting suffering—sometimes deserved but sometimes undeserved—upon the beautiful and the good. So we have here an Ode that is a review of a kind of malevolence or inexplicability of life.

In essence, the logical structure of the four is like this. Man is great, but God is so great as to reduce man to nothing. But passion is above even God. So fate is unpredictable and tragedy is to be expected.

Now we have to think, why did Antigone have to die in this story? Creon's fate is simple enough: he is brutally punished because he defied God's law. That is definitely hubris. That is inherent in the theme; he represents the bad guy in the theme and in the action. So he comes to death; that is no mystery. But why doesn't Antigone, wholly virtuous, emerge triumphant? What is the key to Sophocles' universe that ultimately explains this play?

We go back to the two formulations of the theme: first; the primacy of morality above politics, and second; the primacy of religious law over political law. The first—morality above politics—as interpreted by Objectivists, means that man must obey reality; the metaphysical as against the irrational, the man-made. So the meaning is the value of individualism, independent judgment, self-assertion, and the mind.

But if we take the second interpretation—the superiority of God to man—then the meaning is: man must submit to God, virtue bows to the yoke of the divine. In this case, Antigone's very individualism is wrong. It is an excess; it is too willful an assertion of her own judgment without proper fear of God. From this aspect, you could see Sophocles holding Antigone guilty of hubris. In other words, on the intrinsicist morality which Sophocles holds, self-assertion is not a virtue.

This dilemma is a typically Greek conflict from this period, similar to the conflict in Plato. It is the conflict between paganism and religion. In this respect, Sophocles is like Plato, not like Aristotle who had only remnants of the conflict. He is plunged into the conflict. As to the religious element, remember that Teiresias, the blind prophet, has to be blind to be a seer, according to Sophocles. That is, he has to be free of the distractions of this world in order to perceive the laws of the next. So the very character of Teiresias with his authority and power is further confirmation of the importance of the religious element in the play. That is why the final speech of the play, I believe, is intended to apply to Antigone *and* to Creon. "There is no wisdom but in submission to the gods. Big words are always punished." Antigone's words were also big words so there is a dual factor in the meaning of this play: an admiration of man, of Antigone's passionate strength; and at the same time a putting down of man and, even implicitly, of Antigone.

Sophocles is ambivalent. On the one hand, he believes, as in Ode I, that man is wonderful; that Antigone is and ought to be proud, strong and heroic. To this extent, in common with the Sophists, Sophocles is a humanist, one who emphasizes man and his achievements, powers and skills. On the other hand, Sophocles understands that Antigone is possible only if she is moral. And moral, to him, means religious. This is the only alternative he knew to the amoralism of the Sophists.

Therefore Sophocles is truly caught in an agonizing way. He thinks that if you are man, you can be great. But if you are great, you have to be moral. And if you are moral, you fear and serve the gods. And if you are a servant, then you must obediently accept your superior and his injustices without protests. If man is to be merely a passive, compliant tool of superior forces, then Antigone is condemned because whatever she is, she is not passive, obedient and compliant.

You can look at it this way. The Greeks upheld modesty as a virtue. Modesty for them was like a metaphysical quality. It meant a recognition of the limits of man. It meant a sane, cautious attitude towards life as befits a creature above whom there are such powerful forces as the gods and destiny. Yet modesty so defined is the very opposite of stubbornness, inflexibility, self-righteous anger at injustice, boundless ambition—all of which are essential to the great man, the hero, and especially to the immense larger-than-life Sophoclean hero. So if Antigone was to have gone Creon's way, she would have taken the wrong path. She would have been lost because her pride would have led her to defy the gods' orders. But if she goes her own way by her own independent judgment as she did, she is right, she is great, she is admirable. But she is lost again, because her very virtue opens her to the machinations of a jealous or uncaring fate who wants to keep man small.

She is lost either way—and Sophocles is torn. He admires Antigone as the person she is and, of course, as the dramatist he is, he obviously loves her. But officially he must condemn her. He can't, not as he is supposed to. So in the end he simply cannot bring himself to say yes or no to her. That is, I think, the deepest reason why readers feel baffled; that there is something elusive about this play, about the message, the meaning he is trying to get across. That baffling quality derives from the very ambivalence of his basic philosophy. His dilemma is: man lives in a world ruled by the gods who are good; they are, after all, the source of morality. But they are capricious and often unjust. Yet this is the reality we have to cope with somehow. But how? He thought that we are lost without the gods; we are reduced to the whim-worshipping violence of the Sophists. But we are lost in another way with the gods. We are lost either way, in effect. We can't live without religion, and we can't live with it either. That is Sophocles' implicit agony.

So he comes out as malevolent. Man is doomed to suffer, and to suffer for basically unintelligible reasons, because of some caprice at the heart of things that we just cannot decipher.

Of course, if we could rewrite history as Objectivists, we would tell him the solution to it all is moral objectivity, absolute ethics without gods or religion. But, needless to say, the fifth century BC is too early for that idea to be grasped. And, ladies and gentlemen, speaking on a historical scale, for all we know the twenty-first century AD is still too early for that idea to be grasped.

So let us sum up the overall philosophy of Sophocles, as it emerges in this play. The power of God's will over men, even over great men, means the inexplicability to us of man's fate. Another way of putting it is: in a world ruled by capricious deities, man—despite his potential for passion, for thought, for greatness—faces an unknowable and probably tragic destiny. Or to put it still another way: Sophocles believes that morality is real, that it is important, that it affects man's life vitally—but it is an intrinsicist morality, a morality that flows from the desires of a higher power beyond nature and man. Implicitly, therefore, morality is arbitrary. And precisely because we live in this kind of moral universe, there is also brute unreasonable power in the universe—power, which can take the form of a curse on a family, such as with Oedipus, or a sudden eruption of doom.

So what to do? Well, we should strive to respect the moral. But our virtue, even our highest heroism, will not always protect us from metaphysical disaster. In fact, our virtue, by making the gods jealous, may even invite disaster. This is the basic reason why the Greek tragedies were tragedies and why there were so many tragedies. Malevolence is the essence of the genre with this kind of philosophy.

Greek religion is a lot better than what you know in Christianity. It was weakened by many more rational elements contained in it. For instance, you were expected to fear and obey the gods, but not to love them. It took the depravity of Christianity to expect you to renounce your soul one hundred percent and fall to the abysmal depth of loving the very force that is making you grovel. The Greeks were much too noble and healthy for that. They respected power but they didn't give their love at the point of a metaphysical threat. Of course, there was not much role given to an afterlife. In Sophocles, for instance, the realm of death is just a shadowy underground that holds no real attraction for people—as against the Christian lust to die and go to heaven. So there was a large component of self-respect and love of life built into the Greek religion. Nevertheless religion remains religion and, in some form, necessarily exacts its deadly toll.

That combination of secularism and religion is the best that the pre-Aristotelian Greeks had to offer. Through all of these pre-Aristotelian centuries, Sophocles was the best of the best. *Antigone*, I would say, represents the underground spirit of man rising to its feet at last in the first worldly, philosophical culture of the human race. It is man rising and being admired, exalted, loved—and then, reluctantly being fettered again, punished, struck down. Man was not yet ready to stand erect. Antigone was born too early, and thus she had to die.

One final important aspect of *Antigone* is Sophocles' extravagantly dramatic, purposeful writing; the great clashes of opposite value-judgments and back-and-forth dialogue, where each character tops the other brilliantly by expressing the exactly opposite thought, deliberately using the same, but reshaped words. I would point out to you how fast-moving, how complex yet simple the writing is; and its sheer beauty even in our broken English translations. Consider the description of Creon's wife Eurydice in the last moment of her life: "and she fell, and the dark flowed in through her closing eyes." This makes the dark which is, after all, the absence of light, into a positive force; something moving into her body and seizing her power of sight and life. It is a hauntingly beautiful, tragic image.

Some Objectivists have a tendency to brush aside language—the beautiful, evocative, eloquent, dramatic use of words and imagery—in a rush to get to the theme, the philosophy, the abstract meaning. Please don't do that. You have to treat the words of a play like the colors of a painting; you have to roll in them like a cat in catnip. Relish them, like part of the sexual process. Savor them, thrill to them. Remember, this is a work of art, not a treatise. Therefore, enjoy not only the message but all of its aspects and above all its medium, which is language.

Q & A

Q: I noticed that your statement of the plot-theme of *Antigone* consisted of three key elements. One, the protagonist. Two, the central value that the protagonist is pursuing. And three, the central conflict that she runs into. Does every plot-theme have these three essential elements, and did you deliberately choose the order in which these three elements appear in your statement of *Antigone*'s plot-theme?

A: Okay. That's a good question. Every plot-theme has to make reference to the protagonist because it tells you about some person in conflict with somebody else. If you don't get the person in the plot-theme, there's no story. It does have to imply the central conflict, if not state it. That's why the first thing you read out is: she defies him, he becomes jealous of; you know, whatever it happens to be. He has to kill so and so. So the central conflict has to be there.

You are wrong in saying the "central value." I did not state the central value in the plot-theme, except in the broadest generality. I

said she defies him over a moral issue. But what the issue was—
that she loved her brother, that she wanted him to be buried, even
that she was a moral idealist—I didn't say. So that's already a little
too specific. In some plot-themes you can't get the situation unless
you know specifically what they are after. In others, as long as you
know there's a clash, you can leave it to the development of the plot.

In terms of order, you have to have entity before action. You
have to have a character before he can do something. So the typical
plot-theme is: A does B to C. A and C clash over B.

Q: You say that Sophocles believes that morality is divine. But there
certainly could have been a more religious play. And you say that the
main conflict over morality in those days was between the Sophists
and God. So what was Sophocles' attitude toward the Sophists and
a more secular morality?

A: Terrific question. I just happen to have some material here. Sophocles
liked the Sophists who were, remember, the champions of man and
of this world. All of philosophy has been a false alternative, with rare
exceptions. The other-worldly, religious types who were for moral absolutes and God, and who thought man was low and life was worthless. And the worldly types who said: we have to judge by human
standards; God is a myth or unknowable. But they could never find
any standards, so they were skeptics or subjectivists or brutes.

Sophocles was torn here. I think he would have really gone for
the idea of an objective, absolute moral code that was based on reason
and this life. But he didn't have it and he didn't invent it. So we know
this much: he was much less religious than his predecessor, Aeschylus. He was worldly; he admired strength here on earth. He agreed
with the Sophists for admiring strength and turning the focus away
from the other world to this one. But he couldn't tolerate the idea of
subjectivism; might makes right, there is no morality. Therefore he
felt that somehow he had to put religion into the mix. Of course, what
he is groping for, I think, is an objective approach to morality and he
had no idea how, if you drop God, you could get that.

Now the best way to put it to you, in the way that it actually stood
for the Greeks of that period, is to tell you that in the fifth century BC
the Greeks were wrestling with the distinction between two crucial
concepts: *Physis* which means roughly "nature" or "reality" and is
what we get the word physics from; and *nomos* which means "law."

So *physis* is essentially nature; what's given to us by reality. *Nomos* is law, something which is stated by man or decreed by man.

There was a lot of confusion and people used them in all different terms and contexts. But what it all comes down to is what Ayn Rand called the metaphysical versus the man-made. This was the first groping attempt to make that distinction.

The Sophists at the time were the champions of *nomos* because to them *physis* (reality, nature) was unknowable and subjective. The senses didn't bring you into contact; each man was put in his own subjective world, and so on. Therefore, their attitude was that there's no objective ethics, either. It's a matter of what each of us feels, whatever the state decrees. So if the state decrees that the state is strong enough to impose its will, you have to obey. Remember Thrasymachus: justice is the interest of the stronger.

Sophocles comes in as a defender of reality, *physis*. He says you should obey the law as a citizen. To borrow from the later Bible anachronistically: you render unto *nomos* what is *nomos's*. But you owe your primary allegiance to *physis*, to nature. If men's edicts conflict with nature or reality, then you have to assert yourself and follow reality, even if it means condemnation by mankind.

Now you see, of course he couldn't be consistent with that: it's too early philosophically. But by implication it would imply that a real morality is based on *physis*, on nature, on reality, and not on some decrees of consciousness. Which would have been a total revolution. It was a revolution that even Aristotle couldn't carry out fully, although he suggested it.

So at this point, in answer to what is his attitude to the Sophists: he disagrees with them on this fundamental duality. But he can't let go of either horn of it, and he doesn't know how to integrate it. So Sophocles is caught but it's such a wonderful place to be caught in, because if he could only go the next few steps . . .

Q: I was struck by the applicability of your discussion of the development of a plot-theme in literature to music. You know, the basic set-up and development, resolution. Both music and literature are experienced temporally, in a specific structure. Could you comment on whether you have thought about applying the analysis you have given to plays to great music? Would there be similarities?

A: Well, I could answer your question very simply. Undoubtedly there are similarities, and of the very kind that you mentioned. I have not thought about it. I don't know music that well. Worse than that, I don't know the vocabulary to name these things. So I can't say anything illuminating. I would hope that taking this kind of analysis, someone who really knows music, not only what's written but the technical terms of it—thematic restatement, and so on—could apply the same thing. Only it wouldn't be one for one. There wouldn't be an equivalent of a character. But there should certainly be, for works that take place across time, a structural parallel. You have to start. You have to get somewhere with the rising intensity. And then you have to resolve it. So that much, yes.

I just do not know music that well. Further, I also get into musical ruts, where for two years I only hear one type of music from morning to night. And then I get tired of it and don't hear it again for decades. At this time I am just in the last phases of American jazz, believe it or not, which is not exactly the most fruitful from the point of view of tracing the parallels.

Q: Explain in more detail, please, how most of the characters in the play were determined (by the gods or whatever) but one (Antigone) had free will. Thank you.

A: No, I don't mean to say that this entire play, in my opinion, reflects free will. Not only Antigone. Creon certainly has a choice, he is not cursed. And Ismene certainly has a choice and is shown changing her mind. Haimon has a conflict and is oscillating back and forth. They all have pronounced conflicts and they waver back and forth. There's very, very little indication in this play of divine intervention. There's one passage where they remind you that her father was Oedipus and of the curse on her family, but it's kind of thrown out and then let go. So it's not Antigone versus the other characters in this play. It's this play versus, for instance, *Oedipus* or many other works in Greek drama, in which gods are blatantly part of the scene. They come down—you know, the god in the machine—tell you what's going to happen, and men come across as puppets.

So if you ask me, why he broke free in this play to the extent that he did is because one of its important messages was: the value of man and the importance of the individual. With a theme like that to be ruled by gods pulling the strings would be ridiculous. It would annihilate itself. To be ready to write this theme, you have to believe in free will.

Q: Would you care to comment on the esthetic value of Antigone only scattering a light amount of dust over the body, as opposed to what her other options would have been? Or what the author's other options were? Say, giving him a full burial or something. I thought that was a particularly nice touch.

A: Yes, it's a symbolic touch. We're talking of a great artist here. So the importance of the funeral is the ceremonial recognition and the reverential treatment. It is utterly beside the point to get a gold-encrusted casket, which could be regarded as vulgar. Or to hire four thousand mourners, who could come and weep, which would be a social consideration. All she has to do is strew the dust enough to indicate a cover. After all, that's what the idea of a funeral is: you cover the person and return him back to earth. And particularly within the framework of their beliefs, he was going to go down underground and take up his residence. But it is a more elegant artistic touch to do what Antigone did, rather than to shovel.

You want to see the value beneath the recognition of it. You don't want to have someone pouring heaps of dirt. That's what they would do today, make a mud party out of it; have the guards rip it out of the ground, and have a leg fall off, and slapstick. But that is not the sense of life of this play.

Q: Was the fact that Antigone shrugged off her sister, Sophocles' way of trying to tell us that ethical decisions are not shared; they're an individualist experience?

A: Well, that's part of what he's saying. But I think the stronger thing he is saying is that Antigone is utterly selfish and self-absorbed. She has her own views and her own mission. If you agree with her, fine, you can be an ally. If Ismene from the beginning had said, "Down with Creon, I'm with you to the end, let's go and bury our brother," Antigone would have had a completely different attitude at this point. They would have been comrades in arms.

But Ismene was kind of conventional. She said, "Oh, don't let's start a fight with Creon. Who needs it?" and so on. Suddenly she is overcome by the emotion of the moment and she wants to be with her sister. Antigone is relentless. In effect, she said this is not an issue of personalities, this is an issue of moral principle. You're a nice girl, but this is not your principle. This is not your animating passion, and there's no reason for you to die. I don't want a useless sacrifice. You're not my soul mate. You go off and lead the life you chose and leave me to mine.

So it's absolutely consistent with her character, and if she had done what the Christians wanted and had said, "Oh, sweet baby, come along and die with me," it would have wiped out the character. Because what would her motive have been? It would have made you think, if she likes this wishy-washy sister, who the hell even knows what she liked about her brother? It would have just subverted the whole play. So it's absolutely valid on Sophocles' part, an essential.

Q: A lot of the things that you mentioned today just went completely over my head while I was reading it. I didn't get the thing about the chorus. I certainly couldn't follow the progression. If I were watching the play, I couldn't follow it. The complexity of a great play . . . I am wondering how accessible this is to somebody who is actually watching it, to catch all this.

A: Is a great play accessible? Yes, if you prepare yourself for it. Suppose that I even had the chance to watch it on the stage which, of course, I would because it's a once-in-a-lifetime event today. Ideally, I would never go to a great play that I didn't thoroughly know first. Precisely because there is too much that you cannot get, if they are faithful to the text.

On the other hand, if they cut or simplify the text to make it easily followable, they can eviscerate it of its content. What I suggest, and what I have done for these plays myself, is read it first one line at a time, simply with the standard "do I know what this line means?" And if I don't, I either look it up or decide I don't have to. For instance, if it's a mythological reference, throw it out. This is obviously just an example of somebody that the gods mistreated; I don't care, let's go. Every line I have to know the meaning. Feel free to write paraphrases in the margin. Sometimes I even read two or three different translations until I find one that I can follow.

Read it through slowly and get the meaning. You know, there's a certain automatic reaction that you can't avoid. I regard that as talking with a person in a foreign language. You know, he says,

"Comment allez-vous?" And you look it up in the dictionary and finally figure out that he said, "How are you?" You see? You go through the conversation. Now you know what it is.

Then you start the play a second time. And now you can read it through at a reasonable pace, understanding and responding. It's like you got over the language barrier. And all these plays have a language barrier. Not inherently, but simply because you would have to be as great as the playwright, to take everything that he has done and capture it in a modern vernacular. And yet that's going to have to happen to everything. You people will have to realize that three hundred years from now people will say that they just can't read *Atlas Shrugged* because it's too full of unintelligible references. "Who knows what these words mean? It's so archaic. What is this thing about electricity?" And there would be a footnote: in those days they used electricity to power things. And they'll just have to read through it; there's no other way. Or else some genius will put it into modern Japanese, or whatever the language is at that time.

This is not a reflection on the plays. If you want to preserve these great plays, and if you want to experience and enjoy the up-lifted value they offer, you have to do it yourself. You have to read it once for language. Then read it once for enjoyment, just reacting without any thought: I like this, I don't like that, I hope this happens, I wonder what's going to happen, oh what a horrible ending, etc. And then, when you've enjoyed it, you read it for the third time for analysis. What was the plot-theme? What events stood out? Who are the main characters? What really was the message? What clues were there to the overall philosophy? *Et cetera*. Three readings at a minimum.

Then, after you have all that under your belt, ideally, you go and watch it. And now you can be sensitive to every nuance, every gesture, every word. And it becomes an absolutely riveting experience. The closest we are going to get to that—since we don't have a traveling troupe of performers—is an excellent movie version of *Saint Joan*. And the evening after the day that we do *Saint Joan* in class, we'll watch the movie, if you want to come. You will see what you get out of the movie, how every word is just fraught with meaning. Whereas if you watch the movie first, it could be entertaining but it's just not the same thing at all. *Saint Joan* happens to be the rare case of a terrific movie made out of a great play. That is absolutely not true of most movies. Let me just say that *El Cid* with

Charlton Heston has the same relation to the play we're studying as dead worms have to French cuisine.

CHAPTER TWO

OTHELLO

William Shakespeare

1. Introduction

Of all the playwrights in this course, William Shakespeare needs the least introduction. He is covered everywhere. I assume he is still taught in grade school. He is universally acknowledged as the world's greatest playwright. And in a sense, I think that is true despite his philosophy. His dates are 1564 to 1616, about two thousand years after Sophocles. Elizabeth the First reigns in England, at the end of the Renaissance which is usually dated 1450 to 1600. *Othello* was written in 1601–02, and was first performed in 1604. It is classified as a mature tragedy; a tragedy for obvious reasons and mature because Shakespeare was at the height of his powers.

There is a language problem, which is different from Sophocles, in that it is written in late Middle English. I strongly recommend a book in *The Contemporary Shakespeare Series*, edited by A. L. Rowse. It is Shakespeare translated into English that still follows his line structure, his meter and his images. It just substitutes intelligible English words for Elizabethanisms that have lost their meaning to us. You can read right through it with no difficulty, retaining ninety-eight percent of Shakespeare's language and poetry and none of the obscurity and difficulty of the Elizabethan text. Unfortunately it is not in print anymore, so we are stuck with Shakespeare as he himself wrote it. I recommend Rowse's book if ever you can find it. In any case, Elizabethan English is really not so hard once you read it. You read it slowly the first time, with notes. This is the first of only two plays that are being read without translation in this course.

Why did I pick *Othello* versus the other mature tragedies, such as *Hamlet* or *Macbeth*? A short answer is: this play, in my opinion, has a sympathetic character; one that I can bring myself to care about, and a love story that I can bring myself to care about. In *Hamlet* it is a matter of supreme indifference to me if any of those characters ever rise to greet another day. The same is true of *Macbeth*.

Shakespeare took his political background for this play from a roughly contemporary event, a war over Cyprus about forty years earlier. So it would be more or less like a play today based on the Vietnam War. The personal story of Desdemona, Othello and Iago is not original to Shakespeare. He rarely, if ever, originated his own stories. The idea of creating your own story is essentially a nineteenth-century invention. Sophocles took his stories from Homer, and Shakespeare took just what he found. Shakespeare took *Othello* from Giovanni Cinthio in a work written in 1566. He was a didactic moralist who based his story on an actual murder in Venice around 1508. Basically, as in all of Shakespeare, this is a real-life story with all kinds of changes thrown in.

2. Plot-theme

Let's use the method of blurting out until we reach a valid formulation. A man becomes jealous—we couldn't have this play without that. But as it stands, that is much too broad and generalized. What is he jealous of? His neighbor's money? His friend's social prominence? Is his jealousy justified or not? It is a very different play if he is crazy or if he is right to become jealous. For instance, his wife is really cheating on him and he finds that out. So just to say "a man becomes jealous" tells us no action situation. There is no conflict in that formulation and until there is conflict, there is no plot-theme.

Let's jump to something like this: a jealous man kills his wife. Now we have brought in another person and we know what he is jealous of, presumably. What is wrong with "a jealous man kills his wife?" It is still a summary of the play. It is the final result of the ruling conflict; it is not the essence of the action situation. So that is erring on the side of being too concrete-bound. That he kills his wife is the resolution of the conflict. The plot-theme must give you the essence of the action situation.

Let's approach it from the point of view of what kind of man is acting here. Are we talking about a swine, an average Joe, a fiend? Othello is presented from the outset as rational, self-confident, noble; in a word, a hero. And that is essential to the play. If he is a hero, does it then follow that he becomes jealous of his wife for good cause? Because then it would be a very different story. If he comes in and she is sleeping with Cassio, it is a different play. No, this hero becomes irrationally jealous, blindly jealous despite the facts. To say that he becomes irrationally or blindly jealous of his wife, we have the beginnings of a situation. We have at least a mystery. Why does a hero become blind? That is more intriguing. It is not yet a full situation because it still subsumes too many possibilities to lead to a distinct play.

Why does he become jealous? If that is just the way he is—he is a jealous guy—that would make the play meaningless because then the situation will be "a jealous man becomes jealous." That would sink the play. You should notice that Shakespeare insists—and he is entirely correct in this—that Othello is not easily made jealous. This is demonstrated right from the outset in the opening, characterizing scenes of the play, where Iago is doing everything he can to instigate Othello. Othello is calm and serene. He is just not the jealous type.

Why does this hero become consumed with jealousy? Let's take a page from the latest issue of *Science Magazine*. Maybe he has a jealousy gene; it is an inherited tragedy, his chromosomes are warped for jealousy. That would be an entirely different play then.

What is the essential cause in action terms, not in terms of his soul or character? What in action is the factor that precipitates, brings about, causes, fans, nurtures and inflames his jealousy? The manipulations of an arch-villain. I insist on the word "arch" here because Othello is such a hero that only a uniquely wicked villain could topple him.

We reach a very simple plot-theme: *A hero, manipulated by an arch-villain, becomes blindly jealous of his wife.*

Notice that there are all kinds of conflicts built into this very statement: Othello versus Iago; Othello versus Desdemona, when he becomes jealous; Desdemona versus Iago, who want absolutely opposite things. What is the basic conflict as stated in the plot-theme? There is the hero, and then there is the arch-villain who manipulates him. So Othello versus Iago is the main conflict. Othello wants to enjoy his love; he wants to be happy with Desdemona. What does Iago want in action? He wants to break them up. He doesn't want Othello to enjoy this love; he wants to put an end to it.

From the plot-theme you should be able to tell not only the main conflict, but the names of the indispensable characters. In *Antigone* we have two. We are now reaching a more complex type of play with three indispensable characters. There is no play without any one of them. It is a triangle: Desdemona-Othello-Iago.

3. Plot Development

In working out this plot-theme which he took from Cinthio, Shakespeare took an enormous amount of detail from the original source,
even including the handkerchief. You would be truly astounded at how
little Shakespeare originated in terms of the characters and events of
this story. But Shakespeare did make a few major changes. That is the
difference between a police reporter and a great dramatist. In Cinthio's
version Iago is jealous of Othello simply because he, too, is in love with
Desdemona so it is just ordinary jealousy. It is an innocent and normal
motivation, compared to Shakespeare's brilliant and monstrous picture
of Iago. Cinthio has Iago beat Desdemona to death himself and the
Moor never becomes aware of her innocence. It is just a sordid story of
brutality. In Shakespeare it is a true tragedy; a thing of stature because
the tragic hero himself does the deed and then grasps what he has done.
So this becomes a comment on life—at least life as Shakespeare saw
it—and not just a *National Enquirer* news story.

As always, in a well-constructed play there are three parts. The
first we call the establishment of the situation which brings the basic
action situation of the plot-theme into reality. In this play it occurs in
Act One. You have to establish the lovers and the authenticity of their
love. Othello must be introduced as a calm, confident type; otherwise
there is no play. If he comes off as an easily-enraged, frothing-at-the-
mouth emotionalist, the play is sunk because it is back to "a jealous
man becomes jealous." Iago's hatred of Othello and at least one step on
Iago's part to translate his hatred into reality has to be established so
that we know that this is a factor that is not just an emotion. Remember, just an emotion doesn't carry weight. We want to see it enacted.
As in life, so in theater. A feeling counts when and if you act upon it.

There is a little mini-plot on Iago's part right at the outset, indicat-
ing the pattern of the action and the reality of his hatred. That is his
attempt to get revenge on Othello by enraging Brabantio. It fails but
the basic situation is now set: we have the lovers, the calm tranquillity
of Othello, the hatred of Iago announced right off the bat and the fact
that he is going to act on it. So that is your situation: a hero manipulated by an arch-villain.

Here we have a continuous rise to the climax; it encompasses the
whole of Act Two through Act Three, Scene Three. It starts with the plot
against Cassio, as a means of getting to Othello later on. That plot culmi-
nates in Cassio's dismissal for being drunk and disorderly, and Iago's di-

abolical advice that Cassio appeal to the sweet Desdemona to intercede on his behalf. That framework sets up Iago's direct assault on Othello.

As with any great playwright, you see the actual rise. First, the mini-crime, the attempt to enrage Brabantio. Then a real crime, but against a subordinate, Cassio, as the first step to the major crime. It is like waves of greater and greater hatred in action, building and building. The assault on Othello himself, which is still in the rise to the climax, starts with the beginning of Act Three. Iago brilliantly plants suspicions in Othello's mind, leading finally to what is called the "temptation scene"; that is, Act Three, Scene Three. It starts when Iago says, "Ha, I like not that," as Cassio innocently leaves the scene. He is left with Othello, and he immediately casts the implication: *there's something I don't like here.* Of course, Othello wants to know what and Iago says: *Oh, it is nothing, it is nothing,* and from there they go. It has been likened to Iago as a dentist extracting a tooth from Othello's mouth without anesthetic. It is a careful, gradual surgical operation. A little pull to loosen it, and then a soothing retreat: *Beware, my lord, don't be jealous, I have only your best interests in mind; there is nothing to get upset about here, remain calm. Of course it's true that I saw her do this, but I don't want to speak against her.* And so on and so forth. Another little "yank," and then covered over and smoothed away.

Othello grows weaker and more enraged. Iago continues to protest about the sweet Desdemona and how Othello could think of such things. Until—and this is the brilliant turning-point scene—at the end of the temptation scene, the climax of the play. Remember, the climax is the major event revealing the final outcome. And this is the point at the end of the temptation scene, when Othello and Iago kneel solemnly and pledge the death of Desdemona.

If Othello had said, "Well, you made a good case" and stumbled off the stage, that would not have made a good climax. What makes this so brilliant is that they kneel. They kneel solemnly on the stage— you have to imagine that this is properly staged—and it becomes a religious rite; it becomes a ceremonial declaration. It is the exact equivalent of signing your oath to go into military service or signing away your second mortgage. *The* decision has now been made by the protagonists. Othello says, "Now art thou my Lieutenant." That is it. In principle, now you know that a tragic ending has to occur. That is the climax.

That brings us to the resolution, from Act Three, Scene Five to the end. (I don't count the clowns. I don't read them. To me they are in exquisitely bad taste. Whether to blame Shakespeare or the Elizabethan sensibility for those clowns, I don't know, but I won't tolerate them.)

Even though we already know in principle what is going to have to happen, it has not really happened yet. We do not know *how* it is going to happen, *when* it is going to happen, and we still have not seen it happen. It is not yet a reality. There is still plenty of suspense. Will he really do it? Will something happen to stop Othello or change his mind? Notice that even though we are in the resolution, Shakespeare is still going for suspense and doing it brilliantly. He milks Othello's ambivalence. Will he or won't he? Does he love her or does he hate her? Is he going to see the light or is he not? And then come the series of events that harden him. He has already declared a resolution due to Iago's tissue of lies, the handkerchief, the phony dream. Finally Othello turns and acts. He slaps Desdemona; he calls her a whore. Then, almost without pause for breath; her murder, his discovery of the truth, his suicide. The end.

That is a resolution filled with suspense and action. You must get out of your minds the idea that the resolution means just stating the self-evident after you reach the climax. Usually you cannot appreciate that the climax is the climax until after you finish the play. Then you can go back and see that this is the point at which it was set.

There is a subtlety to a good climax that still leaves you hanging, and only in retrospect do you realize that that was the high point. Even so, you do respond to it at the time.

I want to point out that this play has a beautiful development; very logically structured and each event presupposes the earlier and leads to the next. I have many things against Shakespeare; he is not a favorite of mine. But I will defend him to the death against the following accusation: that coincidence is a significant factor in this play, which is a common complaint of critics. It is not true. This play does not hinge on coincidence at all, not if you are talking in essentials. Shakespeare's whole point is that whatever happens, Iago is shrewd and manipulative enough to seize on it and still make things go his way. For instance, if Cassio weren't an alcoholic, Iago would find some other way to get him in trouble. He is endlessly fertile in thinking of ways to get people in trouble. If Desdemona hadn't lied about the hankie, how easy would it have been for Iago to find some other fib or frailty to hang her? This is highly purposeful drama which, without anything else, makes it high and great art.

Notice that he does this even though plot is not Shakespeare's interest. Nevertheless, he is a master at logical structure. We have all the requisites here for a great plot development: a clash of opposing motives; a structure of rapidly ascending events, one built upon the other. In this case, rapidly ascending crime, intense suspense, and then three decisive blows—the resolution and finale, like the three notes of doom in Beethoven's symphony. Death. Discovery. Suicide. Perfect. It is chilling to watch, if it is well done. It knocks you over and, like the really profound tragedy that it is, leaves you depressed for days.

4. Characterization

The three main characters are Othello, Iago and Desdemona. First, Othello. As always, there are countless interpretations of Shakespearean characters by critics. You could give a fascinating course on just interpretations of Shakespeare, which in itself would be like a history of modern literature. It is commonly said that there is something stupid about Othello. He is too easily gulled. How could Iago get away with taking this calm, serene person and poisoning him so easily? In fact, leftists commonly say the theme of *Othello* is: the stupidity of the military mind.

Dropping this kind of nonsense, the real problem in *Othello* is to balance his gullibility as against his grandeur, because both elements are there together in the one person. You have to observe first his truly heroic qualities which are stressed by Shakespeare from the outset: he is controlled, serene; he has no fear and no anger; he is not seething with violence. If you see any of these modern neurotic Othellos who are foaming at the mouth in Act One, allegedly to show their strength, just stop the film. It is not worth even watching. Othello has to be a truly colossal hero; serenely confident and calm. He has had a life of exotic feats. He is, in effect, a Romantic hero. He is black in his skin color but he is racially insensitive.

He and Desdemona are separated by every known conventional division. Race: white and black. Age: young and old. Nationality: she is from Europe and he is from Africa. Social status: she is upper class and he is a soldier. (Although, if I remember correctly, he has some royal parentage somewhere lost in the background.) The point is that he is a man of self-esteem and none of these differences is even an issue to him. None is important to his love for her.

His love for Desdemona is sexual, but not primarily so. It is not platonic and it is not just lust of the flesh. Its root is spiritual. They love each other's characters. They tell us why right at the outset and they have good reason. Othello is not a man driven by passion or whim; his emotions as presented in Act One are integrated with his thoughts. His love for Desdemona is spiritual and physical; it is a true mind-body integration. Othello is man at his best, according to Shakespeare, and he is wholly admirable in Act One.

It is really crucial for the story that you buy his love for Desdemona, and vice versa. If you do not buy into the love story, you might as well close this play—you won't care. I did. I have, if I say so myself, a well-developed ability to empathize with love stories. And I did in this case. That's what saved the play and made it possible for me to read with suspense and involvement.

I want to point out the technical skill on Shakespeare's part, what a tremendously difficult feat this is. Everything depends on him being able to make the love story real in just a few speeches. Then the love has to endure with the reader for four acts, in which all you actually see is their increasing alienation and distrust. So it is a tremendous literary challenge. It is such a feat that you just have to step back in awe.

I want to give you the speech at the conclusion of what I think was such a fantastic achievement. We are in Act One, Scene Three. The speech starts with Othello about line 128: "her father loved me, oft invited me, still questioned me about the story of my life." Then he goes on to tell all the things that happened to him. Near the conclusion, about line 160: "She swore" [that's Desdemona] "'twas strange, 'twas passing strange. 'Twas pitiful, 'twas wondrous pitiful. She wished she had not heard it, yet she wished that heaven had made her such a man. She thanked me, and she bade me that if I had a friend that loved her, I should but teach him how to tell my story, and that would woo her. Upon this hint I spoke"—and then Shakespeare summarizes it in two lovely, eloquent lines—"She loved me for the dangers I had passed, and I loved her that she did pity them." So it is a love of mutual understanding. She knows his life and she admires him for being the hero he has been. He loves her for being the kind of woman who can understand who he is and what he has done.

What happens to Othello who started on such an exalted plane? At the beginning, he is man at his best and then quickly, in effect, he passes from Dr. Jekyll to Mr. Hyde. By the end of Act Three, he is deranged and brimming with hatred.

It is important for you to note that Iago never offers any objective evidence to support his various insinuations. There is nothing that would stand up in a court of law or to a dispassionate judge. His whole case is made of little impressions, none of which could stand the light of objective scrutiny. Cassio laughs—and Iago makes a federal case out of it. The handkerchief. Desdemona intercedes on behalf of Cassio for mercy. Et cetera. A whole accumulation of little nothings, but Othello never questions the evidential value of these. He never asks any questions. He accepts them at once, as though they are self-evident. In other words, this rational, calm, objective man has lost his rationality. He becomes completely credulous; he is run only by Iago's manipulations. This state of affairs is symbolized by Othello's epileptic fit, the exact opposite of Othello as he first came onstage.

If you know Hegel, it is like the thesis became the antithesis. Then we have the synthesis in Act Five in the murder scene. "It is the cause," he says as he is going to murder her. And what does he mean by "it is the cause?" He means that he is acting from justice, not jealousy or base motives. He is aware enough that there is such a thing as a cuckolded husband who wants revenge. But he tells himself: *I am acting as a man of reason; I am taking an act of justice, not revenge.* So he knows the issue. But nevertheless jealousy is still running him, warping him unknown to himself. He is still torn and ambivalent. You see the two Othellos back and forth; the good Othello pulls back, the bad Othello urges him on. He loves her, he hates her, he kills her.

And then this typical double-meaning line of Shakespeare's, so eloquent. Othello is holding a lit candle and he says, "Put out the light, and then put out the light." And that is the light of her life and thus of his own. Which is just what happens.

So at the start he is alive with Desdemona. That's the good Othello. He sees the world through her beauty and goodness. She becomes, in effect, his view of life. Then Iago ensnares him, and he becomes alive with Iago. And that is the jealous, berserk Othello, a metaphysical change from the preceding. His whole view of life has diametrically changed. He adopts Iago's view of people. Wherever he looks he sees nothing but sluts and crooks. And then at the end he is alive with Desdemona again, but too late. He is aligned with her and he returns to his better self. But by the time he finds out the truth about her, she is dead and he is doomed.

Why these changes in Othello? Why did he succumb as he did to Iago? Why did he find himself again, but too late? Those are the questions we want to explore as we continue.

While Othello is mixed or ambivalent, Iago is not. He represents utter, total evil. He is the blackest character in Shakespeare and, to my knowledge, in all world literature. Notice that he does not start with a specific idea of death for Desdemona. That develops as the play progresses. The start, on page one, is that Iago hates the Moor. The beginning of the play and the key to Iago is that he hates the Moor. What then is the motor of this creature? The poet Coleridge, who was also a literary critic, gave an intriguing but inaccurate answer. He said that Iago is run by motiveless malignity.

Now in a sense this is true. He is motiveless, in a sense, in that all of his stated motives for hating Othello are cover-ups, rationalizations. They are not his true reasons for acting as he does. For example, he says that he is jealous of Cassio's military position but Iago is not motivated by any career interest or passion. He shows no interest in the military field; he even sneers at it. Or again, he says he suspects Othello of cuckolding him with his wife. This is made up out of whole cloth. There isn't a shred of basis for it and he immediately forgets all about it. Or again, he says, I love Desdemona and I'm jealous. There isn't a shred of truth to that. All of the alleged motives that he gives are like that. They are casual, spur of the moment, unreal.

In that way, it is exactly like the arguments you hear against capitalism. You refute one and they come up with three more. Then they drop them under pressure and move on to the next.

What, then, is real and enduring about Iago? He wants to poison Othello's joy. He wants to cut him down, destroy him. For no positive reason, for no reward. He has no loves or passions to achieve. So you can see the plausibility of Coleridge's "motiveless malignity." If we look a little deeper, we will see that Iago is not motiveless. He has no journalistic motive, no specific value that he is seeking. But he does have a metaphysical motive that is driving him. What is it?

Other critics have called him a devil worshipper, a Satanist, a man in love with evil. That gives him far too much credit. Iago is not in love with anything. That is the whole essence of him. What then is his true motive? Well, Shakespeare actually knew it. And one other person since Shakespeare has known it. Ayn Rand said this in "The Age of Envy" and, although it was not written with *Othello* in mind, it is a perfect description of Iago. Nothing less would explain him; nothing else is required:

> Hatred of the good for being the good means hatred of that which one regards as good by one's own judgment. Its exponents do not experience love for evil men. Their emotional range is limited to hatred or indifference. For example, a person characteristically resents someone's success, happiness, achievement, or good fortune and experiences pleasure at someone's failure, unhappiness, or misfortune. The hater has nothing to lose or gain in such instances, no practical value at stake, no existential motive. So what the hater wants is not the values he purports to envy, but the other man's loss of them.

She goes on to quote John Galt: "They do not want to own your fortune, they want you to lose it; they do not want to succeed, they want you to fail; they do not want to live, they want you to die; they desire nothing, they hate existence."

Notice how conscious Shakespeare was. Iago, for instance, at one point explicitly hates Cassio because, he says, Cassio has a beauty that makes him, Iago, ugly. Now I don't think you could give Shakespeare high enough praise for having the psychological insight, the true psychological genius, to grasp such a motive. His depth of thought here, his metaphysical depth, is just truly astonishing. It is an epical feat to be able to think in such terms, to depict a character of such consistency that hadn't been dreamt of for centuries; and that took a world historical genius to define.

So I want to give Shakespeare every kind of credit I can, because in many ways he deserves it. But—and with Shakespeare there is always a "but"—I want you to observe the other characteristics he also gives to Iago, as though they go along perfectly with this nihilism, this hatred of the good. In three words, Iago is also supposed to be the man of *action*, the man of *reason*, and the man of *selfishness*. Now I want to elaborate each briefly.

Iago is the active character. In that sense, regardless of the title of the play, he is really the protagonist, the prime mover. All the key developments in the play are initiated and directed by him. He creates the plot against Cassio, he orchestrates Roderigo's movements, he arranges the handkerchief episode, he plants the doubts in Othello, etc.

Relatively speaking, Othello and Desdemona are passive. They are like puppets—and Iago pulls the strings.

Why does Iago have so much initiative and control over events? Why is he the man of action? That brings us to the second point. He is presented as being free of emotion, free of passion. As he himself says explicitly, "and therefore he can be guided purely by the mind," purely by intelligence. He says in one of his famous speeches, "we have reason to cool our raging motions." Yes, Iago is presented as a man who is intelligent, shrewd. The others live in their dreams and fantasies but he perceives reality, he has no delusions, he grasps the flow of events, he can adapt to events in a second; he is the cool unfeeling calculator, pure thought. And thus, as he says, "the master of himself." I refer you to this speech in Act One, Scene Three, lines 318 to 330, a speech that sounds as though it could have been written by an Objectivist. It is the arch-villain explaining that the way to be a man of reason is to have no feelings. Then you will have free will and be able to be the master of your destiny, as long as you rid yourself of any values, in effect.

It was a baffling speech to me the first time I read it because I asked, does Shakespeare agree with this? Is Iago really the hero? I couldn't make head or tail of it. And then I finally figured it out. The nihilist, the hater of the good for being the good is the source of action, the dynamo. He is the thinker, and he is the egoist. *Iago*, as you may see, is etymologically related to *Ego*. That means he is supposed to value only himself and, of course, "himself" means his whims, his destructiveness.

Notice the stress on Iago's cynicism. You know that a cynic is somebody who believes that virtue is impossible. Nobody is any good, they are all pigs, so I can justifiably do whatever I want with them. I hope you got that message from his famous line about Desdemona. They are saying what a wonderful woman she is and so on, and he says, "the wine she drinks is made of grapes." He means that she is human just like the rest of us, there is nothing so special about her. This exact same line was stated by a commentator that may be before your time. Do you know Eric Sevareid? At the time of man's first launch into space when the whole country was transfixed in watching the screen, Sevareid said, "I don't know what all the excitement is about. These astronauts put their pants on one leg at a time. They're human just like the rest of us." And so that famous line, "the wine she drinks is made of grapes." It is not the nectar of the gods. She is down here in the muck with everybody else. That is Iago's perspective, you see. It is not Shakespeare's perspective. He thinks virtue is possible and Desdemona is an example of it. But it *is* Iago's perspective. And it's supposed to be the real egotist's perspective.

A. C. Bradley, the famous Shakespearean interpreter, wrote this about Iago: (This is how these plays are taught to students to this day.) "In intellect and in will, Iago is great. To what end does he use these great powers? His creed—for he is no skeptic, he has a definite creed—is that absolute egoism is the only rational and proper attitude, and that conscience or honor or any kind of regard for others is an absurdity." Now you see that it is hopeless to teach literature if you don't know Objectivism. You see the importance of philosophy to understanding even the great classics.

Shakespeare gave Iago more lines than any other character in any other play. He was obviously fascinated by this character. But what message does he want us to get from this monster with his mixture of traits? What is the deeper meaning of this portrait? Put that on hold, along with the questions about Othello, while we look finally at the characterization of Desdemona.

Desdemona is the opposite of Iago. She is one hundred percent Christian virtue. She is meek. She accepts anything without protest, even her own murder. She turns the other cheek, she forgives. And, of course, this is essential to the play. If Desdemona were not a thorough Christian, if she were not so intent on forgiveness, there could be no play. Suppose, for instance, when Othello first slapped her or cursed her, she asserted herself, became enraged, and cried out indignantly: this is unfair to me; what the hell is the matter with you? In other words, had she confronted Othello head on and stood up to him, that would have been the best proof to him of her honesty, her innocence, and it would have been a chance to save herself and him. But she doesn't dream of doing this. She is always forgiving, loving, self-denying; whatever he says, it is all her fault. He calls her a whore, and her statement is: "'Tis meet I should be used so, very meet. How have I been behaved, that he could stick the smallest opinion on my least misuse?" In other words, what have I done that he could think this of me? Whatever he does, I deserve it completely. So her Christian virtue is essential to Iago's plan.

So we have the traditional dichotomy. Iago is the sacrificer of others to himself and Desdemona, the opposite: a sacrificer of self to others. Othello, unfortunately, is not a third viewpoint, he just oscillates between the two. So what is missing morally? What third alternative is wholly absent from the characterizations of the play? The man of what Ayn Rand would call a self-sustaining ego, an Objectivist ego of true independence from others. That idea would kill off both Iago and Desdemona, and thus wipe out the story.

Desdemona is a standard Christian heroine. Shakespeare himself was not religious but he accepted the Christian definition of virtue and, of course, non-believers do so to this very day because there has never been another definition for them to accept.

If you want an idea to what depths Christianity has brought civilization, just contrast Desdemona with Antigone, two leading females. One a creature with no spirit, no will, no fire; utterly drab. And you know what I think of the other.

In any event, that gives us the three main characters of the play. They have all been taken, quite legitimately, as Christian symbols. Even though, as I say, Shakespeare was not a believer, Christianity was so built into the culture that even unbelievers used all the symbolism. Iago is the serpent or tempter; he is like Satan. Desdemona is the pure; angelic, Christ-like. And Othello, caught between the two, moving back and forth between them, better than one but not equal to the other, represents man.

This is truly a philosophic play. When you have these kinds of characters, not just as empty archetypes but taking part in ongoing conflicts and suspenseful action, you are talking here about a playwright—and not just a guy that writes plays.

5. Theme

The theme is the abstract message or principle that the events in this play directly dramatize. It is not yet the total philosophy, but the message. Here are some key data for the theme. Iago, who is evil for evil's sake, ends in ruin. Desdemona, who is total virtue, ends in ruin. Othello, the best of human beings, neither angel nor demon, ends in ruin. And no, the message is not the necessity of ruin. The theme is: virtue and vice are irrelevant to life. Or, put another way: moral character is irrelevant to one's destiny.

In elaborating on this theme I have a tremendous advantage that I have with no other play. I was going to teach this play many years ago, and I was unsure about how to interpret it. I had a memorable four- or five-hour discussion with Ayn Rand about it. This play is the only one in this course that I was able to talk to her about and, knowing that I had to teach this the next day; I wrote furiously and tried to be as accurate as possible. I asked her, "What does this play mean?" What follows are essentially her words:

Ariel, the spirit in *The Tempest*, states the essence of Shakespeare's viewpoint and the theme of this play in his line: "what fools these mortals be." Why are they fools? (Speaking for Shakespeare now, she went on.) Some people have the illusion that virtue is important. Others are obsessed with their sinfulness or evil; they think that's important. Whereas I, Shakespeare, am Olympian, detached. I'm wise enough to be above it all, I see the futility of morality. Desdemona happens to be good—it doesn't help her. Iago is monstrous—same end. They are fools because they think their actions, their characters, their decisions matter in life. And the truth is, good and evil are inconsequential. So there's no point in urging virtue or denouncing vice.

I interject here on my own, a contrast with *Antigone* so you are not confused: Sophocles upholds the vital importance of morality. For example, vice is the downfall of Creon who is specifically punished for his evil. Sophocles does hold that there are some unknowable powers at work in the universe but he insists, nonetheless, that morality is one crucial factor in our destiny; that we should struggle to be moral and we would have at least a chance then. He would never say that morality is irrelevant. Remember, he is religious; he is still a moralist as against Shakespeare.

Returning to Miss Rand's analysis, she told me to get Shakespeare's true message. He is not Greek, but nor is he Christian. The traditional Christian would say: life has a moral outcome, if not here on earth, then in the next world. And Shakespeare says no, a man's outcome has no relation to moral character.

So I said, "Well, I guess then Shakespeare believes that life is necessarily tragic, like Byron or Schopenhauer." She said no. Byron or Schopenhauer believed that man is doomed by a hostile universe set against him. "No," she said, "that is not Shakespeare's view because he believes that happy endings are possible; he wrote many comedies. Many of his characters even in the tragedies succeed or end up ahead of the game." For instance, Cassio in this play escapes Iago's net and ends up governor. But the point is: how does he escape? It's not that there is an evil world out to smash everybody. He escapes by pure chance. The point is, some people succeed, some fail, we are not all doomed, but what happens—and this is the key point—is haphazard. It takes place regardless of the merits or demerits of the characters.

So that is a very distinctive viewpoint. It is not synonymous with "everything is rotten."

I'll come back to what Miss Rand said in a moment. But I want to work out in a little more detail how Shakespeare's theme, the irrelevance of morality, is dramatized in the play. He is so brilliant in dramatizing a theme, that you are transfixed with admiration, leaving aside whether you agree with that theme.

First, consider virtue and its irrelevance to life. Virtue for Shakespeare is Christian virtue, self-sacrifice. He has a pretty good thing to do here because we know that that kind of virtue does and must lead its exponents to destruction, so he just has to play Christianity to its natural conclusion. Here is a wonderful quote from A. C. Bradley on Desdemona's plight. This is apropos of the plight of virtue. Bradley, of course, is a thorough Christian. My hair stood on end when I read this quote. "Desdemona is helplessly passive. She could do nothing whatever. She cannot retaliate even in speech. And the chief reason of her helplessness only makes the sight of her suffering more exquisitely painful. She is helpless because her nature is infinitely sweet and her love absolute." In other words, she is so good as to be emasculating—or effeminizing.

Shakespeare applies this same point more broadly to every kind of virtue, including legitimate virtue; in other words, what you in this room would regard as virtue. Every evil scheme of Iago's depends on his victim's weaknesses, it is true, but also on their virtues, their real virtues. For instance, Cassio couldn't be provoked to rage by Iago, if he weren't himself a man of honor. Othello had to be a sincere and impassioned lover or he would have been impervious to Iago's instigations. Desdemona had to want generously to intercede on Cassio's behalf and then to remain loyal in her promise to him to continue pleading his case with Othello. In all these cases true virtue is essential to Iago's scheme. Do you think this is an accident? This is a master we are talking about. Shakespeare tells us flat out in Act Two, Scene Three, line 336. There is a crucial speech by Iago; he makes his plans at that point and then he says, "So will I turn her virtue into pitch, and out of her own goodness make the net that shall enmesh them all."

It is really important that you understand this. A student once asked me, "Isn't this same thing true of Ayn Rand's characters also?" Namely, that the characters suffer because of their virtues, which are exploited by the villains. Now take fifteen seconds to think why this is *not* true of Objectivist heroes. It is the exact opposite situation with

Objectivism. How many are stopped momentarily by this question and don't have an immediate answer? Oh, well, if there are that few people, I guess I don't have to give it. But the actual answer is: Ayn Rand's heroes allow themselves to be exploited because they lack knowledge. It is not their virtues which do them in, but their ignorance. Their virtues are what keep them looking for the truth and eventually make them succeed. Rearden, for instance, is not a victim because he is rational, independent and productive. Those are the qualities that enable him to discover his victimization. He is a victim because he does not know what the world owes him, and his very virtues lead him to discover it.

Shakespeare is the exact opposite here. The very virtues of the characters make them vulnerable. For instance, Othello's passionate love—a legitimate, major virtue—or Desdemona's self-sacrifice, a Christian virtue. It is their virtues, Christian or otherwise, that are the obstacles to their success. To succeed they would need, not more knowledge, but an opposite character. So the virtues here play into the hands of the evil. They make the evil possible, and thereby lead to their own destruction.

Now look at vice. Does that mean that evil is, therefore, all-powerful for Shakespeare? No. And here the key point is the fragility of Iago's scheming. At any moment his plot could collapse, at one question from Othello or Desdemona. Observe the outright stupidity of Iago's final oversight. He neglects to take into account Emilia's entirely predictable reaction, her horror at discovering Desdemona's death. Obviously she is going to immediately tell the whole story. Suddenly a couple of unfortunate letters come to light and bam! within an instant it is all over; it's curtains for Iago. In other words, Iago is a fool, too. And Shakespeare is highly conscious in presenting that. The message is not the power of vice over virtue. Iago is crushed, silenced, and the implication is that he is tortured to death. His machinations collapse like a house of cards and he is ruined along with everybody else.

Still on the theme, I am going back to Miss Rand's words. She told me that Shakespeare doesn't give a damn. He doesn't like Othello or Desdemona; he doesn't hate Iago. He draws black and white characters but they mean nothing to him personally. He is not a cynic; he does not agree with Iago. He has characters that he considers truly virtuous. He is not despairing or rebellious in the face of the tragedy of life; he accepts the tragedy with a smile of detachment. He is not amoral, in the sense of presenting gray characters like today's writers. He is not an amoralist who says, "Who knows the difference between good and evil? We can't distinguish it. Morality is a sham." Then she gave this marvelous description of him. She said, Shakespeare is a special kind of moralist, a psychopathic moralist. In other words, he recognizes the distinction, he writes about it—and he doesn't give a damn about it.

She told me that he is a great poet, a great artist. But if he saw Auschwitz or Atlantis from *Atlas Shrugged*, he would have the same basic reaction. If he saw Auschwitz, he would write beautiful poetry on gas chamber deaths: "oh, mournful, insidious fumes!" If he saw Galt's motor: "oh, glittering, sunken invention that from the bosom of the airy cairn draws forth!" So Ayn Rand calls him a dead soul, a man whose reaction to Galt or Iago is the same.

I have a few last formulations that I copied from my conversation with her. I wish I had thought to do it with every author in history. But at that time I was completely into philosophy. I thought literature was a waste of time. I was saddled with this assignment, so I did it on this one play only. But she was full of these brilliant lines, if only someone had got them out of her. She said to me: "Shakespeare makes a virtue out of the inefficacy of virtue." And then again, "He regards man as important, but denies what is important to him—namely, the power of moral values." The last line I remember from that conversation—"Shakespeare is a great artist esthetically, and I loathe him."

6. Philosophy

We want to look at the context of this idea of Shakespeare's principle of the inefficacy of virtue. The deeper roots of this idea are all over the play and in his other plays, as well. Here are some key ones. The most obvious, perhaps, is determinism. Man has no choice about his nature, whether he is good or evil, and so he has no control over his life; he is helpless. Human helplessness, our lack of choice or control is a fundamental of Shakespeare's philosophy. What is it that Othello says at the end that is a perfect, eloquent summary of it? "Oh, vain boast! Who can control his fate?" And, of course, the implicit answer is: no one.

So morality cannot be a force in human life because, in logic, morality is the means that a volitional being uses to select his course. Without volition, morality is just a redundancy. It has no function. And that is just what Shakespeare holds it to be: a kind of private game of status or emotion that has no role and no effects in life.

Why is Shakespeare so profound a determinist? Why does he hold that man is helpless? One deeper reason is that he is a strong subscriber to the dichotomy of reason and emotion, the mind/body dichotomy. In that sense, he is a faithful Platonist, even though he is not otherworldly. Man, for Shakespeare, is made of two elements, intrinsically opposed. You cannot live with them or without them: reason and emotion. If you try to live exclusively by reason, he thinks, the result is going to be a Hamlet. The indecisive intellectual, always weighing pros and cons, paralyzed because he has no passion to guide him. If you try to live by reason, it is Hamlet or Iago. They are both the intellectual side of this dichotomy. Iago, of course, as we have seen, is the true non-valuer, the true non-feeler of anything; pure calculation. And that is a disaster, Shakespeare says.

On the other hand, if you allow emotion into the picture, then it is going to topple reason. And the result is going to be *Macbeth* where ambition is let loose. Or *Othello*, where love is let loose. And you get dragged into some emotionalist disaster.

So we have the tragic flaw in all of Shakespeare's tragedies—the feet of clay in even his greatest heroes. The flaw ultimately is not any one passion, such as jealousy or anger, etc. The flaw is the metaphysical makeup of man, a creature with two halves at war. You can't live by either half alone. Yet, so it seemed to him, you can't integrate the two into any kind of unity.

The originators of the mind/body dichotomy back in ancient Greece, such as Plato, nevertheless were able to experience hope in this plight thanks to their religion. They thought that one day they would transcend the conflicts of this world for the gods or the next life. But Shakespeare is an early modern. Religion is not a force to him. An afterlife is not an issue. There is only this earth for him but he accepts the legacy of religion unquestioningly; not only the equation of virtue with sacrifice, but the mind/body dichotomy in most of its forms. The result is, he has all the helplessness of the religious view of man without its hope of redemption. He has only the futility. In effect, he feels there is no way to live; the earth is unbearable and there is no heaven to anticipate any longer. So we must give up the pretense of valuing.

This is not Shakespeare's unique evil or error. This was common in the late Renaissance. As men threw over the Christian code, they were not automatically turned into Objectivists. On the contrary, they were left with no code, and they were even more helpless and depressed in many ways than they were during the medieval period. If you want another example from a contemporary of Shakespeare, I suggest you read Cervantes' *Don Quixote*, which was written in Spain at exactly the same time. Cervantes and Shakespeare died on the same day in the same year. And they had the same philosophy. Don Quixote was insane, you know, because he had ideals and he soon learns that he has to come down to earth. You just can't be impassioned for ideals because it is hopeless. They didn't know which ideals to be for anymore. It is a much broader cultural issue.

Stop to think about the famous line from *Othello* which summarizes this: "he loved not wisely, but too well." He loved too well. How is it possible to value your beloved too strongly? Impossible in an Objectivist world. It is just like thinking too well, reasoning too well—loving too well. He doesn't say he loved her inappropriately or irrationally. He loved her without restraints. The thing is that he couldn't, therefore, stand for her to disappoint him. And the moral he draws is: do not be a valuer.

Sophocles, I grant you, implied the danger of love, as in some of the later odes in *Antigone*. But he obviously admired Antigone for her love of her brother and her passion for morality. Sophocles' ambivalence has become Shakespeare's unbreached conviction. It is self-destructive to love—that is his message and that is his philosophy. You cannot care for the good too much, not in a world where it is impossible or irrelevant. If Othello had not loved Desdemona as he did, Iago couldn't have destroyed him. Safety, in effect, consists in not caring; in remaining passive, stoical, resigned, above it all.

So Shakespeare is a thorough malevolent universer. His works are the voice of doom, although not as a primary. It is an effect of all the rest of his philosophy. It is what leads him to this sense of hopelessness. Once the malevolent universe is established in his soul, a vicious circle takes place. The malevolence, once accepted, becomes a self-fulfilling prophesy. It becomes the cause of even more defeats and even more malevolence.

As with Sophocles, I would like to praise Shakespeare as a stylist, as a writer, as an artist. Again, he is so great an artist that to do even cursory justice would take hours of analyzing examples from just this one play. His ability to write great, truly elevated poetry, not merely empty rhetoric; always full of substance and content. His purposefulness, his immense economy of language; every word is weighed and counted. Also the grand-scale nature of his vision and characterizations. The brilliance, the genius, the sensory vividness of his metaphors and imagery. I tried to make a list; it is just impossible. I would have to recite the whole play.

At the very start, when Iago says to Brabantio, "Your daughter and the Moor are now making the beast with two backs." Is that evocative? Do you see it? And all the way through to the very end, to Othello's last speech, "Soft you, a word or two before you go." He tells them to tell his story to the world, and he concludes: tell them "of one whose hand . . . threw a pearl away richer than all his tribe; of one whose subdued eyes, albeit unused to the melting mood [that is, to weeping] drop tears as fast as the Arabian trees their medicinable gum. . . . And say, besides, that in Aleppo once where a malignant and a turbaned Turk beat a Venetian and traduced the state, I took by the throat the circumcised dog and smote him thus"—and stabs himself. That's what you call a death scene.

In the nineteenth century, audiences (you know, the audiences were very restrained and reserved then) during the murder scene would yell out to Othello, "Don't do it, she's innocent." They actually had to watch the wings of the stage because spectators, dressed in ties and tails and so on, would leap onstage to stop him. That is how deep their experience actually went. Despite all the disagreements between Objectivism and Shakespeare, I hope that you too can get as deeply involved in this great play, and that it has added something to your life that you would not have wanted to have missed. I know that it has done that for me.

Editor's Note: At this point in the course, Dr. Peikoff introduced the following list of questions necessary for the final evaluation of the plays, addressed in Chapter Eight.

ESTHETIC EVALUATION

1. Who is the strongest heroine in all these plays? The most admirable hero? The worst villain?
2. Which character has the strongest motivation, i.e., the most intense passion and the most inflexible will?
3. Which character would you most like to sleep with?
4. Which character do you most *like*?
5. Which play has the most ingenious plot-theme?
6. Which play has the strongest conflict?

7. Which conflict has the most gripping climax? The most dramatic ending?
8. Which *story* do you most like?
9. Which play presents the most complex theme?
10. With which play do you most strongly agree? Most strongly disagree?
11. Which play most admirably *integrates* theme and plot?
12. Speaking purely esthetically, which is objectively the best play?
13. Speaking purely philosophically, which is objectively the best play?
14. Taking both art and philosophy into account, which is objectively the best play?
15. Which of the dramas is your *personal* favorite?

I suggest you make a working copy, numbered one through fifteen and after each play—today you have only two plays, *Antigone* and *Othello*—go down the fifteen questions, and write down your provisional answer.

Who is the strongest heroine? Your choice so far is Antigone or Desdemona. It's very easy at this point.

Which character would you most like to sleep with? Very limited choice so far.

Which story do you most like? That may give you more of a pause right now.

Which play most admirably integrates theme and plot? That may give you a pause.

The last four questions are the biggies that we are building up to, because the first eleven are the material for them.

12. *Speaking purely esthetically, which is objectively the best play?*
13. *Speaking purely philosophically, which is objectively the best play?*
14. *Taking both art and philosophy into account, which is objectively the best play?*
15. *Which of the dramas is your personal favorite?*

I allow, as I'll explain, a different answer for that last question from the others. As a matter of fact, I'll tell you that my answers to 12, 13, 14, and 15 are four different plays out of the seven. So it's like Tonys going to all of them.

Try to keep it up to date as we go along. Otherwise, you're going to find yourself the night before saying: Oh, God, I can't remember the characters in this play; I've got to compare seven stories, fifteen characters, etc. And you'll never do it. When you bring in your answers, hopefully you will have some reasons for them so that we can get into some kind of discussion.

Q & A

Before we turn to questions, I want to point out that someone in the audience just handed me this: William Shakespeare's *Othello*, the entire text, unabridged and unexpurgated, in comic-strip form. It is published by—this publisher certainly deserves a plug—Overprojects, Ltd., Cedric and Jackson, 335 Kennington Road, London. They start on the title page with pictures of all the characters. This whole thing is fascinating. It's very easy to read so you may find this takes the curse off Elizabethan English.

Q: I believe it was Aristotle who said that tragedies are written in times of moral upheaval, at a time when people are caught between two moral codes. And I think that would be the case in both *Antigone* and with Shakespeare in the late Renaissance. Do you see that happening here, and is that a factor in both of those plays?

A: Well, let me try to get that down because you have several different points there. Tragedies have been written from the beginning to the present, in all times and in all periods. So it would be incorrect to say they were written only in times of moral upheaval. Certainly when your moral code is ambivalent or uncertain, that in itself is going to give you a tragic sense of life. But if your moral code is completely consistent and is completely wrong, as for instance in the medieval tragedies, that is going to give you a tragic sense of life, which is not changed by the fact that they're going to be happy in the next life; in this world it's still tragedy.

So, in order to write a non-tragedy, you must implicitly or explicitly have an unbreached positive philosophy. You must at least potentially, to some extent, be able to view life as open to man and have a moral code which permits him to succeed. And you know from the writings of Objectivism how rare that is. Even the Romantics in the nineteenth century wrote tragedies, when they believed in human freedom and had political freedom—even they, like Victor Hugo, ended with tragedies. Again, you could say, they had an ambivalent moral code. Well, yes, but then you're not saying anything because you're not excluding anything. They are still tragedies.

And I want to add one further point. Man's ability to achieve his values is not entirely dependent on his own volitional choice. For instance, *We the Living.* It's a tragedy. It's a tragedy even though Kira at the end says that life is still possible; she reaffirms in her soul the possibility of life. But in actual fact, all of the characters die, as in Shakespearean or Greek tragedies. There, though, it's not because of the metaphysics, but because of the political situation.

Nevertheless a tragedy is very, very all-encompassing. And it's a rare feat to write a non-tragedy. So it's broader than what you said. We have some non-tragedies in this course. So just wait for further discussion. But don't be surprised by how many great works are tragedies because mankind's thinking has been in a mess. If you try to write a serious work about life and the universe, with your thinking in a mess, your conclusion is going to be: what a disaster we are facing!

Q: When you said that Ayn Rand was the first person since Shakespeare to understand hatred of the good for being the good, two exceptions came to my mind. And I don't have a question, I just wondered if you would agree with them. One is Nietzsche in regard to *The Antichrist.* He was more focused on Christianity as hatred of the good for being the good. And the other one is Nurse Ratched in the book or the movie *One Flew Over the Cuckoo's Nest.*

A: Well, I didn't see *One Flew Over the Cuckoo's Nest,* but I would be very surprised if that character had the profundity which you suggest. An undeviating hatred can just be an example of modern neurosis. It doesn't have to have the depth of hatred of the good for *being* the good.

Nietzsche in *The Antichrist* is more of an example, but it's so tied into one religion and one narrow view of the good. Nietzsche certainly has the brains for it. Whether his formulations stand up—I haven't reviewed them in that context. I would tend to think you would have to read a lot into it. You know, it's like Aristotle. You can find everything in Aristotle if you read Ayn Rand first. And then you look back: everything, including the omission of measurements as the means of concept-formation is in Aristotle. It's in one of his biological works. But it just so happens that for twenty-five hundred years nobody noticed it. Why did they find it?

I did not mean, however, to make a big point of that. I do not have the knowledge to begin to defend it as an objective proposition: Shakespeare and Ayn Rand are the only two that ever grasped this psychology. That would be a fantastic sweeping statement that I am just not equipped to make. I say that, in my limited knowledge, those are the only two pure cases I have ever seen. One who created the character with the utter perfection of self-consciousness. And one who described the philosophic meaning. If there are others—I mean, it's a type that's been around forever—more power to them.

Q: This question concerns two conflicting theories about the seeming cause of the downfall of Shakespeare's tragic heroes. The most common theory that has been formulated is the notion of a tragic flaw, such as greed, ambition, or jealousy as the primary cause of their downfall. The other one is a more recent view; the theory that the cause that covers all of their downfalls can be reduced to the limitation of human knowledge and that that is what they felt Shakespeare was really trying to imply.

A: You want to say something to make the second plausible?

Q: You take individual cases, like the view that Macbeth was misguided by witches and Hamlet cannot decide because he never has enough knowledge to make a decision.

A: What is Iago's limitation of knowledge?

Q: Iago, I don't think has . . .

A: Oh, you mean Othello just doesn't know what Iago is up to?

Q: That he is misled because he didn't know the truth. The fact is, he didn't know the truth.

A: Well, to make short work of that, I don't attach any validity to that. That is so wrong. You cannot make a tragedy out of a fact of human nature. That is exactly tantamount to saying: man can't flap his wings and fly to the moon, and that's why all Shakespeare's tragedies end in suffering. Remember, art is selective; you are rewriting, picking out what you think is the essence of man's life. If the fact that he is a living being who has to acquire knowledge by his own choice and therefore he only has a limited amount at each step, is what defeats him, it's not. Something else must be motivating him. No one in his right mind could come to this conclusion: man's knowledge is limited, therefore, there's no chance for him except destruction and doom. That would be exactly like saying: you have to open your eyes before you cross Fifth Avenue, therefore you can't get across. You know, because what if you walk into a truck that's coming; you're not all-powerful.

Obviously, accidents and lack of knowledge can contribute. But in all of Shakespeare's plays the characters are not motivated by a desire for knowledge. The reverse is true: the characters are indifferent and hostile to knowledge; you couldn't get through if you beat them over the head with it. Othello doesn't walk around saying, "Oh, God, if only I knew the objective truth." He'd grab anything Iago said; he becomes demonic. The whole thing is, he is indifferent to the knowledge and to the limitation of knowledge. Iago, of course, couldn't care less. Desdemona doesn't care less; she regards her virtue as being true or false; she is no good. If you said to her, "Your self-analysis is going to depend on objective knowledge," she'd say, "What are you talking about? I'm no good no matter what, that's what my Christianity lies in."

Any one of these characters is oblivious to knowledge. You could hit them over the head with this whole lecture, and they would still go about their business. Iago would explain that it was all part of the scheme on Cassio's part to confuse Othello. And Desdemona would say, he is selfish, don't listen to him. I mean, I don't agree with that theory.

Q: I had a question about the way you analyzed the play. I wanted to know how you came to the conclusion that these six points are the points by which you should understand the plays.

A: Well, that's a good question. I'd like to have given a lecture on methodology. It's not really six points because the introduction is just general cultural knowledge so that you have some idea that it's ancient Greece rather than modern England or whatever. You don't have to know the dates of the playwright; you don't have to know his name even; you don't have to know that this is his thirty-seventh play. All of that is just thrown in as background.

So the actual analysis is really only three things because I don't have time for style. And style is a very treacherous and difficult thing. To do style, you have to go far beyond the play you are reading. You have to read that play; you have to know all the other main plays of the author so that you can abstract. You can see what is true of him generally and not just in this play. And then you have to know his contemporaries, so that you can say, "This is distinctive to Shakespeare here, and it is not true of Marlowe or his contemporaries and so on and so on." If you don't know that, you may be giving Shakespeare praise or blame for something that was inherent in the whole Elizabethan era.

That's why I have to frankly admit to you that I am not knowledgeable enough to comment intelligently on style. All I can say with regard to style is, "I like this for these obviously good reasons," but I haven't thought about what is distinctive about any of these. So taking away introduction and style, the three things that I talk about are really plot, characters and meaning. And then it becomes a simple question. Those are the three levels. If a play doesn't have any one of those three, it's out as far as art is concerned.

It has to have action. Otherwise, it's just philosophy; it is not fiction. Action has to have actors—so there must be characters. And if it means nothing, then literally, by implication, it's not art. Art is by its nature implicitly philosophical. I happen to have chosen plays that are more explicitly philosophical but you can't have art without meaning. So those three you can't escape. Action and characters are unavoidable in any art, and theme; meaning in art.

Now meaning has to be last. It has to be last because on what else are you going to base it? You can't just come in and say, "I've just read a speech by Iago on the importance of reason, therefore Shakespeare is in favor of reason." You can't take that speech out of context. Who is Iago? Why does he do it? *Et cetera*. So meaning has to come at the end.

Where do you have to start? Your choice to start, therefore, is action or characters. Now can you start with characters? No. I agree with Aristotle one hundred percent: the most important thing in literature is action. We hold values for the sake of achieving them in action. Our characters are the automatized values that will guide us in behavior. Therefore, the thing that counts in life and in art, the metaphysical primary, the important thing, is what we do. Not a primary in the sense that it has no cause, but a primary in the sense of its importance. If you sit back and study Objectivism until you are blue in the face and you express passion for it and so on, but when the time comes you vote for Hitler and shrug, your previous behavior doesn't make any difference. That one action wipes out all the rest.

If we showed you throughout your whole life studying and praising Ayn Rand and so on, it wouldn't be your character. It would only be your character if that was your action. We'd have to know your action before we could know your character.

So we have to start with action. It would have to be, in order: action, and then, what kind of character could perform this action? And then, what does it mean? Those are the three things. Then we divide up. What is going to give you the action? It can't simply be a synopsis. So you develop the idea of the plot-theme, the essence of the action which then leads you to: how is it structured? Those are my first two. Then the characters—which are read off from that—who are essential and what their motivations must be given the action. And then meaning. But meaning we do in two stages; the direct, explicit meaning given in the text and then the wider framework which we have to infer from that.

So it seems to me inexorably logical to follow the structure that I am following.

Next, *Le Cid.*

CHAPTER THREE

Le Cid

Pierre Corneille

1. Introduction

I am happy to introduce you to a Frenchman most of you probably don't know, Pierre Corneille, seventeenth century, 1606 to 1684; a lawyer, a highly productive author, father of seven children and an immortal French playwright. He is regarded as a Classicist because the French Academy at the time was issuing a set of stern, concrete-bound rules that every play was supposed to follow. Corneille followed some of the rules but broke others—he is freer than the typical Classicist.

He is often linked with the slightly later French Classicist playwright, Jean Racine. To help you understand why I like Corneille so much, I am going to read you a few comments on these two writers from their contemporaries, and you can try to guess why I picked Corneille for this course and not Racine. "Corneille depicts man as he ought to be; Racine depicts him as he is." Or this from somebody else—this is wonderful and true—"When one has seen a play by Corneille, one has the desire to be virtuous; when one sees a play by Racine, one is pleased to see that others share one's weaknesses." So you get an idea of what the difference is and now you know why I picked Corneille for this course. You haven't lived, dramatically speaking, if you don't know this playwright.

The play that I chose, *Le Cid*, is, in a way, his most famous. It is a medieval romance late in the Middle Ages, around 1100 AD in Spain and it tells the story of El Cid, a legendary Spanish hero, who conquered the Arabs at the time when they were a major threat in the West and who thereby saved the West from becoming Islamic.

Cid is transliterated Arabic for *lord*, so El Cid means literally "the lord"—the master, the emperor, the conqueror of the world is the idea. As is usual for writers before the nineteenth century, Corneille did not invent the story; he took it bodily from an earlier source and then reworked the material, giving it his special magic.

This play was performed first in 1637. That happened to be the same year that Descartes published *Discourse on Method*. It was common in France at this time to stage medieval romances. It gave playwrights a chance to write about the unusual, the adventurous, the idealistic, the passionate; such as the feats of the knights of the past. Remember, this was the Age of Reason, the seventeenth century. So, far from being a repressed period, audiences of the time were hungry for this kind of play. And I quote from a historian: "The [seventeenth-century-French] public adored the strong man, the dominating woman, the excessive, the fantastic in art as in life. People demanded the heroic, and heroes appeared to answer the demand." In parentheses he adds: "today we are suspicious of the hero." Then he goes on: "Problems of personal honor obsessed aristocratic society. Never did the duel to the death so flourish as in those days."

A student of mine compiled this statistic: in the last ten years of Henry the Fourth's reign, four thousand young French nobles died in duels, so there is a "naturalism" to this situation.

The historian concludes his quote: "Today we find honors, scruples ridiculous. The seventeenth century would think our rejection of honor ignoble." It gives you a feeling for the period.

Although *Le Cid* represents, in a way, the traditional medieval romance, it is a highly unusual play. It was incredibly popular and inaugurated a new era in French drama because it did not just use the romantic conventions. It was filled with youthful passion and exuberance, and combined that with total mastery of the literary and dramatic form. It was an epic-making play, because it was extremely controversial. In other words, it was so free, relatively speaking, it broke a lot of the rules of the French Classicists who insisted on strict propriety on stage. For instance, when Rodrigo comes to Chimène's home at night to visit her, the critics at the time were utterly scandalized because, not only did she meet her father's murderer, she did it at her home unsupervised in the dark. You get the idea.

One more preparatory note. We have had two heavy tragedies, *Antigone* and *Othello*. So I wanted you to have a chance to see a new dramatic form. This is a form originated in France some generations earlier, but Corneille is a master at it. For the first time elements of tragedy and comedy are united and given the unwieldy name "tragicomedy." I paraphrase one commentator (His sentences are too complicated but this is his essential idea.): In comedy the characters are not heroic; they are ordinary, bourgeois, contemporary people. They generally struggle with domestic problems or the pursuit of love in such a way as to bring out the ridiculous side of their natures or contemporary customs. There is no danger of death and there is always a happy ending. That is the formula for comedy, ancient and thereafter. In tragedy, which is considered a much higher genre, the characters are heroic. They usually belong to the race of princes or are great politicians or warriors. They are often borrowed from Greek or Roman antiquity or from the Biblical past. And they are prompted by noble interests; such as political, military, dynastic and/or by the passion of love in adventures that always resolve in catastrophe.

Tragicomedy, by contrast, gives you the best of both worlds, at least if you are an Objectivist. Like tragedy, it has heroic characters pursuing noble values. They are not ridiculous; it is deadly serious. There is a danger of real loss or death but, like comedy, it has a happy ending. So the traditional dichotomy of tragedy versus comedy really rested on the malevolent universe idea: either you had serious values leading to misery, or ridiculous characters who end up happily, so their happiness was meaningless. But the common denominator was the idea that serious values must lose.

Tragicomedy is the discovery in the theater of the benevolent universe premise. It is interesting that it occurred during the Age of Reason. And *Le Cid* is a marvelous, although not perfect, example of it.

I want to offer one last preparatory warning: the play is written in French verse, with a highly complex meter and a special rhyme scheme which gives it a haunting beauty. To my knowledge, it is impossible to reproduce this in English. I have never seen a translation that even begins to capture it. Those who try to capture the rhyme in English usually do so by sacrificing the sense or the meaning to the sound of the poetry. I strongly believe that if you have to choose between meaning and poetry, you have to take meaning. Give up the poetry is my advice, if you don't know French. As great as it is, I do not know a translation which captures both the meaning and the poetry.

Read the prose version which I recommended. It still has a few extra lyrical passages, which had to go into rhyme, so you will get just a faint taste of it. Maybe someday, if you like the play enough, you can learn French and read the original—it is definitely worth learning French for and I say that with my very inadequate French. It is a very special experience to hear an expert in seventeenth-century French read this play aloud and follow the text. It is a chilling experience you simply cannot capture in English.

2. Plot-theme

My standard method is just to plunge in with something, blurt out something and then refine it. *A man is killed in a duel.* Well, that's not going to get us too far. What kind of man? Why was he killed? Who killed him? It's a dead end. This is actually historically how I got to these plot-themes—I am recreating my mental processes.

I try again. I bring the lovers in. *Two young lovers face major problems.* That's no good. What problems? Why? That's not an action situation.

So I jump to a completely different thing: *a princess gives up the man she loves because he is a commoner.* And then I think: No, that is completely beside the point because the Infanta, the princess, is a subplot. It is not essential to the action; it is dispensable to the play; it is merely a variant to help stress the theme. It is unnecessary to the plot situation or to the play; it would have been the same play without it. So we are going to drop the Infanta right now.

Let's try to get a more plausible idea. We have to get a man and his sweetheart, and a duel. How about this as a beginning? *A man kills his sweetheart's father.* Now that is better. But why does he do it? Does he do it out of fear? Does he do it out of greed to inherit? Does he want the freedom to elope? These plot-themes would all result in different plays; it is not yet a definite situation.

Let's try it like this then. *A man kills his sweetheart's father in order to defend his own honor.* That is much better. A real situation is starting to emerge. I asked myself just as a matter of logic: would it have had to be her father for it to be the same play? Theoretically, it could have been her brother or a revered teacher, someone who was a tremendous value to her. But the point is, it had to be a major value to her if we are going to have a major conflict. You would never have this play with something such as: *in order to defend his honor, a man breaks his sweetheart's china.* That would sink it; there would be no play. Theater is drama and that means, in the end, it has to be life or death. Life is irreplaceable; when it is lost, it is gone forever. *It* is what counts; *it* is what must be at stake ultimately. And that is why in tragedies they all die, because of the idea that life is the supreme value that is at stake.

We have an interesting conflict suggested. We have a man defending his honor so he would have to have some kind of noble motive, it would seem. But it is a terrible action: he is killing his sweetheart's father. So what's up? What does this mean? If you can state a plot-theme that has a mystery like that, that is already good. It's an intriguing plot situation. And ideally, if you are writing a great play, this very statement of the plot-theme should perk up your ears and say, "God, that is a situation! What's going to happen?"

I want you to notice that he is defending his honor, not his father's. Of course, factually he is defending his father's honor, too, because his father was too old to fight. But the real fact is that he is defending his own honor, because it is his obligation and his responsibility to step in at this point.

The big question now is: have we named the essence of the plot-theme by saying "to defend his honor, a man kills his sweetheart's father?" I would maintain—though this is controversial (but everything is controversial)—that this is not an exact statement of the plot-theme. We owe it to the play to make our statement as universal as possible, while retaining the specificity of a concrete action-situation. After all, we want to see if our play has a universal meaning applicable to all men and all eras, or whether it's restricted to being a period piece, good only as description of a limited era.

A great play, in my opinion, has to have a universal meaning. It has to apply to all times and places, such as the meaning of *Antigone* or *Othello*. But if we define the man's motive as defending his honor, I think that is going to be too narrow a concrete. It smacks of the feudal code, dates the play and obscures its deeper meaning. So I suggest that what is at stake here, and the proper way to formulate it, is not the man's honor but his morality. Morality is a much broader abstraction than honor: it is timeless and universal. And, it is applicable whether a feudal code is or isn't in existence.

I would therefore put the plot-theme as follows: *A man can remain moral only by killing his sweetheart's father.* This formulation dispenses with all references to feudalism, the honor code, dueling, etc. You are entitled to ask: can you really do it? Can you take this story, *Le Cid,* and set it in the twentieth century, make it revolve purely on matters of morality, with no references to an honor code, and still keep the same play with the same essence? And I say, yes you can.

I did an experiment: I took the liberty of re-conceiving *Le Cid* as a contemporary story. In fact, I got so involved in it that at one point I decided to write it and submit it to a TV network or a movie studio as a movie based on Corneille. You will see it is exactly the same story, with only the feudal material dropped. I am just going to give you a taste of my story so you see that it can be done without any problem. And it is a terrific story, I think.

Imagine two lovers today in the United States, a young woman and a young DA. She loves him because he is a crusader with a passion for justice. And he loves her because that is what she admires; it reflects her character, too. She is not satisfied with an average guy, she wants a moral hero. Then the girl's father commits a debatable action, a controversial crime. It's justifiable from one viewpoint, but dead wrong from another. Now it can't be a flat-out, unequivocal evil, because then we'd have no sympathy for the girl. Nor can it be an utterly innocent action, because if the father were purely virtuous, we would have no sympathy for the DA out to prosecute him.

So let us imagine, for instance, that the father is a medical doctor who commits euthanasia on a patient of his who is undergoing extreme suffering. He is moved by pity; he thinks the situation is hopeless and the patient just does not want to go on. Yet there is an objection to his action. He is accused of moving too soon, of acting rashly at a time when the disease was not provably fatal—and let's just say, to make the situation real, a cure is actually discovered a month later.

So we have this state of affairs. The DA, with his love of justice, is indignant at the doctor and feels that he has to prosecute him. And let's say the penalty is the death sentence: it is a capital crime to take an innocent person's life. What is the DA's dilemma? I must prosecute, but she will hate me. Well then, I can't prosecute; I'll look the other way. But then I won't be the same kind of man, I won't respect myself, and the basis of her love for me is destroyed. She'll disdain me—properly.

Meanwhile she has the same torture. Don't dare prosecute, it is my beloved father. On the other hand, you must prosecute. You are a man of justice, and that's what I love. If you default, you are going to torpedo the whole basis of our love.

So he prosecutes and wins the case. She demands revenge. He loves her and says, "I couldn't have done any differently. But I know I've killed your father, so take revenge on me, etc., etc., etc."

Now I submit this is the exact essence of Corneille's play, especially if you make the DA's own father the euthanized patient. So the DA is, in part, avenging the premature death of his own father.

At one point I was all gung ho to write this for Hollywood with due credit to Corneille. I do want you to see that this is a wonderful plot situation. (I mean Corneille's, not mine.) It is utterly brilliant and by far the most complex plot-theme that we have had so far.

The others have been very simple: a girl defies somebody, a man becomes jealous. Here we have a whole structure of conflicts deliberately constructed to milk the main conflict. And, as I say, it is not dependent on the feudal code. I can't tell you the admiration I feel for somebody who could come up with a plot situation like this because that is just as hard to do as you can imagine. And Corneille just tossed them off. I don't know how many plays he wrote. He is a tremendous person to plagiarize, if you are inclined in that direction.

I hope you see the universality of this play. I am going to follow the actual concretes and talk about honor and duels and the feudal terms, just as the play does. In essence, to enjoy this play you must be able to see the feudal situation as a symbol of a universal moral situation. If you can, you will be entirely hooked and in suspense. If you can't see it as universal, you will turn away and say, "Oh, it's old-fashioned, feudal junk and it just means nothing to me."

This is my statement of the plot-theme: *A man can remain moral only by killing his sweetheart's father.*

Observe the conflicts rife in this terrific situation. What is the major conflict? The man versus his sweetheart. Here for the first time we have the defining conflict occurring between two characters who are both one hundred percent good. That adds a lot, as you will see. Up to now we have had good versus bad, or mixed versus wicked. Now we have two good characters in mortal conflict. They are both motivated by the same inner conflict. Both of them are idealists and strong moralists. They both believe you must do the right thing no matter what; whether it is he avenging his father and killing hers, or she avenging the death of her father by him. Both are passionate lovers, who are tempted to place their love above what is right. Since their love is based on their virtue, their love will not allow them to evade virtue. So their love demands the very virtue that is going to sabotage it.

That is what I call a great situation. There is seemingly no way out. If the hero practices virtue, he loses the girl. If he doesn't, he loses her. But he is a great conquering hero and nothing can defeat him. What will he do? Can he win? How? All of that should be stirred up in you by the statement of the plot-theme, and it should show you that you are really getting into something of an immortal stature here.

3. Plot Development

I am dropping the Infanta as a mere subplot. I always drop subplots because they require much more time to go into than we have; a complete additional lecture. A subplot is a story tangential to the main story, but united by the same theme. It is like another angle on the main theme and helps to develop that theme. For our purposes, we just have to strip the subplots away.

We have three parts, as always, in plot development. First, the establishment of the situation. That takes place in Acts One and Two where we learn that Chimène and Rodrigo are in love; the two fathers quarrel; there is a slap in the face to Rodrigo's father and Rodrigo must avenge him because his father is too old to avenge himself.

We have to sympathize a bit with both sides to get into the play. You have to recognize that the honor of Chimène's father has actually been insulted by Diego's statements. In turn, Diego's bravery has been insulted by a slap in the face. Therefore by their code (which we are here respecting just as a symbol) Diego's slap has unintentionally provoked a duel. Both men, in effect, lost their temper vying to be the bravest and the most honorable. Neither is a villain; that would destroy the play. We would not, then, be able to sympathize with their defenders, their children.

To fully plant the situation, we have to add that the king is angry at their quarrel. He has decreed who is going to be the tutor, and this is defiance of his will. He says there is to be no duel. We have to plant one other thing: the dread Arabs, the Moors, are around and ten enemy vessels have been seen in the vicinity. (These are the same Moors of which Othello was a hero but this is a different time.)

The situation comes into existence as Rodrigo kills the count and Chimène demands vengeance.

The rise to the climax, the second part of the structure, starts from the beginning of Act Three and continues through Act Four, Scene Two. Rodrigo comes to Chimène to surrender. "Kill me," he says. Qua moralist he feels he deserves a medal, but qua lover he deserves to die.

In an ordinary play, that would be it. She would either say, "Oh, it's okay, I forgive you. You had good motives." or if she was bitter and modern and hostile, her psychiatrist would advise her to kill him and work out her catharsis. And that would be the end. But we are talking about a master of drama here. This is the beginning, not the end. It keeps getting worse before it gets better. This is what we call the rise in intensity. And this rise, if it is to be a great play, has to be logical, not arbitrary. So what does Corneille do?

Well, Chimène neither forgives nor kills him. She rejects the whole idea. She rejects the offer of suicide. And she says with perfect logic: you *live by the code of honor, and now* I *do. Honor demands that I see you face a worthy adversary and die properly, morally, struggling to remain alive. Otherwise your honor is insulted, and worse, my father is thereby being insulted. If you are a worthless suicide, he will have been killed by a wimp.* This is tremendously logical; it is utterly consistent with her characterization and with the basic premise of the situation.

So what is he to do now? She won't accept his life, he can't give her up and he can't have her. There is only one choice: he is going to die for her, but properly, nobly, in an even more monumental struggle for honor. The Moors are coming. Great! If I die a noble death, then I will die with my honor intact. I will have behaved well. If I win, which I am certainly going to try to do, the king will be grateful, Chimène will be overruled by the court, and maybe, just maybe, I will win over her heart.

So we go to the top of the rising action, a vast battle with the Moors which is not allowed to be shown on stage by the rules of Classicism. It would, however, be an essential part of a movie. It is total victory, full heroism. Rodrigo comes to court afterwards and the king proclaims him Le Cid; the lord, the all-conqueror. And that I think is the climax.

We know that he has to win out somehow in the end because he has achieved in action the utmost in honor. He has carried it to its ultimate form and is recognized around the world for it. And that takes place at Act Four, Scene Two.

That brings us, therefore, to the resolution, the third and last part. If this was an ordinary play, Chimène would capitulate here. She would say, "Okay, he is a great hero, a man of honor. I love him." The end. But not Chimène. She is truly a woman of iron, utterly and totally admirable. She says at this point: *I'm sorry but the Moors are irrelevant. He's a great guy, I love him, but his risks in wartime are not enough. Even if he had died in that war, it wouldn't be enough.* Remember, she is an idealist and she is concerned about avenging her father as a matter of moral principle. She doesn't want Rodrigo's death as a wimp nor as an act of glory either, in battle with the Moors. She wants his death as an acknowledged criminal. She wants him to die by execution to avenge her father, not as a great man saving his country. Of course, she also wants him not to die because she loves him. Thus, her response is absolutely torn and completely logical.

So what is the resolution to be? He is going to win somehow, but the question is how. Chimène demands a final combat with a volunteer that she hates but she hopes that he won't defeat Rodrigo. The king decrees that the winner is going to get Chimène. And that ends Act Four.

Again you think this has to be the end. Rodrigo is going to win the battle, get Chimène and achieve a happy ending. But another brilliant, breathtaking turn by Corneille. Rodrigo won't fight. He says that he won't shed her champion's blood. You see how logical again he is. After all, Chimène is in the right morally. Again he offers his life, and again she won't take it. (Voltaire said the flaw in this play is that Rodrigo offers suicide too many times.)

But Chimène remains adamant to the very end. Even when the king has ordered her to marry Rodrigo, her last words are: "Should I be the reward for what he does, and be delivered to the eternal shame of having bathed my hands in my father's blood?" In other words: marry my father's killer voluntarily? And the king mutters, "Leave it to time, your valor and your king." Curtain.

This ending is not, in my opinion, exactly perfect. In fact, it is very controversial as to how to interpret it. It is not explicit enough as to what the final state of the lovers is. Some people actually regard it as an unhappy ending, and they think the lovers will never be reunited. But I disagree with that. The vast majority of critics regard it as a happy ending, and they think it is just a matter of time before their reunion. And there are some people who think it is deliberately unresolved: that Corneille just could not go either way with it and, therefore, left it implicit and up in the air.

My first reaction on reading it was disappointment. I felt that Corneille wanted it to be a happy ending but could not, within the logic of the setup, justify or explain a happy ending. I could not imagine anything in logic that could ever satisfy Chimène. It seemed she had to see him dead or she would just never be satisfied. And, therefore, I felt at first that he left it unresolved with merely a suggestion that they would be happy later. In other words, I took it as a weakness in the ending. He was unable to deliver the happy ending which his structure called for but which logic seemed to prohibit.

But I have since strongly moderated my original reaction. In talking with several French scholars that I respect very much, I have been universally told that Corneille, if he were resurrected, would answer the logic issue. They explain that English does not make it as clear as the seventeenth-century French does (on which I can't comment), but I know that it is possible for something to be untranslatable. Corneille's answer would be: Rodrigo in the final page of the play is being given a mission of atonement for having killed the count. This mission is aimed specifically at glorifying the count. In other words, he is undertaking the conquest of the entire world in the name of the count's memory and as a tribute or monument to the count. If he is successful, he will have avenged the count, made him an illustrious name in Spanish history and therefore freed Chimène of the need for further vengeance.

On this theory the reason that the play ends without a final embrace on stage—which I always strongly feel the need of in any type of play—is that Rodrigo has to do a year of military battle before they can reconcile. By one of the Classicist conventions at the time, a play had to elapse within exactly twenty-four hours. Corneille was not allowed to stage a scene occurring a year later, so he had to leave it off-stage.

This viewpoint, put forth by French scholars that I respect, seems plausible to me now and makes the ending substantially better than I first thought. But I have to confess that I still feel that, inherent in the theme which we will be discussing shortly, there is a conflict that cannot really be resolved. And this contributes to the uneasiness of the ending. As much as Corneille wants to, there are philosophic reasons why he cannot bring the two permanently and happily together. I just can't imagine Chimène, adamant and logical as she is, dropping the issue of honor even if Rodrigo defeats the entire world for her father and places placards everywhere. There is an inherent clash there, never fully, finally solved. That is an unsatisfactory note to me. I grant a happy ending, mostly explained, but a residual logical doubt about the structure and the characterization, and a deeper feeling on my part that there is a philosophic explanation for this residual hesitancy.

4. Characterization

How many indispensable characters are there? You really need the pretext for the situation, which is the father who gets killed off. But in terms of enduring characters, there are really only two, and those are the two lovers. The father is just an excuse to get the war going.

I want to develop the theme I mentioned earlier, that both of these characters are completely good. They both have enormous stature: they are strong, admirable, heroic. There is not an evil character in this play.

It's fascinating to me that it developed in this way given the benevolent universe intention of the play, because the conflict is between the good and the good.

That same principle animates all of Ayn Rand's novels. She, of course, has highly developed, evil characters but she always said that the essential conflict in her novels is between the good characters. For instance, in *The Fountainhead* between Roark and Dominique or between Roark and Wynand, not between Roark and Keating or Roark and Toohey; or in *Atlas Shrugged* between Galt and Dagny over the strike. Or Galt versus Dagny and Rearden, not Galt versus Wesley Mouch. She always insisted that in her novels the key conflict was between the good, and that is what gave such a powerful sense of a clean benevolent universe: that both sides of the central conflict were admirable. So you came away with the sense of the cleanliness and stature of men fighting for their values. As against having the whole focus and essence of the novel as Roark versus Keating. What metaphysical power that would have given Keating—and the same if it were Galt versus Mr. Thompson.

Here Corneille and Ayn Rand are in exactly the same esthetic position, in contrast to Shakespeare who could not dream of a situation of that type. For instance, Iago is just the antithesis of that. What conveys the enormous malevolence is that the potent force in the conflict is depravity.

Here the two characters are utterly innocent, seventeenth-century French romantics and it completely changes the universe.

Continuing with characterization, the essence of their conflict is: their love versus morality. Notice that it is not, I repeat *it is not*, a conflict between mind and body. It is not physical love for a slut versus spiritual love of virtue. If you thought it was the mind-body dichotomy, you might as well throw out the play and resign from the course because that misses it utterly—and that's putting it mildly.

Each of these characters has a spiritual love of the other as the fundamental, and, of course, they want to sleep with each other as an expression of that. So it is an integrated, mind-body love of each other as against the demands of morality on both of them. You can put it this way: it is love of virtue as against love of the other person, who is the human embodiment of virtue. Both sides of the conflict, in both characters, are noble. Both of the things each of them want are good—and, therefore, it is an agony that they should be in conflict with each other.

Corneille's great achievement was the intensity of the conflict he was able to dramatize. I would like to make a quick aside here on conflict in general because it is a defining characteristic of greatness in the theater; in literature more broadly, but certainly in the theater. That is why I always stress: what is the conflict? A play without conflict is nothing, you might as well throw it out. Conflict means value-clash, and that's what leads to excitement, to suspense. Who will win? That is what justifies the very name *drama* for this form.

Value, particularly if we are speaking of an all-positive context of good characters, implies a real valuer: a man or woman of purpose, stature, strength. In other words, conflict developed like this implies man as a hero; the very kind of man that can fight for his values and remain true to them no matter what the conflict, no matter what the obstacles. And this is precisely what Corneille specializes in presenting.

If we studied this play one point at a time, there is conflict everywhere; the same kind of grand-scale conflict on the major and minor characters alike. The Infanta, the subplot, has that. Rodrigo's father has the conflict: *I must fight, but I can't.* Chimène's father has that conflict. Rodrigo and Chimène, of course, have it. It is not that the same conflict is repeated boringly over and over. No, it is presented in many variants; all, one way or another, stressing virtue versus love or sometimes even versus life. We will come back to that.

To develop further the characterization, let us ask of the two leads in conflict here: who is the strongest? Who is the real protagonist? Usually you can go by the title of a play but not always. For instance, Iago is definitely stronger than Othello and is the mover of the action. I think that here you can make a case that the strongest one is really Chimène. She is not given as much action, and therefore, it is not really her play. I mean, you have to consider that Rodrigo defeats the Moors and the whole world. You can't get more action than that. But Chimène is not merely a character in love. She has a whole moral perspective and is willing to take on the king and the entire country. It is her rock-hard adamancy that really drives the action. Rodrigo conquers the world, he lays it at her feet, he offers his life to her over and over and he still can't satisfy her. So he is mighty strong, but I think she has an edge in sheer tenacity of will.

You decide later, when you are going over your assignment, who is stronger: Antigone or Chimène. (Desdemona doesn't even enter the picture.) I happen, for reasons which will undoubtedly baffle you, to like plays which have strong women in them. You are going to get yet another one, besides these two. But to decide between Antigone and Chimène is already a problem of objectivity.

I am discussing these two characters together because they have the same character. I want you to note that, as passionate as they are, they are the opposite of whim-worshippers or emotionalists. This is the Age of Reason and these characters reason out what to do at each stage of their dilemma. What is so fascinating is that you see them reasoning onstage, logically wrestling with their crises.

Take any modern play where the hero—if you can call him a hero—does something. Why did you do it? "I don't know, I just felt that way" is the most they can say, if they can even get to such a crude question as why. Contrast that with the syllogisms flowing on the stage before the action. He is figuring out: if this, then this; if this, then this and this, but what about that? On top of that, even in English, the translation is beautiful.

I am going to give you a few randomly chosen excerpts here, one from Rodrigo and then from Chimène. I want you to notice the passion of these characters, the agony of the conflict, the beauty—so far as it comes across in English. Above all, observe the logic, as they confront their dilemma and try to figure out what to do.

In Act One, Scene Three (page twelve of the book I assigned), note the eloquence and simplicity of Rodrigo, just before he duels with Chimène's father: "A war is in my heart. Against my honor now my love takes part. I must avenge a father, lose my love. One fires my courage, one puts out the flame. The dreadful choice is to betray my love or live in shame. An infinite harm both courses now present. O, God, the dreadful pain! Must an insult have no punishment? Must I punish the father of Chimène?"

This man is fabulous. "Father, mistress; love, fame; . . . My fame will tarnish or my pleasure die. One brings me misery, the other shame. . . . Better by far to die. . . . To die unsatisfied!"

He goes on in this vein and he finally decides logically that his debt is to his father. This is volitionally what is up to him to do. He is going to avenge his father and suffer the consequences. Once he realizes it, he is "ashamed that I have wavered for so long. Let me not stay in pain, because today my father suffered wrong. His injurer the father of Chimène." You see? So he's off.

In Act Three, Scene One (this starts on page twenty-nine) Chimène has just learned of her father's death. "Eyes, weep your fill, and drown yourselves in tears! Half of my life has put into the grave the other half." That is an immortal line. "Half of my life"—her lover—"has put into the grave the other half"—her father. If you can write one line like that, it does not matter what the rest of the play is, you will survive.

"So that I must avenge, after this deed, what I have lost on what remains to me." But a dilemma—"What can I hope for, except an eternal torment, if I must pursue a crime and love the criminal?" You see the incredible clarity; it is like it is written in flashing diamonds.

Later she says, "Despite my passion which resists my anger, I will do all I can to take revenge. But yet despite the strictness of my duty, my sole wish is that I accomplish nothing." Now that is what you call an inner conflict.

Observe that the Infanta at one point tells Chimène to cool it; in essence, telling her that it is more noble to self-sacrifice than to pursue personal vengeance. Her exact words are: "It is yet more noble to give up personal vengeance to the public interest." You obey the king now, cut this out, and think of the well-being of your country. Just sacrifice yourself a little for the public welfare, and stop thinking only of your own revenge and your own concerns. But Chimène is unyielding: *it's MY father, MY honor, MY love.* In other words, there is a pronounced selfish quality to both sides of the characters' dilemma. Their sense of honor is not presented as a demand for selflessness on their part. On the contrary, they are presented as having a true hero's love of morality for selfish reasons, as a goal and expression of their personal nature. By the same token, the playwright doesn't sneer at their love on the grounds that it is personal and selfish. It is not a conflict between altruism on one side and egoism on the other side. It is a conflict between two selfish loves: the love of honor or the honor of love.

There is implicitly a very selfless element in this play. But what I am telling you now is that it is only implicit. Explicitly, it is not there.

Rodrigo and Chimène are two examples of what has been called—and it is a common term in scholarship now—a Cornelian hero, the hero as presented by Corneille. The essence of the Cornelian hero is that he is a self-made man and a being of iron will; not only free will, but the capacity for tremendous courage, passion and rational judgment. Corneille's heroes have great self-esteem, but they exert Herculean effort to deserve it and maintain it in the face of tremendous obstacles.

I am going to give you a few quotes from commentators, so you will see how widely recognized this aspect of Corneille is. That will perhaps explain to you why you never hear of Corneille anymore; not in the theater, not in colleges, not in the movies. He is absolutely non-existent. One obscure commentator that I dug out of the library stacks says, "Fortified by their own energies, the Cornelian heroes have nothing to fear at the hands of destiny. They will parry its blows or bear them uncomplainingly. Fate may dog their steps, but for them it is powerless to force an entry into their hearts and alter their resolve. Man is entirely free and fully responsible."

In 1963, Robert J. Nelson wrote a book on the Cornelian hero, *Corneille: His Heroes and Their Worlds*. It is a mixture—like many good books—of excellent things and nonsense, in consecutive sentences. The whole trick is to figure out which is which. You remember Ayn Rand's definition of value: that which one acts to gain and keep. And you remember the essential argument against altruism: life depends on achieving value, not sacrificing it. Here Nelson gives Corneille's definition of value: "Value in Corneille is something to be realized not denied." Nelson knows nothing about Objectivism, of course, but talk about Objectivism centuries before.

Later he writes this: "Corneille's heroes are always on their best behavior, for this is the only kind of behavior of which they are capable." Here is the true Romanticist credo, taken from Aristotle and practiced by Corneille in the seventeenth century, at least two hundred years before Hugo and the other avowed Romanticists. "Corneille shows men, not only as they ought to be, but also as they might be, as they would be, as they could be, and as they have to be." And he means *have to* morally, not deterministically.

It struck me in working on these lectures that there are four great thinkers/artists through the ages—and only four that I can think of— that have been united, whatever their differences, by the view of man as a hero, and specifically a hero unafraid of the gods or society; completely self-willed and master of his destiny. Those four through all of Western history are: Aristotle, with "the great-souled man"; Corneille, with the Cornelian hero; Nietzsche, with what we call "the superman." You should note, by the way, that Nietzsche was personally influenced, partly directly and partly indirectly, by Corneille's individualism and hero-worship as against the enshrinement of mediocrity. Nietzsche is often referred to as a disciple of Corneille. So I say there are four: Aristotle, Corneille, Nietzsche and, of course, Ayn Rand.

I think you see more fully why I chose Corneille and why I think it would be a tragedy for you to go through your life without knowing a playwright of such enormous value.

5. Theme

But—shifting gears—he is not an Objectivist and he has problems working out his plays and his characters because of this. That brings us first to his theme. We are now getting into murkier waters, more unpleasant waters.

What is the direct message of *Le Cid*? The primacy of honor or, if you want to take the more universal view, the primacy of morality. I'll use those as interchangeable for this discussion. So, the superiority of honor or virtue over even the noblest, most spiritual love and even over life itself. Rodrigo describes himself in the third person in Act Five and captures the whole theme. This is what he wants posterity to remember: "to avenge his honor once he lost his love; to avenge his mistress he has quitted life." In other words, he sincerely offered suicide. "Preferring, whatever hope had ruled his soul, his honor to Chimène, Chimène to life." And that is the theme: the primacy of honor over love and even over life itself.

A sympathetic French scholar writes: "Here is a world in which personal honor is not a chemical reaction of gland secretions, but a self-instituted, self-administered rule of life. A world in which nothing—not even life and love—is so precious as one's honor as a man."

So the clash, as we said, is love versus honor. Spiritual love, with its appropriate physical expression in sex, versus spiritual honor with its appropriate physical action. The question I want to ask you is: how can you explain such a clash between love and virtue? We have already established that it is not a clash between mind and body. If it is not a clash between mind and body, how can there be a clash between love and virtue?

You might think that perhaps Corneille holds that love is irrational, that it is inherently capricious. We already know that is not true because their love is founded on their perception of the virtues of the other person. But just to hammer this point home: Corneille does not agree with Odes Three and Four of *Antigone* or with Shakespeare's view of love in *Othello*. He does not believe that love is irrational. The whole seventeenth century, especially in France, rejected the idea that there was a dichotomy between love and reason. This was the Age of Reason and Corneille believed with his century that love is an expression and consequence of one's moral evaluation.

One scholar pointed out that there was something in common in the Cornelian psychology and the Cartesian philosophy; namely, the intellectualistic conception of love. By that he means that love must be tied to the knowledge of the merit of the loved object. Then he gives two ringing formulas in French that capture this. "It is impossible to love what one does not value." And the other famous one: "Love never takes to itself contemptible things, but always that which is rarest, most valued, and most exalted." This is the literal antithesis of Christianity, of the idea: love your enemy, love weakness and love need. This is the idea of loving value, and it was the formal view of the French in the seventeenth century.

For Corneille it is an act of intellect, an evaluation according to a code of values, which produces and justifies love. In other words, love is an expression of reason. So the conflict is not between love and reason nor is it between love and sacrificial duty.

So it is really baffling to try to put your finger on what the conflict is. It is between two kinds of love; love of virtue in oneself, and love of the very same virtue in one's beloved. That is a puzzle as a theme. How can virtue come in conflict with a rational love of virtue in your partner? Or to put this another way, from this viewpoint, how can love of virtue in oneself (that's what honor is) come in conflict with love of virtue in another (which is what falling in love is)? You see, you have a real intellectual problem here to understand this theme. To understand it is to penetrate into the essence of Corneille's official philosophic thought.

The first thing to notice here is that under Objectivism this theme would be impossible. Literally impossible. You could not write a play on this theme. I hope you are not confused by the modern play I invented at the start, because that play hinges entirely on our ignorance of scientific facts. That is why we can be morally ambivalent about the doctor. We don't really know—even if I say that a future cure is possible—how much effort it would take to cure the patient or how much future pain on his part a cure would entail. Is there really objective proof that a cure is possible? How much has the man already suffered? How old is he? What is *his* preference? There are a dozen other things I deliberately blurred and left out. But once all the facts are known, the doctor in my story would come out either right or wrong. It would be clear-cut, and that would be the end of the story. The whole conflict in my contemporary version rested on our ignorance of certain medical facts.

In Corneille, however, the conflict does not rest on ignorance but is inherent in morality itself. The conflict is fundamental; the same issue dominates all of his plays. He believes, in some way, that, in pursuit of morality, you will necessarily clash with others, even though they pursue and embody the very same morality. In other words, morality is an ideal for which rational heroes have a selfish passion, and yet it often unavoidably leads to agony and even tragedy.

6. Philosophy

How do you explain this kind of conflict? Obviously it depends on the content and deeper context of your code of morality. To understand Corneille's theme, we need to look more broadly at his wider philosophy.

Let us start here with an analysis of the concept of honor, which is his symbol of morality. So far I have taken the term loosely as pride in your virtue, but we have to be more specific. What values, according to Corneille, comprise honor? What specifically should you take pride in? What virtues in content make a man moral?

I did a fair amount of research, and my own analysis of the meaning of honor for Corneille involves three unidentified components, each basically different from the other two, and all put together by Corneille and commentators alike as one big package without analysis or distinction.

First of all there is an objective component in which Corneille agrees with Aristotle and with Objectivism: honor involves pride, self-esteem, strength of purpose and will, and rationality. All of that is obviously to the good. But these are abstractions, and they leave open what specific moral code to follow. You are supposed to have strength of purpose—fine, but what kind of things should you take as your purpose? You are supposed to have strength of will—but what should you direct your will toward achieving? So all of these are generalities which acquire meaning only in conjunction with something more specific.

That brings us to the second element that comes under honor. And here, unfortunately, we have to say, without resorting to symbols, that Corneille in *Le Cid* does accept the feudal code. Remember, he has just come out of the feudal period and he is a strong moralist. Christianity is weakened but he needs a feeling that there are still strong moral principles. And he, like Shakespeare, did not know where to find them. Shakespeare gave up, some others turned society into God. But Corneille did it by looking to the feudal period.

To him, morality was a series of commandments binding on an individual, because they flow from the class in which he was born. For instance, the Infanta's dilemma: she can't marry outside of her class. That is simply a categorical imperative. If she does, she demeans her honor. Another such categorical imperative is: you must duel to the death if you are insulted. There is a whole set of these, if you know the feudal period.

How do you know that you are supposed to follow these? They are not revelations from God. How do you know? It is in your blood. In other words, there is a definite element of biological determinism here. It is not sufficient to be born into a noble caste to be moral, according to this viewpoint. But it is necessary. If you are not born into a noble caste, then you don't have these inner imperatives of how you must behave. And, in fact, they wouldn't be applicable to you. You then act the way the peasants act or some other division acts. But if you are born into the nobility, your choice is to obey the feudal code which springs from your high birth—or to flout it and be ignoble.

So, sadly to say, for all of his stress on self-assertion, when you push him to the wall, the Cornelian hero does not survey the universe independently and choose his values by his own independent, rational judgment. He is born obligated to obey a set of commandments, which he had no part in choosing. And this is a tremendous and tragic limitation on his autonomy.

The third factor in the package-deal (which is not emphasized, but *is* there) is that honor also involves the opinion of others, your status in their eyes, what they will think of your behavior. You notice how the characters are concerned with how posterity will remember them. Here is a trinity tossed off in the play as though they were just three synonyms: his dignity, his reputation, his honor. Could you say Roark is concerned for his dignity, his reputation, his honor? It is really fantastic to stick "reputation" in there.

So you see that *honor* is what we would have to call a huge package-deal. It includes many good, real virtues plus some arbitrary commands plus social approval. Or, putting it more broadly and using terms that I think you are familiar with as Objectivists: to have honor you must practice certain objective virtues, you must follow many intrinsicist commands, and you also have to gain subjective social approval. What we have here is a mixture of the objective, the intrinsic and the subjective that no one but an Objectivist could even untangle.

If this is your package-deal approach to morality, you obviously have plenty of room for conflict within and between individuals. Arbitrary commandments are necessarily going to clash at some point with the requirements of survival and reason. If honor involves intrinsicist commands, then to that extent the individual must place something above life and reason: he must be obedient to those commands. That is the very opposite of self-assertion or individuality. He has to, in effect, do what his socio-economic class at birth dictates. Period. If we toss in that he also has to gain posterity's approval, it is still worse. The self that he is asserting turns into Peter Keating.

So we have a tragic mixture here: a selfish, individualistic passion for morality defined dominantly in feudal social terms. Here again you see what happens to a noble mind and soul without a moral code. There is no Christianity anymore—and there is nothing else. What to do? They just don't know. And that is the downfall time after time, before Christianity and Sophocles, and after—the desperate need for a moral code to implement their exalted sense of life. And they can't do it because they don't have it.

I want to make sure that you understand here the contrast between Corneille's view and Objectivism. I'll put the question to you this way. Would John Galt ever say: my honor is more precious than my life? Using those terms, he would say, "Life is impossible without honor." In other words, virtue for him is a means of survival. It is not a form of bravery that may defy your own safety.

Corneille, for all of his selfishness, does end up, despite himself, saying: sacrifice. He says, in effect, sacrifice your life as necessary for the sake of obedience to an arbitrary code imposed on you. That idea is clearly at war with the individualistic, moral self-assertiveness of his better intention.

You can probably understand and not be surprised to know that Corneille was born Catholic and he was a good Catholic all his life. His plays never got him in trouble with the Church. He was accepted as a good Catholic, despite his utter repudiation of Original Sin and his heroic view of man. I think you see now that there is enough of an element of intrinsicism and of sacrifice in Corneille so that he was not regarded as a threat to his religion. You see how he struggled to combine his Catholicism with his individualism.

Let me ask you to be sure the contrast is clear. What is the proper Objectivist response to a slap in the face? Is it a duel? It is not a lawsuit—that's the American response to everything. What is the one word that you would have to say if I asked, "What is the proper response to a slap in the face?" Context; what is the context? What if it is Francisco and Rearden? The proper response of the one slapped is to turn away and say, "Within your knowledge, you are right." Or the proper response, if he is bigger than you, might be to run for your life. Or call the police, etc. But there is obviously no absolute mandate that you must avenge your honor even if it leads to your death, which is the feudal idea, the intrinsicist idea. On that kind of premise everyone's honor is a danger to everyone else. For example, I get mad at something you did. Well, that's to my credit. You insulted me, and I have the honor to protest. Then I strike you as retaliation, which is honorable. And you demand a duel, which is honorable. In other words, every falling-out or heated disagreement entails the ultimate death of one of the participants.

On this view you can certainly believe that there has to be conflict among individuals, all of whom cherish and practice the same moral code. This is why I feel that the ending of Le Cid is, unfortunately, oblique or, at best, implicit because the underlying philosophy doesn't lead to a happy ending.

Here is the paradox of Corneille: the play situation is so complex, the obstacles to true love are so diabolical, that it would kill the play if the lovers simply gave in and separated. So, for drama, they have to win out. On the other hand, the philosophy which sets up the situation doesn't really allow them to win out. Corneille is trapped between his own drama and sense of life on the one hand and the logic of his implicit theme on the other. That explains the peculiarly mild, implicit, somewhat ambiguous ending.

Now, just a few concluding remarks on Corneille's philosophy. On the one hand, he is a strong champion of what we could call the benevolent universe. As one of the commentators puts it: "He wants to inspire in his audiences, not fear or pity, but hope and admiration." To this extent, he is the opposite of a Catholic believing in Original Sin. But, in total, he is torn between religion and this earth; between man, the pawn of destiny (in the case of this play it is not God, but socio-economic fate) and man, the self-directed hero.

In this broad sense you could properly compare Corneille to Sophocles. You can't compare him to Shakespeare, because Shakespeare gave up all hope of man as a self-directed hero. He just wrote it off so he has no real conflict. But Corneille, like Sophocles, is still fighting for human dignity, but hasn't broken through to a code of values that would make it consistently possible.

Here is his philosophy in a nutshell: man is a hero, the universe is benevolent, reason is our guide, passion is its expression, morality is a supreme value. However, he has no code of morality except fierce pride in obeying a package-deal, resting ultimately on sacrifice and social status. I think of him like a bird born to soar, actually soaring and fighting to stay aloft, but with a broken wing. I think he is happier than Sophocles, thanks to the Renaissance; that he is less dominated by God but philosophically he still has a very long journey to travel. Despite this, however, Corneille is capable of affording immense pleasure and inspiration, if you read his works, which I hope you will.

Q & A

Q: Was Ayn Rand inspired by Corneille as she was by Hugo?

A: Well, I don't know her own knowledge of or reaction to Corneille. I think, from her extensive education combined with the fact that she read and spoke French fluently, that she would be familiar with him. And I don't believe she would disagree with anything that I said. But, if I regret anything in my life, it is thirty years of incredibly long conversations with her in which I never discussed theater, only philosophy. So it's not fair for me to ascribe to her what I don't personally know.

She did not have Corneille in her works in French in her library. But she had a tremendous education in Russia. For instance, she read all of Shakespeare in Russian before she left Russia. Everything. So I wouldn't be the least bit surprised if she knew Corneille.

I never knew that she liked *Monna Vanna* during her lifetime. I found out just by accident through her correspondence. We had a very delimited relationship. I always came in with a hundred philosophic questions. And then there were the hundred questions that those questions generated. I really regret that I never found that out.

I know what I would ask her second, if she came back to life, and it would be about the theater. The first thing I'd ask her is what she thought of my book on Objectivism.

Q: Do you see a similarity between the endings of *Le Cid* and *Night of January 16th* in terms of their ambiguity?

A: No, I don't, because the ending of *Night of January 16th* is deliberately left to the audience to decide. They're supposed to use their sense of life to interpret what went on. So the evidence is deliberately left equally balanced, and the verdict is up to you to decide. That's a stunt. That's not a philosophic ambiguity on her part.

This is a different thing. Corneille's heart wants him to have them come onstage after all of it, with a final embrace, a huge kiss and a fading into the sunset. And the problem is he can't do it—partly because he's not allowed to keep them on stage that long. Secondly, I don't think they're allowed to kiss onstage. Thirdly, because he has the philosophic problems that he can't fully resolve. So he has a problem as an author. It's not a stunt.

Q: I am casting myself in the role of a Cornelian hero here, because I do have a criticism of your critique. And despite the slings and arrows that are likely to rain down upon me, I just want to express this. My problem is this. You made the comment that all the characters, within the terms of the time, were good. I question that, because there's no mention here about Rodrigo's father being a quadriplegic, they just mention that he was old. The point here is that he could have fought—but he would have lost. Further, what he then does is put his own kid in the front line instead of fighting and losing, despite the fact that he knows that his son's love for Chimène would be irretrievably damaged, however it turns out. So the points are: one, the father was not a good character under the terms of his own time, because he won't fight because he'll lose; and two, if that point's conceded, then how to proceed from there?

A: All right, I won't rain down arrows on you for that question, but I would regard that as a textbook example of what I would call pettifogging—that is, taking a tiny and highly debatable point and turning it into an essential.

As I interpret it—and undoubtedly Corneille does—the father is really too old to fight with dignity. Remember, it does not satisfy the code to strap him, teetering from Alzheimer's, onto the back of a horse and run him through. That would be farce. He's got to have enough vitality so he can put up a fight. And this is a young, strapping, new right-hand man of the king. It would be so unbalanced that it would be a violation of the feudal code for him to do it. So he's put in the position that it is just beyond him.

Having said all this, I have to say that it really is a trifling point. Because we simply have to get to the point where the son has to do it. And I think the father makes very clear that he would do anything if he could.

Maybe this is the place to invoke the fact that these are meant to be acted, not read. What I am doing, basically, is reading aloud the score to a concerto or a symphony. And I'm saying, "A flat follows B minor," and so on and so on, rather than playing the music for you, because I have no orchestra. And that's all we can do in this course. My title is "Seven Great Plays as Literature and as Philosophy," not as *theater* because we can't act them out. So it's like great scores but not as music.

If this thing is properly acted, then this gentleman has to be cast so that the contrast between the two would be such that you don't have to wonder if he's a coward or whatever. It becomes obvious, by looking at this old, gray-haired man, bent over and so on, that he couldn't possibly engage in combat.

Let me now raise a question. This is something I cut from the lecture, but happily there's time to put it back in. I want to be sure that you make a clear distinction between identifying somebody's philosophy and evaluating the philosophy from the point of view of Objectivism. In other words, there's a big difference between naming the philosophical theme of a play and evaluating that theme from the point of view of Objectivism.

The philosophic theme of a play is an objective fact. It's the same for everyone regardless of their philosophy. The evaluation of that theme will vary from person to person, according to what the evaluator's philosophy is. Now I want to show you on this very play why you must not mix these up. Otherwise you'll never have an objective interpretation of a play. You'll have only "the play as interpreted by Ayn Rand" or "the play as interpreted by St. Augustine" or "the play as interpreted by Kant"—but not the play.

Now if you don't have the play, that means there is no interpretation; that everyone is living in his own interpretation. That means there is no reality. In this play, for instance—to make it very brief—Corneille presents a partly intrinsicist code and an unresolved ending. Let's just take those two points. His explicit message is: honor comes above life. Now that much is entirely objective, it's not a matter of interpretation.

Now comes interpretation from your own philosophy. Let me give you three different interpretations with identical facts; with complete agreement on the theme and the problem of the ending. One: an Objectivist watches this play and says, as I did in the class, "Well, it's the intrinsicist element in his moral code which leads him to uncertainty and potential malevolence."

In my preliminary seminar, I deliberately included some non-Objectivists because I wanted to get a feeling for the reaction to these plays among people who weren't Objectivists. A gentleman who I very highly respect and like, who is in his own way a relativist said, "The trouble with Corneille (and the reason we had this long discussion about the ending) is his absolutism, which is causing the problem with his ending. Because absolutism is just not applicable in reality; it's impracticable. And that's why the characters just can't resolve the situation at the end." Now you see, I would never dream to come up with that interpretation, but that is a legitimate interpretation if relativism is a correct philosophy.

We still agree on what the theme of the play is; what the problems of the play are. But now he comes in with an entirely different philosophic explanation. And I had to say, "Well, I disagree with your explanation because I disagree with your philosophy but we agree on the facts about the play." So I am not saying that your interpretation is subjective or arbitrary. But I am saying, you have to keep an absolute line in your mind: what does Corneille represent? what does he say? what is his theme? versus, what do I, as an Objectivist, think of it? And how do I interpret the flaws and virtues that it makes possible? You have to know whether you are identifying his thought or yours. And if you don't keep that line clear, you have no hope of ever reaching an objective assessment of a play.

Now there are other interpretations. For instance, if we brought St. Augustine in, then I have no doubt that if we watched this play and asked him how he would explain the ending, he would say, "How do you ever expect people to achieve happiness or fulfillment if you ignore God? This is a completely secular play; of course they are going to end up frustrated and unhappy." You see what I mean? Here again he would see the same theme, the same events, but he would have a completely different interpretation.

This kind of disagreement does not show that you can't know the objective analysis of a play. But it does show that to do it, you have to know the facts first and keep your evaluation distinct.

Having said that, I'm going to ask you a question that I was asked in the preliminary class, which really blew my head off. I mean, I really couldn't believe this question. So I hope the person who asked this doesn't hear this on the tape. But this is the question I was asked, and I wanted to be one hundred percent sure that everyone in this room understands the fatal error in this question. It's on this very same point of the distinction between the play and your interpretation of it.

This was the question. We had just done Shakespeare, and then Corneille—just as we've done here. He said, "Shakespeare said that morality is irrelevant to life. Corneille says that morality leads to agonizing conflict and possibly tragedy. Can we not then conclude that Shakespeare and Corneille agree philosophically? Because, after all, if morality can lead to conflict and tragedy, who needs it? For life's purposes, it's irrelevant."

Did you get that question? Shakespeare said that morality is irrelevant. Corneille said that it leads to conflict and probably tragedy. Well, if so, who needs it? So practically speaking, for Corneille, morality is just as irrelevant as it is for Shakespeare, and therefore Corneille and Shakespeare agree philosophically. They have the same theme and the same viewpoint.

I just fell out of my chair when that question was asked. I never heard such a disastrous question. Now why is that bad? I don't mean morally bad, but what is the tremendous error of that question?

He's combining two different views—two opposite views—by the fact that, from the point of view of Objectivism, they're ultimately going to lead to the same thing. But that is completely unfair. He is making their thought something that you can't grasp except through the Objectivist Categories. And that amounts to saying: There are only two themes in world literature or in all thought—Ayn Rand and everybody else. You know, that's just like the mentality of the guy who burned the ancient Alexandrian library on the grounds that if it's in the Koran it's superfluous and if it's not it's heretical, so get rid of it. He just burned everything. Now that is dogmatism to the core.

What I'm trying to show you is that you have to appreciate, if you read this play, that Corneille does not sneer at morality, Shakespeare does. Corneille thinks it's the primary value to which men should aspire and Shakespeare says "what fools these mortals be." Corneille reveres virtue above all else and wants a world where virtue is rewarded which is the opposite of Shakespeare, who presents morality as utterly impotent—any morality, any virtue or any vice on the part of any character.

It's a completely distinct fact that Corneille's moral code doesn't work, that it isn't practical. And you, from the outside, can say, "Well, his code, since it doesn't work, is going to lead people to the idea that morality is irrelevant. So he is going to inadvertently, unknowingly, end up giving support to Shakespeare." That's your side commentary, as an Objectivist commentator. But this is utterly different from saying, "this is Corneille's meaning or message." Do you get this point? It's very, very important that you not make this error.

Q: Without the package-deal of honor, wouldn't there have to be far less conflict in this story?

A: Yes.

Q: If that is the case, what would it do to the hypothetical modern version of this story?

A: Well, that's a very good question. If I did this play—the modern one—without the package-deal of *honor*, where would I get all the conflict from? Well, as I said, all the conflict hinges on ignorance. And the problem would have to be creating an emergency situation where they have to act without the knowledge available to them. But that is what would diminish the play. And the thing that actually stopped me from finally doing it was that it would lose a very significant resonance or universality. It would become a kind of odd case. You know, what happens in a crisis? It could be exciting and so on, but it would not have—that I could see—a universal theme. Because as soon as I tried to make a universal theme out of that clash, what would I be clashing with? I couldn't make it "love versus honor." And if it's "love versus justice," the resolution, in Objectivist terms, would have to finally be: well, what are the facts? When the facts come out, then justice and love have to point in the same direction. If he's innocent, then don't prosecute him, and they should love each other. If he's guilty, then you have to prosecute him, and the woman has to say, "my father is guilty of a crime; I don't hold up for his vengeance just because he's my father."

So in that sense, if you held an Objectivist code, on this situation even as modernized, you could only get away with it by making it an emergency and withholding the final resolution or the facts from the audience. And that would blunt the importance of your message. That's one of the things that stopped me. It would be like a gimmick that you could get away with for TV, you see. I never thought of it as going as far as the movies. It would be like one of those *Twilight Zone* episodes; you know, where you have a twist and then fade-out. It would be a thirty-minute thing and if you tried to drag it out too long, you'd be sunk by your own problem.

So that's a very intelligent question. That's what happens to you when you try to adapt somebody's play to your own terms. I only did it to show you that there is a wider meaning, but to actually carry it out is a different thing.

Q: What is the philosophical origin of this intensive personal code of honor?

A: What do you mean by *personal*? You mean the feudal idea? He's asking me for the philosophic origin of this idea of honor. Now you don't mean personal honor in the sense that Aristotle or the Roman heroes had a definite code of honor. We're talking about the feudal sense of honor.

That goes back to the breakup of the ancient world, inherent in the very dichotomy between noble and commoner, which did not exist in the ancient world. They had master and slave in the ancient world, but they did not have noble versus peasant or noble versus commoner. That distinction actually originated in the breakup of the ancient world, when the barbarian tribes were pouring in. Law and order had basically collapsed. And your only way of survival was to ally yourself with some powerful warrior—powerful strictly in terms of the number of horses and men and muscle he could put on his side. And they came to be regarded as noble strictly by courtesy of physical brutality. If you were the physical champion, you were the lord. And if you were dependent on him, you were just the commoner.

And that distinction of nobility and superior class actually goes back to physical warfare for survival. So what we call noble is the most materialistic of concepts, in the crude physicalistic sense, in terms of its historical origin.

The nobility you get many centuries later, when it's hallowed and sanctified by the Church and you mix into it that they don't do any work, and they're educated, etc., takes on a different and higher meaning. But actually the philosophic origin of the concept of a sense of honor as a nobleman goes back to the lowest brutality.

Q: The hero killing the heroine's father takes place very early in the play, and it's the action that sets up the conflict that occurs between the two main characters for the rest of the play. Why do you state the plot-theme in terms of that original action, which more or less just sets up the situation?

A: Well, because that's what a plot-theme does. The purpose of a plot-theme is not to tell you what happens, but to tell you the situation. The plot-theme is not a summary of the action. The plot-theme is: what is the central action conflict? What is the kind of event on which the play revolves?

Now in this case the situation is precisely: he has to kill her father to retain his morality. Whether we put in the plot-theme "he does kill the father" or "he has to kill the father" doesn't make any difference. Because the action follows immediately on the decision, and then the whole play revolves around that action. You see what I mean? The whole play actually begins from the moment when she says: *My God, he killed my father.* And he says: *My God, I killed her father.* And then they go from there.

Let me put it to you another way. The fact that something is early does not disqualify it from being a plot-theme. The plot-theme has to be established at the beginning. And therefore, in every case that I can think of, a major event must take place in order to establish the situation. For instance, Creon has to decree the crime and she has to bury the brother, before you've got them engaged. And the same is true, as you'll see, throughout the various plays.

As a matter of fact, in *Don Carlos* there is act after act to get the situation established. There are subplots. You don't get the situation established until well into Act Three.

So whatever is required to get the characters engaged in a conflict goes into the plot-theme. But what happens to that conflict, what further actions, is not part of the plot-theme. That's the development.

Now let me conclude here with a word on Classicism, just to give you a little background. This is the only Classicist in our course. Classicism consisted of concrete rules—usually applied to buildings, theater, music—allegedly taken from the Ancients, and rules that had to be obeyed no matter what the subject or theme.

You know that as far as the standards of art are concerned, philosophically there are three different approaches. There's the subjectivist who says, "There are no rules, anything goes, whatever you feel." There's the Objectivist who says, "Art has to be created and judged by abstract principles, which have to be defended by the essential nature and role of art, but they have to be applied within the context of the theme and the subject." And then, of course, there is the intrinsicist in art, who says, "There are specific rules derived from authorities, apart from context, apart from any discussion of the nature or purpose of art." It's like the Ten Commandments of esthetics.

It shows you a certain consistency here. In ethics, as we've seen, there's a large element of intrinsicism in Corneille, in the feudal commandments. And so he is consistent in having a large element of intrinsicism stylistically in his Classicism as well. They go together as a certain kind of mentality which is trying to uphold standards—as against subjectivism and skepticism—but does not know how to do it except by ultimately going back to authority, although Corneille breaks those rules freely in both cases, to breathe life and heroism and beauty into the work.

If you looked at the actual rules of Classicism, they're basically like the Ten Commandments of the Bible. It's a mixture of good points, silly points, overstated points, points that are ambiguous and need interpretation. I am going to mention in closing, just one from seventeenth-century French to give you an idea: A play must be dignified. That sounds good to me. And you can see what the reasoning was: they wanted a value-oriented, rational world. They didn't want anything debased; they wanted something dignified. Now what did that mean? Here was a list of what was prohibited by that principle: no foul language, no colloquialisms, no mention of low objects (like handkerchiefs, or even daggers), no violence, not even a duel. No details of everyday life: you couldn't eat onstage, drink onstage, sleep onstage. You see the furor over Chimène's meeting with Rodrigo at night; that is just simply not dignified.

That gives you a taste of the kind of thing that Corneille accepted—or accepted at least in part—in the name of staying true to a rational, orderly, logical universe. It's another example of the difference between rationalism, which dominated France at this period, and reason.

Despite all this, I still want to restate in conclusion that Classicism made possible some great poetry and some great plays. And in my judgment, *Le Cid* is among the immortals in those respects.

CHAPTER FOUR

DON CARLOS

Friedrich Schiller

1. Introduction

Intellectually, we now move into the Age of Enlightenment, the eighteenth century. Otherworldliness, and specifically religion, is substantially down; it's on the defensive. Skepticism, the kind of skepticism we saw in Shakespeare and the Renaissance, is down. Reason is up. There has been a century preparing the ground for the takeoff of reason, and now it has finally reached its climax in the West. Politically, therefore, as you would expect, it is a revolutionary age because when reason is up, freedom is up. Thus the American Revolution in 1776, culminating in 1787 with the Constitution. And that happened to be the very same year as *Don Carlos'* premiere. The French Revolution is only two years away, in 1789. So we are in a great era of human thought and human freedom. In a way, we are at the climax of the West, because it is downhill, intellectually speaking, from here.

Germany, you know, is one of the most philosophical countries, for good or evil, in all of Western history—and Friedrich Schiller is the best representative of the German Enlightenment. He is more philosophical then Goethe, and intellectually—well, on a scale of one to ten, he would be a half point higher than Kant so wherever you put Kant, Schiller is half a point higher.

Schiller did not live very long, he died in his forties. He was born in 1759 and died in 1805 so almost all of his works are youthful. He started *Don Carlos* when he was twenty-three, which was the same age that the real Don Carlos died, some two hundred years earlier in 1568. It took Schiller four years to complete this play; he started it in 1783 and completed it in 1787. That is going to be relevant to understanding the play.

His great compatriot in literature was Goethe. These are the two great German poets and playwrights of the German Enlightenment.

They happened to be friends and professional allies in the theater of Weimar in the last decade of Schiller's life. Later, after World War One, the Democratic Germans wanted consciously to start a new regime, having overthrown the Kaiser's, and to base it on true freedom. They called it the Weimar Republic because their motto was "Back to Schiller and Goethe." This was the truly exalted, freedom-loving era of Germany.

You know from having read my book, *The Ominous Parallels*, what unfortunately happened to the Weimar Republic. You will see even a bit more fully, having analyzed Schiller—who was *the* best thinker in the history of Germany—why the Weimar Republic went the way it did.

This is a somewhat negative way to start. I wanted to start on a positive note. I want to quote a Schiller scholar, Charles Passage, who gives the following very accurate and factual evaluation of Schiller's importance. This is not a blurb, this is a historical truth. "Schiller is the greatest writer of serious drama between the death of Racine in 1699 and the emergence of Ibsen as a master in the European theater around 1880." So he is the top writer of serious drama in a two hundred year period. The quote goes on, "This statement regards the intrinsic merit of Schiller's plays, their immense and extended popularity and performance, and their influence on subsequent dramatic and non-dramatic writers."

If you want a capsule cultural commentary on the state of life and thought in America today, I will simply point out to you that you cannot find Schiller in bookstores in Southern California. He is just simply unavailable; you have to go to libraries or specialized reading shops in New York. This is a horrifying and eloquent sign to me of the emerging barbarism and the loss of great classics.

That quote expressed how influential he was, and I am sure you must have heard of some of his followers. For instance, the opera composer Verdi was a follower of Schiller. When he wrote *Don Carlo*, which was his version of this very play, he was taken tremendously by the Grand Inquisitor, who is fantastic in the play, as we will see, and in Verdi also. Dostoyevsky, the famous Russian novelist who was highly admired by Ayn Rand, wrote a book of which the outstanding sequence includes the Grand Inquisitor, inspired directly by Schiller. Those are just two of the kind of giants that sprang from Schiller and particularly from this play.

Schiller himself was a professor of history (all Germans are professors) and a writer of philosophy, especially in the field of esthetics, beyond being a playwright and a poet. He had definite political ideas, but he was not an activist; he did not believe that his social ideals could be achieved in that period of time. The establishment, he thought, was just too entrenched. His goal was to bring about political action in the future through philosophical education now. He wanted a thorough reform of political thought and life to be achieved basically through the education that he would put forth in his plays.

Don Carlos is set in the sixteenth century, although it was written in the eighteenth, and it is allegedly the story of Don Carlos, the son of Philip the Second of Spain, a powerful absolute monarch who ruled much more than Spain. I indicated to you that the real Don Carlos died in 1568 and, as far as I can make out, the real Don Carlos was a very unappetizing creature. He was a halfwit, a sadist, a womanizer, ugly, mentally unbalanced—and, in despair of what to do with him, his father locked him up in a room, in which he alternately starved and gorged himself, a kind of father of bulimia, and then died.

In the Protestant world, which was politically and religiously opposed to Catholic Philip and to Spain, a myth arose about Don Carlos' heroism and of the vicious king who killed him. This myth was gradually elaborated and was summed up in a widely believed story about Don Carlos, written by one Abedus San Royal. The San Royal story was Schiller's point of departure. He believed that it was historically accurate.

2. Plot-theme

This is an extraordinarily long play, one of the longest in history. It is twice the length of any Shakespearean play, which Schiller himself concedes is a problem with it.

Here is a standard description you get among commentators. See what you think of this: "a tragedy of hopeless love." Would that you could do the plot-theme of this play in five words. Obviously this is completely inadequate. There is an element of that, I suppose, between Don Carlos and the queen. But the idea of hopeless love goes all the way through literature. It is in *Othello*, for instance. It is in *Wuthering Heights*. It is in *Gone With the Wind*. So we have to do an awful lot to turn a tragedy of hopeless love into *Don Carlos*.

Obviously, the first thing we have to do is add a political element to our statement because there is a fight for liberty against an absolute monarch. You may be tempted to say that that's just background for the love story or that's just really the abstract intellectual theme. But

I would say: no, this fight for liberty actually motivates much of the action. It is a literal part of the exquisite motivation of the leading characters. So it is not simply a background or a side message. It is part of the actual story; in a way, it is the actual story. The test is: does it motivate their action or do they just talk about it in the drawing room? And here it motivates their action, so it cannot be omitted from the plot-theme.

What about: "a story of tragic lovers engulfed in a passionate struggle for liberty?" Or more briefly: "doomed love in a dictatorship" with the lovers doomed because they are trying to challenge or overthrow the ruler. No, that is no good as a statement of the plot-theme. Ayn Rand's *We the Living* is exactly "doomed love in a dictatorship." *1984* by George Orwell is the same. Even *Antigone* you could say is doomed love in a dictatorship.

In *We the Living, 1984* and others like it, however, there is this difference: the lovers' primary goal is their love; they fight the dictatorship as a means to achieve this goal. In other words, they want to escape from servility so as to be able to enjoy and fulfill their love. So they go on loving each other romantically and sleeping together until one or both are destroyed physically or spiritually by the evil tyrant.

In *Don Carlos*, by contrast, the love relationship between Don Carlos and the queen is not the primary concern of any character, including Don Carlos and the queen. In fact, the characters all say that love is an obstacle to what they want, and therefore they renounce their love virtually from the start and then again officially later. It is an obstacle to their higher value, which is, though it sounds odd to say, the liberty of the Netherlands. We are going to call that world liberty because the Netherlands (or in another context Flanders, which is called Belgium today) was the center of the Protestant world. That meant that if they were free, the whole rest of the Protestant world would be free and it would theoretically overturn the Catholic world. So it comes down to, their highest value is really world liberty.

Note that it is not King Philipp who ends their love. The queen and Don Carlos end it as an act of virtue, of nobler consciousness, of deliberate commitment to world freedom. They renounce their love before they even sleep together once. If the essential of this play were a love story, it would be a disaster as a play. It would be a love story without love; or with only Platonic love, which is even worse.

Of course, the love story does somehow fit into the plot-theme, but still deeper is the fight for world freedom against a tyrannical king. Where are we now? We can't stop with just a generalized statement. Let us try to approach it from the point of view of the protagonist. Who is fighting this king? Who is the chief initiator of the action, the chief hero, the chief emotional focus of the play? Obviously it is not the queen and just as obviously it is not the king, because he and his court are against freedom. The two real candidates have to be Don Carlos and Posa, his associate. Is this, then, a joint equal battle among equal partners or is one of them dominant in the fight for liberty over the other? At the beginning of the play, it seems pretty clear that the protagonist is Don Carlos; the play is called *Don Carlos*. For over two acts the story revolves around his passion to unite with the queen and his fear that the king is going to find out. It is Don Carlos who has been asked to be leader in Flanders. All this time Posa (Roderick) in action is merely his friend, his confidante, even his gofer delivering notes—albeit with some strong speeches. Think over the first half a little more deeply. Who is it that convinces Don Carlos and the queen to forget their love life in order to fight for mankind's freedom? Posa. Don Carlos and the queen are sunk into passive misery until he comes along and awakens their ideals. So he is the real—even if only implicit—mover of the action in the first half.

In the second half, his role becomes blatant. Posa openly takes over the play and the political action. He is the one who beseeches the king to reform. He becomes the king's agent. He plots each step of the future, leaving Don Carlos at certain points completely baffled, a mere reactor. Posa even sets up his own death and its aftermath. In other words, Posa becomes the actor, the initiator, the protagonist.

What are we going to make of this? Is Don Carlos a red herring? Before we pronounce on that and before we make a final decision here on the plot-theme of this play, I want you to observe another new element introduced in the second half of the play besides the ascendancy of Posa to the position of protagonist. A second love triangle is featured. The emphasis is no longer on Don Carlos, the queen and the king, although there are still scenes about the king's jealousy in regard to the queen. From early Act Three on, from precisely the point when the king says "Give me a man," that is to say; a man I can count on, there is a major shift in the love story. The king grows to love Posa, as the focus of the story; and the queen drops into the background. The king makes Posa his spy and Don Carlos begins to suspect Posa of betraying him to the king. Remember the portfolio that he gave to Posa and somebody sees Posa giving it to the king. Don Carlos begins to agonize jealously over his lost love, namely Posa. Then Posa tells Don Carlos that he really loved him all the time; the king was merely a tool of his plan. The king discovers this truth and is insanely jealous and crushed.

In other words, the play stresses the rivalry between the king and Don Carlos for Posa. When the king realizes that he has lost Posa, he goes after Don Carlos' life as vengeance because of Posa's betrayal of his love.

By this point the king's jealousy of the queen has basically vanished. The queen had confronted them earlier, cleared the air, and that was the end of that story. In other words, the final outcome of the play is related to the second triangle, not to the first.

I would like to look at the second love triangle for a moment because we need to have some understanding in order even to state the plot-theme. This triangle sneaks up on you and it is not exactly your most conventional love triangle. One intelligent Schiller scholar puts it this way: "Carlos' denunciation of the king in the presence of Posa's corpse is the frenzied taunting of a rival in love. Similarly the king's monstrous behavior after he finds out the truth betokens a subconscious erotic jealousy and a ghastly rage over betrayal in love. Nowhere does the text suggest any fleshly expression of passion on the part of any of the three male personages in question. Yet in 1788 [that's the year after *Don Carlos*], Schiller began planning a drama in which three figures predominate: a father, a son and the son's friend with an exalted male passion explicit between the son and his friend."

What do you make of that? Is this homosexuality? Do we have a play about gay relationships in eighteenth-century classic German literature? It's a very contorted question. I don't think so, but I do believe it is still love that is being portrayed here. In other words, Schiller intends something more than strong, warm, close friendship. He does want to depict real male love in some romantic sense, even though he does not believe that that entails sex or even sexual desire.

Does that baffle you? How many find that incompatible with Objectivism? I want to read you a quote from Ayn Rand now. This is from an unpublished letter of hers written in 1944. It is written about *The Fountainhead* with, of course, no thought in her mind at all for *Don Carlos*. It is to a fan. I will just read a self-contained excerpt, which you will either consider as self-evident or as a revelation.

"You ask, is anybody in *The Fountainhead* in love, besides Roark and Dominique. Oh, my, yes!" Then she goes on to talk about Roark and

Dominique, Wynand and Dominique. And then she writes these words, which I will quote without any comment right now. "But above all, and greater, I think, than any other emotion in the book, is Wynand's love for Roark. Wynand is in love with Roark in every way except physical. It is not a homosexual feeling, but it is love in the romantic sense and in the highest sense. Not just affection or admiration."

This is exactly what Schiller had in mind. I would like you to ponder this, so you won't be too scandalized by Schiller here. He holds—and obviously Ayn Rand agrees with him—that a passionate, even romantic male relationship is possible between heroes; and even between Objectivist heroes. So you have to be sure you know what you object to if and when you attack gay lib or male lovers. That is another subject I would be happy to comment on in the question period, if you feel this is not self-evident. For now I want to go back to Schiller on this intriguing note.

We are still plodding along, trying to get the plot-theme here. Go back to the protagonist. It's pretty clear the protagonist is Posa. But why was it so difficult to find out? It took Schiller four years to write this play and he underwent real personal changes while writing it. He started at twenty-three and finished it at twenty-seven, which is a very, very fertile period in an intelligent person's life. We undergo great changes in our early-to-late twenties. Basically, what happened is that he outgrew the character of Don Carlos, with whom he could identify at the beginning, and came to admire Posa, a much more philosophical and long-range character, as the hero.

One accidental factor was that in the middle of the writing, after he was half-finished, he discovered that San Royale's story about Don Carlos was a total invention. Therefore, the biography on which he was allegedly basing the play was just wrong. That helped him further to lose interest in Don Carlos, the character, as a primary focus.

So he wrote the last two acts with Posa as his protagonist, and with just enough skillful continuity so that every once in a while he would bring in the changes this imposed on the king and the queen and Don Carlos to avoid it being a blatantly different play.

Why didn't he rewrite Acts One to Three accordingly, from the point of view of his new and more mature perspective? Unfortunately, something stopped him from doing that. The first three acts had already been published, one act at a time, in magazine form. So, as he saw it, the choice is: abort the play or skillfully weave a new second half onto the first half. And that is what he tried to do.

From Act Four on, it is basically Posa's story and the story of the second triangle with the first triangle thrown in only occasionally for continuity. By Act Five, the best act in the play, the first triangle is simply dead as a dramatic issue. All the key actions flow from the second triangle.

Schiller himself drew a moral from this crisis in his play's creation. He put it very aptly: "a play should be written in one summer. I spent too long on it." God knows that is true and that is the big flaw in the play. He just could not stop; then he changed it in the middle and made it a great play in the second half but he had to tie it onto the first half.

The change comes exactly (and all Schiller scholars know this) at line 2940. You can just draw a line because that is where the play effectively starts when the king says, "Give me a man."

Judging now from the total work, I think you have to say that Posa is the protagonist even from the start. He supplies the play's ruling motive. The first love story is basically only an obstacle to Posa's ideals. Posa wants Don Carlos, as the legal successor to Philipp, to drop the queen, not risk a breach with Philipp, and devote himself to the fight for liberty. The love story about the queen is, therefore, really only a relationship to be used by the playwright and then thrown away for the sake of the ultimate concerns of the story.

So here are the elements of the plot-theme, the longest we are going to have. A plot-theme is like a definition: the briefer, the more essentialized, the better. But in this play it is a paragraph. These are the main elements: a man fights for freedom, and it has to be world freedom to have the stature of a great romantic play (a secession of Staten Island wouldn't qualify). He fights against a tyrant who loves him (Schiller has to make the point that the tyrant is in love with him because that will bring in the second triangle) by backing the king's son as the next ruler in the succession. It so happens that the son is in love with his father's new queen. All these elements are important to the play. Add the play's length and Schiller's change of mind during the writing and we have a very complicated plot-theme.

The play has a real flaw in that it is just too convoluted for a play or even for anything. This is the price you pay for genius. If Schiller had stayed on the level of the first three acts, I would never have assigned this play. Act Four and particularly Act Five are what make this a unique masterpiece. Here then is my official statement of the plot-theme of the total play. I was able to get it into three lines of type, by the judicious use of punctuation. *A man fights for world freedom against a tyrannical king who loves him, by backing the king's son and heir: a prince passionately in love with his father's new queen.* Now that is a mouthful. As a plot-theme it has virtue only in relation to the mammoth size of the play. For an ordinary play this would not fulfill the function of a plot-theme because there is just too much in it. In this play it is not a synopsis; this is just the situation.

This formulation permits you to enter the essence of the play. All the major motivations, personal and political, are implied in it and, above all, all the crucial conflicts. What is the major conflict? The first question we always ask after the plot-theme is the defining conflict of the play, and from the plot-theme statement you should be able to read it right off. What is the decisive conflict? Posa versus the king.

Of course, as in all great plays, variants of this conflict or derivative aspects of it, rage throughout the work. There is Posa versus Don Carlos over the ultimate goal to pursue. And the king versus Don Carlos over the queen. And then the king and Don Carlos over Posa and, of course, over freedom. And the king versus Posa, when we get to the second triangle. And Don Carlos versus Posa over the king. There is just a tumult of violent conflicts which is a great virtue of Schiller. He specialized in plot-themes with multiple passionate inbuilt conflicts. And therefore he could write passionate, highly exciting, dramatic plays.

One final note as we leave the plot-theme. I have omitted Princess Eboli from our discussion. The reason is that I do not regard her as an essential of the play. She is a side issue, a subplot only, even though she takes up a lot of space in the first triangle. She is, in effect, a go-between relating other truly major characters. Thankfully we can drop her as of now; we already have a huge plateful to deal with without her.

3. Plot Development

If you understand the plot-theme, the development is very straightforward. All of the plays I have chosen have an exquisitely logical development. If they didn't, I would not have chosen them. So they are all perfect in structure, absolutely logical.

1. The establishment of the situation

In this play the establishment consumes a lot of space because of the change of triangles. The second triangle must be established before you really have the situation and can rise to intensity. In my opinion the establishment includes all of Acts One and Two, and Act Three through Scene Nine. By the way, according to whether you get an American or a Continental numbering, the number of the scenes differs from edition to edition. So I can't say Scenes One to Nine, because in different editions it is broken up differently. But it is Scenes One to Nine in The German Library translation that I assigned. That is what you need to get the essence of triangle one and its complications, and get triangle two started. Basically the establishment is over when we get to: *I need a man, send me Posa.* That gets the ultimate play going.

2. The rise to the climax

This goes from Act Three, Scene Ten through Act Five, Scene Three, which is the death of Posa. In other words, all of the milking of the Posa triangle—Posa's fight for world freedom against the king; his plea to the king to reform to give us a new age; Posa's takeover and the arrest of Don Carlos to save him, all the way to Posa's final recognition that there is no way out except through his own self-sacrifice. If he is going to save the heir to the throne, he must go instead of Don Carlos. Finally he tells the whole story to Don Carlos and, as he is talking, there is a shot through the door. Posa says haltingly: "He is very quick, this king." Posa is dying: "I hoped—for more—Consider your escape—you hear?—Consider your escape. The queen knows everything. I can no more." He dies. The king enters with his court. That is the climax of the play, in my judgment; the death of Posa.

I will give you a slightly different definition of climax now. It occurred to me that you can define climax in epistemological or metaphysical terms. We have been using an epistemological definition: that event from which you can tell how the ultimate resolution is going to come. A metaphysical definition seems more clarifying for this play. They come to the same thing, but this is perhaps a better definition of climax: the event which directly, although not necessarily immediately, dictates the final outcome.

In a good play every event implies the outcome, but it does it through all the intermediate events. The climax is the event at which you could say: the next causal step is the outcome but it doesn't happen immediately. It could take a long time and that causal step could be presented in a lot of substeps. That is basically the same idea of a climax, only instead of saying "the event from which you can figure it out," it really goes a little deeper. You can figure out from the climax because that is the event itself which leads to the ultimate resolution.

I find that in some plays the epistemological formulation is more helpful and in others, such as this one which is so convoluted, you cannot quite figure out what is coming next. However, when you look *back* on it, you can see that this is the event on which it all turned.

Let me explain why I call this the climax. Does Posa's death actually determine the final outcome of the play? I say yes because, once Posa has died, a tragic ending is necessary. Why? Because Posa is the protagonist, the mainspring of the action. After he dies, that mainspring is broken. Don Carlos can only react to the loss.

Of course, in theory Don Carlos could escape and carry on Posa's work. But then so could Kira have escaped in *We the Living*. In both cases, it would have been simply accidental. If we go by the essence of the situation and the characters, Don Carlos was never a prime mover. His energy was Posa's energy and, without Posa, we could not expect him to determine events.

Similarly, the king's only redeeming features were brought out by Posa's love or seeming love for him. When Posa is gone, the king turns into a monster. The situation is that when Posa dies, Don Carlos is prostrate with grief, the king turns vindictive, and the writing is on the wall: the destruction of the good forces is inevitable.

I want to pursue this issue of climax for a moment because this is our section on the logic of the play. That is what the development covers. I would like to ask you: why did Schiller have Posa die? Maybe you see with me that once Posa dies, that foretokens tragedy. But why did Posa have to die? Why did he have to fail in his quest? Wouldn't this play be fine with a happy ending? Both Posa and Don Carlos escape, riding off side by side into the sunset for Flanders, leaving the king behind to gnash his teeth.

I would say no, you are not talking about the same play at all then. What would the meaning of that play be? Remember, you judge meaning by action. You do not judge it by speeches, unless those speeches are integral to the action. If they could ride off into the sunset and save Flanders, the meaning would be: tyranny and the Inquisition are not so powerful; they are not so terrible. All you need is a little commitment and the whole free world out there will rise up and welcome you. If that were the situation, why in heaven didn't Posa and Carlos ride out in Act One, instead of staying with Philipp and arguing with him, and all the complications that that involved?

Remember, the heart of Posa's plan, which is to back Don Carlos as the heir, as the successor of the future, necessarily puts off success to the next generation at least. Posa's mission in the play is not to *establish* freedom, but to fight within the system to convert Don Carlos. He actually sends Don Carlos away only when things get desperate, and by then it is too late to win. The reason for this is that Schiller wants to show in this play the kind of character necessary if a new era of freedom is ever to be developed. He wants to show the evolution of Don Carlos from a passive, self-absorbed creature to full decisive maturity at the end; this is why he called the play *Don Carlos* even with the new protagonist. But Schiller had no intention of showing that character in successful political action.

Schiller wrote a series of very famous letters about this play in answer to critics the year after he finished it. The reason I picked this translation is that for the first time ever, these letters are all included in the back in English. (Of course, this edition went out of print as soon as I assigned it.)

In any event, in his letters he says that it is simply too soon in history—this is the sixteenth century—to expect that actual freedom could be established. Real-world freedom is for a later era. He says he is simply showing how someday the world is going to get there. And it is going to get there with the creation of characters like Don Carlos and their education into the kind of hero who will then ascend to the throne and create a revolution.

The climax of this play is consonant with Schiller's strategy; his intention is Posa's failure, at least in concrete terms. In other words, his inability to establish the perfect political system. In other words, his defeat by the incumbent system. In other words, it means, dramatically speaking, his death. This is an absolutely logical climax, inevitable by the structure of the play.

I know a lot of you have the idea that it would be a much better play if only it had a happy ending. You cannot throw a happy ending on a play, unless the play requires it and builds up to it and can cash it in. A play like this with a happy ending tacked on would be an absurdity. It would have no conviction and no reality. You have to earn a happy ending. A happy ending is like becoming a billionaire. It doesn't happen to you without blood, sweat and tears, and without every part of your structure, your characters, your plot leading inexo-rably to that happy ending.

3. Resolution

This is commonly called the denouement, a synonym for resolution. (By the way, it just happens that all these terms are French.) In my judgment, the resolution is by far the greatest, the most exalted and magnificent part of this play. It is the only reason I chose this play. If we had had to go through the first three acts only, I never would have chosen it, although it does have a lot of virtues. It is just a good romantic play up to there with some confusions, typically Germanic, and it is overlong. But from Scene Four of Act Five to the ending, you have an unprecedented dramatic spectacle.

Ray Cole told me he cursed me while he was reading this play: why did I make him go through these hundreds of pages? But he had to agree with me that when you get to Act Five, any price is worth it to be able to read and enjoy the last act of this play. Starting with Don Carlos taunting the king after Posa's death, then the king's love of Posa turning before our eyes to pure hatred for humanity, with fabu-lous lines like the king saying: "He [Posa] sacrificed me to humanity. Humanity shall make atonement." Now they are going to get what is coming to them, the bloody race, you see. Soon all the proofs of Don Carlos' disloyalty flood in and the letters of Posa are intercepted. And then—I make this as a flat statement, I don't even say it is my opinion—the greatest, the most dramatic, most philosophical scene in all world theatrical literature. And that is the Grand Inquisitor Scene.

The Grand Inquisitor is called in by the king for guidance about what should be done about Don Carlos now that Posa's dead and Don Carlos is still plotting rebellion. The king wants guidance, and boy, does the Grand Inquisitor give him guidance. We will go over that in some detail shortly. Directly after that, Don Carlos' fate—a powerful staccato burst. Don Carlos is flushed with excitement over his plans; he is finally going to Flanders and leading the crusade. He is finally going to come out into the open. As a symbol of this, he will take off his mask that has hidden his identity from the queen's guards. He says to the queen, "My wish is that there shall be nothing more between us that is secret. . . . Let this be my last deceit." And he starts to take off his mask.

The king has entered unseen, steps up to him and declares, "It is your last!" Queen faints. Don Carlos: "O Heaven, O earth! Then is she dead?" King, coldly and quietly to the Grand Inquisitor: "Now I have done my part. See you do yours!" Curtain.

Now *that* is a finale. I couldn't restrain myself. When I read that, I wrote in the margin: like a knife in the chest. The most powerful ending.

I am saving the Grand Inquisitor scene for discussion under Schiller's philosophy. It is that scene in conjunction with the immediately following arrest of Don Carlos that is what is so fantastic about this play.

4. Characterization

How many major characters? We have a long plot-theme so we have four major characters: the queen, Don Carlos, the king, Posa. Those are all in the plot-theme.

The queen does not have to hold us for long. A relatively weak character, she initiates no action. Sweet, gentle, passive—more or less like Desdemona. Certainly a much lesser creature than Antigone or Chimène and the least important of the major characters, she gets dropped by the time the play really gets started. Good bye, queen.

Don Carlos. What is his central character trait as presented in the play? Is he a crusader? Is he primarily an idealist? No. He doesn't have a lot of ideas but he is not primarily second-hand. Using Objectivist terms which are not Schiller's, he is an emotionalist. He is a whim-worshipper, if you wish, until the very last scene. He has a lot of the qualities of the villains in *Atlas Shrugged*. He suffers a lot, but he doesn't do very much about it. He is a man of feeling; passive, sensitive, even helpless apart from Posa. He walks around asking everybody to love him; Posa, the queen, even the king. He says: just don't hate me, and I'll love you like a child.

There are constant eruptions of sudden passion on his part, where he drops all context and jeopardizes his plans. For instance, at one point he breaks into a fit and antagonizes Alba until the queen has to command him to come to his senses. At another point, he gets deliriously happy when the secret note comes from Eboli; he thinks it is from the queen and the page has to tell him to shut up. So he is, in effect, a reckless emotionalist. Apart from Posa, his life is empty, melancholy, inactive—and he is getting pretty bitter, too.

He does have good attributes. He is shown to be intelligent and brave. For instance, he did take the punishment for Posa when they were children. He is idealistic. And he is capable of being converted to a passion for world freedom. He needs to grow, to become steady, mature and think long-range. He needs to develop his virtues and correct his flaws. That was Schiller's intention: to show, in effect, a playboy becoming a hero. Not a playboy in the gross sense of sleeping around, but what we would call a whim-worshipper.

What is the main flaw he needs to learn to correct, according to Schiller? What is the main weakness of Don Carlos that Posa struggles to correct in him? In a single word, selfishness; the desire for personal romantic happiness. What does he have to learn? He has to learn to place his passion at the service of the world. That is a theme we are going to return to shortly.

Let's turn to the king. The king is a mixed character: evil but with an idealistic side. An interesting character, he falls somewhere between the Grand Inquisitor on one extreme and Posa at the other. He is jealous, weak, melancholic, and with a real potential to become vicious. On the other hand, he is intelligent, he aspires, and he is even capable of being large-hearted and magnanimous. For instance, he forgives the Spanish Armada for its disastrous loss. It is skillful on the part of the playwright to throw in a few concretes like that, so we can really get a feel for these characters. The king, like any mixed character, is a hotbed of contradictions. He is animated by power-lust and, at the same time, really admires Posa's independence. He sneers at the human race and, at the same time, feels painfully alone. He needs a friend, a man to love and communicate with. He sneers at emotions; considers them unmanly and weak. On the other hand, he needs love authentically, and he cries when he doesn't get it. So he is a contradictory, malleable man. He is the true gray man. Or, if you want, he is the mixed economy of the spirit. He can be shaped, temporarily at least, by a better influence but at the end and at bottom he is going to become a tool of evil. This is because any so-called mixed economy, as you know, will turn inevitably black and disastrous if it is not radically cured. That is just what happens to the king. In the last act we actually witness his love for Posa turn to hate and see his willing conversion into a puppet of the Grand Inquisitor.

That brings us to Posa, the real hero, on whose character the whole interpretation of the play depends. What central fact have we already seen about him? He has to fail. So far we have looked at this issue externally. In other words, given the playwright's viewpoint and the structure of the play, Posa has to die. That leaves open a crucial question. What within Posa himself causes his failure? What makes it believable, understandable, inevitable? What is the inner logic of his failure and death? Is Posa just a helpless victim of evil or does he contribute to his own downfall? This is the question that takes you into the heart of the message of *Don Carlos* and the philosophy of Schiller.

First of all, Schiller writes about this extensively in the play itself and in the twelve famous letters that are appended at the end. No, he says, Posa is not just a helpless victim of evil. Posa has an Achilles heel; he is defeated by something within himself, something in the very nature of his character, something good. Something in the nature of his virtue brings about his downfall, according to Schiller. Now what could it be?

Let's say some positive things about Posa first. What good traits does he have? He is long-range, purposeful, passionate. He is resourceful, daring, eloquent, very philosophical and grown-up in contrast to Don Carlos, although they are the same age. What is the essence of his motivation qua hero? He is a crusader for mankind. His primary value is dedication to the well-being—the Freedom of the Whole according to German philosophy. And the decisive action that he takes? He sacrifices himself. Not for his friend, not for Don Carlos, but for the ultimate sake of fostering the course of world freedom.

And in fact, Don Carlos' legends and plays have been done many, many times in theater over the centuries. The first thing that occurred to Schiller and made it of interest for him to write this play was the idea that Posa would rescue Don Carlos by an act of self-sacrifice. Thereby, in Schiller's own mind, Posa will inspire Don Carlos to emulate him and also to sacrifice: become a lover of the world, grow up, sacrifice his private cares, and live for mankind as a whole. So the genesis of the play historically in Schiller's mind and his unique twist was to have Posa sacrifice himself.

This certainly suggests that Posa is the opposite of an egoist—and that is something that is all over the play. He is an altruist, his concern is the welfare of the world and the evil of selfishness. Here, for instance, is a quote from the play. Posa is disappointed at this point; he sees Don Carlos pining away for the queen. He wonders what happened to his childhood idealism. "We were both going to save the world," he says. "All of that is gone, devoured by *one* emotion, the victim of one small and selfish interest. Your heart has ceased to beat. There are no tears left over for the wretched fortune of the province, not one small tear is left. Oh, Carlos, you are desperately poor since you love no one but yourself." And this goes on, over and over, in the play.

Now let's go a bit deeper into Schiller's thought on this subject. He is very anxious that Posa's motivation not be misunderstood, so he goes to great lengths in his letters to clarify exactly what moves Posa and why he had to fail—by the very nature of his virtue. Here are some highlights from Schiller's own analysis. I am excerpting about a hundred pages into two, but it will give you the idea.

First, he stresses that Posa is not primarily Don Carlos' friend. He is not anybody's friend because friendship is not an important value to him. His concern, says Schiller, is not some one individual, but the whole. This is the same country, you know, that gave us Hegel and Marx—and Schiller is definitely German. In relation to the whole of mankind, says Schiller, "Every limited, smaller condition vanishes." In other words, every individual vanishes. Posa's primary identity is not a friend of anyone but a crusader, a revolutionary, a servant of mankind. So Don Carlos is, therefore, not the man he loves, but rather an indispensable tool for Posa's political ideals.

That is to say, the basis has been laid in the play for Posa to have a pretty damned cavalier attitude toward Don Carlos. Schiller understands this and it is very deliberate. Remember, whatever you think of his ideas—and I do not think much of his ideas—he is a philosopher-playwright. He doesn't write for CBS. He knows what world-love as a primary means. The hero must be willing to renounce and sacrifice any personal love on behalf of the whole. He has to be indifferent and even callous to the needs and welfare of any one individual, including his dearest, closest friend, if he thereby fosters the well-being of the species. In other words, he has to be a true exponent of German philosophy.

Against this background, let us look at Posa's most controversial action in the play, for which the critics descended on Schiller and on which the whole complication of the last part of the play depends. Question: why did Posa not tell Don Carlos right off the bat in Act Three of his new relationship to the king? Why did he let the second triangle develop at all? Why did he keep Don Carlos in the dark about his real intentions, leaving him feeling suspicious and jealous? Why did he say nothing? A word from him would have brought Don Carlos into the light; he would have known what was going on; there would have been no misunderstanding. Don Carlos would never have had to rush to Eboli as his only friend left. Then there would have been no need to arrest Don Carlos to save him from himself. There would have been no need for Posa's sacrifice. In other words, the whole disaster would not have taken place.

Schiller himself is a very honest man. When the critics put this question to him, he rewrote it in even stronger terms and then gave his answer. It is really fascinating to see someone answer, rather than evade, a major question—even though the answer is even worse. Schiller himself says that the reserve of Posa (reserve here means he is not telling anyone, including Don Carlos, about his plan) is "the single source of all the subsequent confusion." He goes on. Listen to this; it is really well-written. "Many people have reproached [Posa] that he, who fosters such a high concept of freedom and is incessantly talking about it, should nevertheless assume a despotic option over his friend. That he should guide him *blindly*, like someone underage, and precisely for that reason lead him to the brink of destruction."

In other words, the critics got a massive contradiction: this freedom-lover who is treating his friend as though he is dirt, doesn't bother to enlighten him, and is just moving him around like a puppet. So why does Posa act like that? Is this inadvertence on Schiller's part? You can be sure that in four years he figured it out. Obviously his Achilles' heel is at work; the inner defect which leads to his ruin and to a tragic ending for all the good characters. Something makes him secretive, even despotic, over other individuals, even his best friend. What could it be?

Remember, he has no friends. That is the key here. Only mankind as a whole is his concern. Individuals are mere means to this end. So what do you expect? If that is his hierarchy of values, isn't it to be expected that he would treat everyone, including Don Carlos, as puppets on strings to be pulled by him? In other words, wouldn't he treat Don Carlos as a means or a tool or, even implicitly, a serf?

Schiller says it openly. I am going to give you some excerpts to show you how he himself puts the point in his letters. His grammar is Germanic—there is nothing I can do about that. There are long sentences but try to get the meaning. "The most unselfish, purest, and noblest person very often, because of enthusiastic devotion to *his idea* of virtue . . . , is very often displayed dealing just as arbitrarily with individuals as even the most selfish despot." Do you get that? Now listen to this one. "True greatness of mind [in other words, one hundred percent altruism] often leads no less to the violation of the freedom of others than does selfishness and the lust for power." Did you get that? Even while a hero operates with constant regard for the whole, the smaller interest of the individual is only too easily lost in his broad perspective. He goes on a little later, "I chose a totally benevolent character, completely above every selfish desire; I gave him the highest respect for the rights of others. I even gave him as a goal the creation of the universal *enjoyment of freedom*, and I believe I do not find myself in contradiction . . . when I allow him, on the way to that goal itself, to stray into despotism. It was part of my plan that he should be caught in this trap that is set for all who find themselves on the same path with him."

I have to say I fell out of my chair when I read that. If I ever heard propaganda for Objectivism, that's it.

Let's just make the grammar and the language here a little simpler. In other words, ignoring and sacrificing his friend and doing it, in effect, heedlessly, even needlessly, is in the nature of his ideal—altruism. Any single person is just unimportant and not worth considering. This is what leads to disaster. Does Schiller, who is a philosopher, then conclude that there must be something wrong with altruism, if it leads to destruction even when practiced by its purest exponents? That is what his play demonstrates perfectly; it is like a textbook on the disaster of altruism.

If Posa had thought of his private, selfish relationship with Don Carlos, of his special, personal feeling for Don Carlos, then he would have felt it his duty to Don Carlos to keep him informed. He wouldn't have treated him as a cog in a cosmic scheme. The disaster would never have occurred.

If I had written that, my conclusion would be, "Geez, I have to switch my moral code completely then. I have to adopt egoism and start over." But what does Mr. Schiller conclude? The problem here, he says, is not a flaw in altruism, not at all. This is simply a demonstration of how wonderful a code altruism is. It's a different problem, which we just simply can't escape; that's life. Guess what the problem is? Moral versus the practical; the ideal versus the realistic. His very morality is going to necessitate practical disaster. Of course, you know that is inherent in altruism anyway. That's why he held it.

The way Schiller puts it: there is the theoretical reason, which gives us abstract theories of good and evil and there is the practical reason, which gives us guidance directly from the heart. Did you ever hear that one before? Who said that? Immanuel Kant.

Altruism stands in Schiller's mind like this. Altruism is the theoretical ideal; it motivates the hero in the play. The play's moral essence is the lesson Don Carlos must learn to be a fit ruler, the lesson of service to mankind. And yet the practice of that very ethics necessarily leads to disaster. So Schiller concludes that theoretical ideals can't be consistently practiced. In effect, all we can do in real life is act, not by reason, but by our innate, subjective feelings.

That is more than enough of Schiller's philosophy to give you some insight into Posa.

5. Theme

What is the primary action concern of Posa and the key value explicitly motivating him? In a word, freedom. World freedom. So the first statement of the theme would be: the value, the importance, the primacy of *freedom*.

The word is used in a generalized way but Schiller seems really to mean it. He gives freedom a content. It is not a bromide, the way it is in the mouth of Stalin or Clinton or equivalent individuals. To Schiller, freedom means freedom from arbitrary governmental authority; it means the right of the individual to live his life as he chooses. It means a republican (with a small *r*) form of government, as against tyranny, monarchy and so on.

In other words, he really does believe in political individualism and in the rights of man. And there are major eloquent expressions of this in this play. For instance, in Act Three, Scene Ten, when Posa first meets and beseeches the king to give his subjects liberty, there is a famous individualistic passage where he pleads with the king: "Then lead the way for Europe's kings. A single stroke done by your pen and newly created is the earth. Give us the right to think with freedom."

Note that formulation: to think with freedom. This is one of the earliest, most impassioned statements in Western dramatic literature demanding the right of free thought. And it resonated long after Schiller died. As late as 1935 a German audience, under the rule of the Nazis, broke into spontaneous applause when this line was stated in *Don Carlos* at the theater. The next day the Nazi paper formally rebuked them and reiterated the evil of freedom to think, actually denouncing it as a debased Jewish ideal. So Schiller was a rallying cry for liberty for a long, long time after his death.

So far we haven't captured the full theme. The primacy of freedom, yes, but over what? It is not so much directly over tyranny. What is the obstacle to freedom as presented and dramatized in the play?

What is Posa's virtue? What makes him able to be a world fighter for freedom, and not sink in his own little romantic escapades? The fact that he is a selfless crusader. What is the evil of Philipp, the Church and the Grand Inquisitor in terms of the play? They want power. For whom? Themselves. What is the lesson Don Carlos has to learn? The renunciation of personal love. So from every angle the message is: the primacy of freedom over selfishness.

If I could interject a comment as an Objectivist: what a tragedy that this is his theme, the dichotomy of freedom versus selfishness. How could a man be free without a self? And if he is selfless, won't he then be docile to some authority eager to sacrifice him? But, of course, you know all this.

6. Philosophy

A philosophy, according to Objectivism, has three central issues. Ayn Rand always summarized Objectivism as reason, selfishness and capitalism or freedom. And that is, in other words, epistemology, ethics and politics, with metaphysics being implied in epistemology. What is Schiller's trinity? Freedom? Yes. Selfishness? No, the exact Kantian opposite. But what about the third issue, reason? Remember, we are in the Enlightenment and the play gives you an explicit answer. Even aside from the Grand Inquisitor scene, there is another character—the religious priest, Domingo, one of the villains and the enemy of Posa and of freedom. He is made to say explicitly and disparagingly about Don Carlos: "his heart is glowing with a newer virtue [that is, newer than piety] that, proud and certain and sufficient onto itself, will not be beggar to a faith." Then he reveals the identity of this monstrous new virtue in two fabulous words: "he *thinks*! His head burns with a strange chimera—'Tis mankind that he worships."

In other words, the objection, from the point of view of the Church, is that Don Carlos is concerned not with God but with man, not with heaven but with this world. And that, of course, is the true Enlightenment spirit: it is reason, man, nature; this life against religion, revelation and faith.

Now Act Five, Scene Ten: the Grand Inquisitor scene. After our analysis, I urge you to reread it again at your leisure and see how stunningly complete it is as a scene. A total philosophy, on every key issue, not stated as a speech, but dramatized in the context of a power struggle. The king trying to stand up to the Grand Inquisitor, the Grand Inquisitor asserting himself over the king and crushing him down to a position of abject obedience. A brilliantly logical scene in the course of which the Grand Inquisitor has to come out against nature, reason, freedom, the individual. And he does it all righteously and proudly, on principle. He comes out against independence, against personal value-judgment. He covers the waterfront, from metaphysics to politics in a total, integrated viewpoint—and as an absolute story necessity.

This is the scene which I regard as unequalled in world theater for the combination of profundity and drama. By profundity, I mean the breadth and totality of the philosophy and its consistency. By drama, I mean here the ability to integrate that profound and all-encompassing philosophic view into moment-by-moment action on which the fate of the characters and the lives of the heroes are going to depend. It is, on the face of it, an impossible assignment. To be able to do it is something I think you will never find anywhere else within theatrical history. (You'll find it in the novels of Ayn Rand but that is not theater.)

Let's just look at this scene to get the idea how it covers the gamut philosophically and does so out of necessity of the logic of the structure. That is what is so incredibly difficult to do. From the very opening, this scene takes off when the Grand Inquisitor comes on stage. He is ninety and he is blind. Who does that remind you of? Teiresias, right? He is leaning on a cane; he is led by two young kids. But he has on his side a power much greater than eyesight. He has the power of philosophy.

Right from the very opening Philipp is on the defensive. The Grand Inquisitor comes in and says, "Do I stand before the king?"

The king says, "You do."

"I could no longer tell." This has a double meaning. He is blind so cannot see; and you are not acting like a king. Wonderful double meaning, which is one of the greatest feats of dialogue, if you can do it.

Then we learn that the Grand Inquisitor knew everything from the outset. He berates the king: *You knew about Posa's liberal leanings* ["liberal" in the pro-freedom sense] *so how could you be friendly with him?* Then this statement from the Grand Inquisitor, "If *one* finds mercy, why would we have the right to sacrifice ten thousand?" Which is what they are doing regularly at the Inquisition. So he is a true man of principle. He asks: how could you be friendly with a creature— Posa—whom God sent "to make a show of ostentatious reason?" In other words, God sent him to show us that reason is mortal sin, so that the Church could punish him and teach mankind something about faith and duty. The king says: *Forgive me but I am an amateur at ruling.* And the Grand Inquisitor says: *You certainly are.* "Do you really know so little about the minds of innovators and of dreamers?" Notice the evils: innovation and dreams, as against obedience to the long-established decrees of the Church.

The king says, "I looked around to find a man." The instant comeback, "What are, then, men to you but numbers, nothing more." What does that mean? What is an individual? All that counts is the group, the collective.

It is all part of the same philosophy and it comes as a matter of necessity as he is knocking down the king. Only the collective counts. Men are nothing but numbers. The king says: *Yes, I know but* "I am a little man." *I'm not up to being a king.* And the Grand Inquisitor says: *Don't try to deceive me. In courting Posa you were trying to escape the rule of the Church, you had a personal agenda.* "The Holy Order's chains had weighed you down; you wanted to be free, unique."*You wanted to carve out your own values in your own realm. And that is sin.* The king is silent.

And the Grand Inquisitor turns the knife. He tells the king that Posa was killed by the Church really as a punishment for the king's sins. *Now I would like you to thank us for it. Kneel down before me. Lick my boots for having killed the man you love.* Unconditional surrender. This is pretty powerful stuff.

The king says: *What about Don Carlos, my son? He plans to lead the rebels.*

The Grand Inquisitor says: *What's the problem? Give him exactly what he deserves.*

The king is stunned at the idea, and he says sarcastically, "Can you establish a new faith for me that will defend the murder of a child?"

The Grand Inquisitor doesn't bat an eye. "The Son of God died on the Tree to make atonement to eternal justice." Why not your son?

The king says: *It's unnatural, what you are asking, for a father to kill his son. I would be offending the voice of Nature.*

The Grand Inquisitor: "No voice of Nature is of any worth before our Faith." So much for metaphysics.

The king says: *Well, I don't know what to do; who am I to know? You decide. Can I withdraw completely as a judge in this matter?*

The Grand Inquisitor says: *Oh, yes, you can abdicate your power of judgment.* "Give it me."

The king has a last pang, a last pull to his human status and he says, "He is my only son.—For whom have I then gathered?" I have all this wealth and power for whom?

And then the climactic line of the Grand Inquisitor: "Better to destroy than to make free."

Do you understand that line? This does not mean he is a nihilist. The Grand Inquisitor is not a nihilist. When he says it is better to destroy than to make free, he is talking about two different orientations. Making free, in his mind, stands for: oriented to yourself, your own desires; what is called the pursuit of happiness. As against being oriented to God, faith, obedience, on your knees. And Don Carlos has proved recalcitrant. So the choice is to let him be free—which means an affront to God, to virtue, and to the nature of reality as the Grand Inquisitor has just demonstrated—or else destroy him. There is no other choice.

I hope you see from this quick sample what a brilliant scene this is. Every word is necessitated by the action, by the ruling situation. There is no extraneous philosophizing and yet all the bases of philosophy are covered, and an entire view of the world is dramatized—and it is dramatized in a passionate confrontation, not over theory, but over the life and death of a hero.

This is a feat that just simply cannot be overestimated. It is pure intellectual and artistic genius on Schiller's part. As far as I'm concerned, I am content to just relish and admire that scene forever. There is just nothing higher that theater can offer than that scene. This is not the greatest play, but if this is not the greatest of all philosophic scenes, I can't think of what its competitor would be.

Do you see why I chose this play, despite what you have to plow through?

As to the content of the philosophy, as against the genius of his dramatization of it, I have to give a very different estimate. What is the philosophy that Schiller wants the reader to come away with? Well, of course, we come away with the idea that the Grand Inquisitor is wrong about reason; he is wrong about nature; he is wrong about the individual; he is wrong about freedom. There is only one point that he is right about; sacrifice, the need of serving something beyond yourself.

If you are an Objectivist, you know the tragic self-contradiction of Schiller. His trinity is: reason, sacrifice, freedom. Yet, as you know from Ayn Rand's writings, sacrifice makes freedom impossible, and it makes reason impossible. More than that, Schiller demonstrates both those points in his play himself. He gives you the data to conclude that by enshrining sacrifice, he is laying the basis to destroy both reason and freedom. The end result is that the Grand Inquisitor mentality is going to win out the world—as, in fact, it has.

The primary villain, needless to say, is not Schiller. I quote: "Schiller's debt to Kant is a commonplace of intellectual history." Even though Kant's *Critique of Pure Reason* was not published until a few years after *Don Carlos*, Schiller had studied Kant's views at university very early, even before Kant was widely published and known. Schiller was, in effect, the first Kantian in history; one of the very first of Kant's disciples. Intellectually, *Don Carlos* is a perfect statement of what you get when you merge the best of the Enlightenment spirit with the purest of Kantianism. You could say, there could be no such merger, and yet that is just what this play is. What you get when you merge them—although Schiller never knew it—is the total triumph of the irrational.

I want to say in conclusion that, despite the corruption of the ideas and the flaws in the play's construction, I hope that you were able to enjoy the unprecedented values that this play offers. Even more simply, I hope you were as thrilled by the last act of this play as I am. I know it is a lot of work, but I thank you for reading it and giving me the very enjoyable opportunity of discussing it.

Q & A

Q: Why do you not include the Grand Inquisitor in your statement of the plot-theme?

A: Terrific question. My answer to that is: that is Schiller's problem, not mine. In other words, the Grand Inquisitor was not integral to the story as told by Schiller. The whole story would hold even if there was no Grand Inquisitor scene. It is not a story about the king's relation to the Church. It is not a story about Posa's fight against the Church.

Of course, the Grand Inquisitor scene is logical and causally related. It is certainly not an arbitrary addendum. But to be part of the plot-theme, it has to be inescapable and inevitable in the core of the action. And it is not. It's in the nature of a brilliant afterthought, when Schiller was really steamed up and going. But he did not have the Church or the Grand Inquisitor or anything representing him as a major element. Domingo, who was the only character representing religion in the play, was just like Alba representing the nobles; he was not a major figure.

I'll give you this analogy. If you are giving a plot-theme for *Atlas Shrugged*, you would certainly include Galt, even though he doesn't appear till the end. That's because Galt appears in a hell of a lot of the actual novel. But just imagine that there was no hint in the novel; there was no unknown inventor; there was nobody asking "Who is John Galt?"; there was no Dagny looking out and wondering where was the ideal man at the end of the tracks, etc. All of that was gone, and the story went on. Suddenly out of the blue, she opens the door and there stands John Galt. She would say, "Who the hell are you?" Even if he was a great character, you would have to say this wasn't part of the story. It wasn't an ongoing thing. It was an afterthought; it wasn't integrated into the total.

It would be like one of these James Bond movies. While he has been fighting Dr. No all the way through, at the very end we find out that he has been financed by General Motors. All that does is put in an anti-business swipe. It doesn't do anything for the story. That's the way the Grand Inquisitor is. It is of tremendous thematic significance, but it is not a plot necessity.

Ideally the plot and the theme should be integrated: the theme should necessitate the plot and vice versa. This play is a failure of integration on Schiller's part, specifically the flaw of not integrating a fabulous character, who is crucial to the clarity of the theme, into the structure of the plot-theme.

The reason that he didn't is not that he couldn't. It is that he got the idea too late, after he was already on another play. In a sense, he outgrew the play; became too brilliant too soon for this play. So I think, esthetically, it is a flaw but I am certainly prepared to live with a flaw of that dimension.

Q: It is difficult to ask this question; I am trying to formulate it. Given the state of professional philosophy during the eighteenth century, do you believe it was possible for the non-philosopher, the statesman, the artist, the serious thinker who was not a professional philosopher to really identify the contradiction between altruism and the notion of freedom and benevolence and reason?

A: You don't have to be a professional. Professional means you make your living at this field. Kant was sometimes regarded as the first professional philosopher because he was an actual professor who gained his livelihood this way. You certainly do not have to be a professional philosopher to challenge the tradition of the ages that ties altruism in with all good things. But I do concede that you do have to be a philosopher. An ordinary artist, businessman, statesman, etc., however sensitive, who was not a philosopher with an original philosophic mind, would never think to challenge that combination. Even Jefferson did not think to challenge it. You have to go to the very, very roots of the West. You have to go all the way to Christianity and Judaism versus paganism, which didn't have a whole code of ethics either, and reconceive from scratch. That requires a philosophy.

The thing is, Schiller was a philosopher but he was not an epochal philosopher. You need for that a philosopher who could shape a whole epoch, who could challenge down to the base. There is no predicting when that's going to come; it is not a product of social circumstances. It could have happened at that time, but it didn't. It could have happened in our time, and it did. We would have been saved a tremendous amount of time if that kind of challenge had been raised right at this time: at the time of the American and French Revolutions and before Kant was institutionalized. We would have Utopia. It would have been a battle, but at least there would have been somebody battling. Unfortunately, that never did take place and Kant became entrenched thereafter.

I am not blaming Schiller. You can never blame a man for not being an epochal genius. That is just ridiculous. It is like blaming a man for not being able to serve faster than Bjorn Borg. You cannot do more than you can do.

Q: I believe you said that double meanings refer to the highest feat of dialogue, if you can do it. Would you talk about the value of double meanings, please?

A: Well, the value of double meaning is really very simple. You get two for the price of one. What is terrific on stage is to have a character say something and the audience knows more about it than the character he is addressing. You have the tremendous joy of watching the one meaning and at the same time you get the deeper level. Or maybe the other character gets the deeper level, but he is not allowed to acknowledge it. So you have a much richer and fuller presentation.

Let's put it this way. The whole thing with art is integration and integration involves tremendous condensation. You want one element to carry as much as possible. Every element has to carry the plot, the characterization and the theme. Within that, therefore, the more dense the work; that is, the more eloquent and powerful it is, the more it is able to carry because art is the opposite of something diffuse. You don't want a whole bunch of things strung out. Even in a play, you want only a few images that will condense and give you a visual reality.

Double meaning is one brilliant technique within the theater of doing this, because it conveys a deeper form of the reality in a condensed, economical fashion. That is one of the hallmarks of Miss Rand: the ability to use dialogue or gesture with double meanings. You know who else in this course is excellent at double meanings? Maeterlinck. If you reread the end of *Monna Vanna*, there is a whole passage when Monna Vanna is making a speech to the king, which he understands in one way, and we understand that she has an entirely different meaning. She is supposedly denouncing Prinzivalle to her husband, Guido. In fact, she is denouncing her husband to his face and he doesn't get it. There is a tremendous tension and interplay which is extremely elegant.

Q: Speaking of double meanings, I have a different interpretation than you of the line from *Othello*: "put out the light and put out the light." Mine was basically the murder of Desdemona and pride at putting out the light of her eyes.

A: I guess you could put it that way. He is holding a candle which he snuffs before he kills her so I think the traditional interpretation is truer to the action. What is good about the traditional interpretation is that it is a percept—art has to be perceptual. You see him putting out the light and it is not so much putting out the light of her life but of his own life. He is snuffing out all value in the act of snuffing out the candle.

Q: Can you describe your preparation for this course, both in terms of the tasks and the time involved? I would be interested to know what went into it.

A: I started preparing for this course in September and I did one play a month. For a complexity of reasons I was able to work only two days a week, approximately six to eight hours a day. I did each play, including the lecture in about eight or nine days of full-time work. That included, first of all, picking the playwrights. You really have no choice here; if you are going to do great playwrights, they just name themselves.

The harder task was picking which play. I had to skim the leading candidates and make a decision on which play. I had to read the play and make notes on what it meant. I had to simultaneously scan three or four other translations to try to find one that was easier and more accessible. Then I buried myself in secondary literature, six or eight library books out of the stack and swallowed it in, until my head was just bulging.

That is about three or four days of full-time work so far across several weeks. My focus was: what is this play about?—not the theme but the action. From the beginning, I always tried to work out: what is the plot-theme? I would constantly be writing notes and across several weeks, the plot-theme would fall into line.

Once that happened, it was a breeze. I would make notes in the margin and just collect them. I organized all the notes with scissors and paste; under *Characterization* one big pile, under *Plot* one big pile, under *Theme* one big pile. Then I just sat down at the type-writer and sorted through them in order and typed it all out. That was basically how I did it.

I would say I worked a total of sixteen to seventeen hours per play, counting the writing of the lecture. About one half was spent on immersing myself in alternate texts and research to figure out the plot-theme and the other half in batting out the rest.

Editor's Note

At this point in the course, Dr. Peikoff introduced a simple grid to facilitate the retrieval of information to be used at the end of the course in the evaluation of the plays.

> *Antigone*
> Characters: ANTIGONE; (Creon)
> Plot-Theme: A young princess defies a powerful king over a moral issue.
> Climax: Antigone is led away by guards.
> Theme: Indiv/State; God over Man
> Philosophy: Religion$^+$/Humanism

Just before we plunge in, I want to call your attention to this little chart I put on the blackboard in preparation for our final class where we have to make comparative, objective judgments on all these different plays. I found it very helpful to capture the entire course and content of all the plays on two pieces of paper. You can see how, for the crow epistemology, you can condense all the key points that you need, and then you just have to run your eyes down. First, I list the main *characters* in capital letters, the ones that might conceivably qualify for the questions asked; the strongest heroine, the most admirable hero, the worst villain, etc. I put in parentheses any minor characters that might conceivably qualify—like, who you most might like to talk philosophy with or whichever. I know this is all that *Antigone* has to offer, as far as characters are concerned, so I condensed down to that.

Then I include the *plot-theme* exactly as I dictated it. That's the only one I don't synopsize, because there every word is crucial and must be a full sentence. Next, I put *climax* and a brief way to capture what it is. Antigone is unyielding in this case; it's not a very pronounced climax. In some cases it's a full event, like Posa is murdered or whatever. Next is *theme* and since I know that very well—it's just philosophy—I condensed that heavily. "Indiv/state." And that tells me "individual above the state" or "moral above political"; just anything to capture in my mind what the play is talking about.

And then I write the final *philosophy*, the big abstractions, summarized briefly. And in this case for *Antigone* I have "religion/humanism"; with the idea that Sophocles has one foot in the religious camp, and one foot in life on earth, and a little plus beside "religion" to indicate that it's definitely prominent, not vestigial.

That's it. That is the total play of *Antigone* as far as needed for the assignment. Now you can easily get seven of these on two pages of paper. Do that with each play—and that's just a condensation of the notes that you should already have been taking. So when you get to these questions, such as "with which play do you most strongly agree?"—you don't have to sit back and say, "Oh, my God. Now Antigone said this, and Othello said . . ." You just zip through: "individual above the state," etc., etc., etc., and it comes right out at you.

Or "which has the most gripping climax?" And you try to remember which climax was whose. Whereas here you just zip through the climaxes. So I recommend this very strongly to facilitate your judgment in the final lecture.

CHAPTER FIVE

An Enemy of the People

Henrik Ibsen

1. Introduction

*A*n *Enemy of the People* by Henrik Ibsen is the first modern play in this
course and the only one set in the modern era. (Both *Saint Joan* and
Monna Vanna, though modern plays, are set in historical eras.) On top of
that (I don't think I'm going to spoil too much by saying this), its philosophy is essentially unimpeachable across the board. Therefore, this is without doubt the easiest of the plays. There is no difficult language to get used
to, no historical period to worry about, no contradictions on the part of the
author that baffle you. That does not make it necessarily the best play, but
it doesn't make it *not* the best play either. I am not foreclosing that question.
It definitely makes it the easiest play for us, although in a thousand years it
won't be that easy. Right now though this is like eating ice cream, so you
should be able to just sit back and get pure pleasure out of this play. It in
no way upsets, baffles or antagonizes you. I thought you should have the
experience of one utterly unobstructed, but still great, play.

Ibsen's dates are 1828 to 1906. He's a Norwegian author of a lot of
poetry and twenty-six plays, including some very famous verse plays,
such as *Brand* and *Peer Gynt*. His most famous works are his final
twelve prose plays, which are generally regarded as a single cycle,
having a special unity among them. There are people who will not
study any one of them without doing all twelve works. However, I do
not take that view.

An Enemy of the People is number four of Ibsen's final cycle. It was
written in 1882 when he was fifty-four. In the United States, Ibsen is
most famous for his play *The Doll's House*. It has been his biggest play
here because it is alleged to be a feminist play—which it is not. Ibsen
has a much greater importance in the history of the theater. Can you
remember in which fiction work of hers, Ayn Rand came out with a big
plug for Ibsen? In *The Fountainhead*, Ike the Genius was showing his

manuscript and Toohey tried to explain to him that there was no room in the theater for him and Ibsen both. If Ike was to be enshrined in the theater, Ibsen was the one that had to be destroyed. That is pretty clear evidence that Miss Rand was a great admirer of Ibsen, which she was. He is correctly called the Father of Modern Drama—in a good sense of modern drama—for several reasons, one of which I am going to touch on at the end.

Just to orient you from the outset, he is an exponent of the well-made play. He is a romanticist who avidly read Corneille, Racine, Shakespeare, Byron and Hugo before he was twenty. Obviously he did not have an American education. He is an extremist in what I personally identify with and regard as a very good sense. He has been widely praised and criticized throughout his career. As one commentator put it, he has had a sad fate because he is "too radical for the nineteenth century and too conservative for the twentieth." That is very hopeful from our point of view.

In terms of historical context, we are in the late nineteenth century, a hundred years after our last play by Schiller. At the time of Schiller, political freedom was just erupting, in the sense of the American and French Revolutions. And of course, technological progress via the Industrial Revolution and capitalism then took over. That was accompanied by a full-fledged Romantic development in art, where artists were concerned with self-made heroes. There was wide-spread intoxication with freedom—both in the sense of the idea of free will and man's self-determination, and in the sense of political freedom, the untrammeled freedom to do with your life what you decided.

People held the idea that under these fantastic conditions, in every day and in every way things would get better and better (to borrow the formulation from Coué). They came to the idea that progress is self-evident and automatic, an idea of which the twentieth century would have disabused them entirely. The idea was that all change would be a gradual change toward improvement. Thus "evolution" became the byword of the period. Evolution did not become the byword because of Darwin; Darwin became the byword because of evolution. He is the one who took the idea of evolution that was in the atmosphere and gave it a scientific base within the field of biology. It had been essential to Hegel's philosophy before Darwin. I cannot think of a thinker influenced by the nineteenth century who was not an evolutionist in one way or another. Even the religious people thought that we evolved in understanding God's word. Ibsen also comes out for evolution. When you read nineteenth-century writings, you pretty much have to discount evolution as a theory of what they believed, because everybody believed it. It was like motherhood.

Ibsen has to be understood in this context, not that he is at all difficult to understand. But the overall message of his total body of work is that man is free but he doesn't use his freedom intelligently. We need the freedom to break with the past, to start over, to throw off the establishment, to think things through afresh and from the beginning. Who does he remind you of in the seventeenth century, the early Modern period? It is the same view that Francis Bacon and Descartes held: sweep everything aside and start over from the beginning. It is always a hopeful note when that is somebody's viewpoint, because they are throwing out all the prejudices and errors and trying to start over rationally.

Ibsen is therefore a thorough iconoclast, an idol smasher, but that does not make him a nihilist or a skeptic. A skeptic would say that freedom is impossible because man isn't good enough for it, which is what they all say today. Or, that freedom is a threat because we don't know how to use it, which the Existentialists in the fifties used to say. Ibsen believes man's mind *is* capable of governing him and directing his actions, but that man is not using the powers he has; that all of his institutions are warped and corrupted and have to be reconstructed from scratch. He comes across as attacking everything: marriage, "morals," even liberalism and reform, to say nothing of conservatism and reaction. Since everything is pretty rotten, you can almost always sympathize with him.

An eloquent touch of capturing his perspective are the final words he uttered on his deathbed. He was in conversation with someone and his last three words were: "on the contrary." (If you are going to die, it is very important that you figure out what your last words are going to be—and then stop after you have said them.)

The plot of *An Enemy of the People* was based on an incident which Ibsen had heard about. In the 1830s, a German doctor warned the people at a spa that an outbreak of cholera had occurred there. The season at the resort was ruined, the townsfolk stoned the doctor's house and he had to flee. That was the germ of the idea for this play. There was also a case in Norway of a chemist who had denounced the Oslo steam kitchens for neglect of the poor. When the chemist attempted to read a prepared speech repeating his earlier attack, the chairman tried to prevent him from speaking and the audience forced

him to withdraw. This is very similar to what happens to Dr. Stockmann in Act Four of the play. So here again, even though it is the
nineteenth century, he is taking his main plot situation from events
that he heard, and transforming it into a profound piece by his genius.

2. Plot-theme

I am going to give you an example of what a nominalist would say
about the plot-theme. A nominalist is someone who, on principle, rejects essences and abstractions; who can do nothing but recite concretes. That is the great majority of literary critics and commentators
through the ages. You may have heard of Carl Van Doren (the uncle of
Charles Van Doren who was tainted in the quiz show scandals of the
fifties).This is his brilliant statement of the essence of *An Enemy of
the People*: "this play is the story of a man who learns that the water
of the municipal baths in a town in Norway is infected, supposes that
the authorities will at once move to do away with the public menace,
finds that because of the necessary expense they refuse to pay any
attention to him, tries single-handed to correct the abuse, is defeated
and mobbed, and has to take refuge." He goes on and on like that.

And then he gets to: what does all that mean? It doesn't mean
anything whatever, because it is just a string of concretes. Van Doren
says, "The misfortunes of the play are too highly individualized to be
looked upon as allegorical, symbolical, or even typical." Armed with
that wonderful overview, the student is supposed to go in and read
this play. In other words, there is no wider meaning, no theme, no
message, no significance. I thought I would give you this as a horror
example as to why you have to grasp the essence, which is the plot-
theme. Otherwise, you have nothing except a recapitulation of what
happens in the play, with no insight into it.

The plot-theme functions to a play the way a definition does to a
concept. It gives you the essence of the play condensed in a way that
contrasts it to other plays and relates it to those plays which are closest
to it. In just the way that a definition gives you the genus which tells
you the category that is most similar to the thing being defined; and
then the differentia, what sets it apart—so too with the plot-theme.
You have to give it in such a way that you bring it in conjunction with
the plays it is closest to, and then say what sets it apart.

What I think we should do is define the plot-theme in this case in
relation to *Antigone*. In both we have a common genus of the individual

directly challenging and disobeying authority. (I am using *genus* here met-aphorically.) They are basically the same kind of play. The best way to capture *An Enemy of the People* is simply to differentiate it from *Antigone*.

Here are some of the key differences, none of which change the fact that it is basically the same situation as *Antigone*. Antigone directly challenges the authorities over a moral issue; the refusal to give her brother proper burial. Tomas Stockmann confronts authorities first over the issue of factual truth: are the baths poisoned? Only as the con-flict deepens does it become a moral issue. Of course it is not the same moral issue as in *Antigone*. The moral issue in this play is: to accept the truth at any price or to evade, fudge and compromise it for the sake of "higher" concerns. In this play the conflict is first over the content of truth; then over the value of truth; and only finally over freedom, the freedom necessary to pursue the truth. So that is one difference in con-tent of the challenge.

There is also a more modern element to the challenge, beyond the issue of the content. Tomas Stockmann is a modern experimental sci-entist. He is not an ancient princess. Antigone is a moralist who had no objective proof of her morality, of what the gods really expect us to do with the corpses of the dead. But Tomas Stockmann (I always refer to him as Tomas because of his wicked brother. Let's just make the rule: if I call him Stockmann, I mean the hero; if I mean the bad one, I'll say Peter)—the scientist, has objective, experimental proof of what he stands for. And so his mission takes on the meaning of the man of reason against the passion of the mob. From the very nature of his clash, you can already see emerging Ibsen, the secularist and atheist, in contrast to Sophocles, the religionist. It is a completely this-worldly play. By the nineteenth century, God has dropped out altogether. God comes back in Shaw in other forms, but he never comes back the same way that he was in the past.

Another difference with *Antigone* is the nature of the authority being rebelled against. Antigone defies the corrupt ruler in a mon-archy. Tomas Stockmann takes on the entire society in a democracy. What does society fight him over? It is to be contrasted with what society fought Socrates over in the ancient world; his religious con-victions and society's, such as they were. Socrates, they thought, was impious; he worshipped false gods; he corrupted the young; etc.

There is no such ideology on the part of society in this play. On the surface the fight is over money. The people keep talking about the fact that cleaning up the baths is a two-year shutdown, vast sums of money will be lost, it will mean economic ruin. But money is not really the issue. Two seconds of thought would convince them (or you) that in the long run they are going to be doomed financially anyway, because when the tourists come and start to die in droves, obviously the word is going to get out. If money were really the issue and they wanted to be dishonest, the most these people would do is rush to clean the premises on the sly, so no one would ever know. If they were motivated by money, their dishonesty would never get farther than hiding the truth while they were busy trying to get rid of the poison.

But Ibsen's point, of course, is that these are short-range mentalities. They are non-planners, non-copers, non-thinkers. They simply do not want to face the problem; they want it to go away; they want to evade. There is nothing on their side but numbers. Their attitude is: we are the majority and that decides the issue. If we *want* it to be that way, that is the way it is going to be.

In other words, this is a modern society. It is not a society that has religious convictions, however false, and persecutes the martyr who disagrees. It is a society of short-range relativists, compromisers and evaders. This is another reason why Ibsen is the Father of Modern Drama. He captures this type of society with great skill.

I think with those contrasts we can just dictate the plot-theme without batting an eye here. It is a very simple and straightforward plot-theme: *an idealistic scientist champions truth against a society of compromisers.* That seems to me perfectly straightforward. The very nature of that situation, if you are sick of the quality of the contemporary world, is calculated to make you lick your chops in anticipation. Unless, of course, they are going to defeat him. The plot-theme doesn't tell us what happens, just the nature of the conflict.

What then is the essential conflict that we read off from the plot-theme? Tomas Stockmann versus society. That is the conflict in this play and, appropriately, the two come face to face at a certain point. Throughout the play, society has to be represented by various characters, so that in concrete terms the conflict is: Tomas Stockmann versus his brother Peter, the mayor; Tomas Stockmann versus Aslaksen, the printer; Tomas Stockmann versus Hovstad, the editor; Tomas Stockmann versus Kiil, his father-in-law. And then all the other conflicts within the establishment that this central one entails, like the editor versus the mayor, or the editor versus the publisher, or Kiil versus the mayor. Further, all the conflict between Tomas Stockmann's allies and the establishment figures. For example, Horster, the sea captain versus the ship owner who fires him; Petra versus the editor; Petra versus her employers who fire her, etc.

The message I am trying to hammer home is: as in any great play, there is a central, ruling conflict and then an abundance of derivative clashes. That makes for a passionate, suspenseful, exciting, dramatic play. When the establishment is split, we have the drama of each of them being at each other's throats. When the establishment coalesces and unites, we have the virulent ferocity of the mob against Tomas Stockmann. So either way there is something riveting going on.

3. Plot Development

First, the establishment of the situation takes place during Acts One and Two. In Act One we learn that Dr. Stockmann is happy and sociable; he expects praise for having discovered the poison. In Act Two he seems to acquire allies, but the mayor surprisingly declares war and Stockmann is indignant and amazed. At this point the situation is established: there is going to be a fight. By the end of Act Two, for the first time, we have a situation.

The rise to the climax is Acts Three and Four. Now we watch as Stockmann is, step by step, stripped of all illusions of support from different factions in the community, until there is nothing left for him but to appeal, one on one, against the whole society. I hope you see the necessity of his defeat and disillusionment at first in the development of the play. He cannot fight for fundamental social change as long as he naively misunderstands the essence of his society; as long as he doesn't realize how deep the corruption goes. It takes him through Act Two to reach this point. Then he has to see, at the editor's office, his allies collapse, the mayor convert the liberals, and society become a unified front. At that point, enraged, he has no option but to confront, as the last court of appeal, the assembled mob.

In other words, the conflict is introduced in Act Two, and broadened until it reaches the maximum conceivable intensity and scope in Act Four, which is the climax; the high point of the conflict and the point from which the ending has to directly follow. As I have said several times, if we call something a climax, it does not necessarily mean that we can predict the ending. But when you reach the ending, you should be able to see in hindsight that it followed inevitably from this climax. It is often the case that the climax is identifiable only retrospectively. The essence of the climax here is: Tomas Stockmann, silenced about the baths, tells the moral truth about the society to their faces. He denounces the authorities and the public—the compact majority, as he calls it—and he receives the final sentence from the supreme court of democracy, the mob. He is, they claim, an enemy of the people. So he is the lead character and that is his ironic title in the play. The people, with great logic, turn ugly when he tells them what he thinks of them and take out after him.

That leads us to the third and last part of the play, the resolution, which is Act Five. Here again, as with any great playwright, the resolution doesn't just meander to a close. It itself has tremendous suspense and structure. Stockmann's attack on the authorities has escalated, as we saw in the climax, to an attack on the whole society and all the citizens. So logically now, he has to end up alone, alone with a few allies. In the resolution, the situation is brilliantly milked. Every kind of temptation is dangled before him, one after the other. The mayor offers him his job back, if only he will recant. Kiil offers to make his family rich but if he doesn't give in, his family will be paupered. The editor offers him all the support and publicity he could ever want. It is like they take him up to the top of a building and show him all the world can be his, if only he will recant.

But he is adamant. He doesn't bat an eye at the fact that he is condemning his children to starvation and poverty. Too bad for them, is his attitude. He has nothing but scorn for all of the people that did not dare do otherwise: the school that dismisses his daughter, the landlord that cancels his lease, the ship owner that fires his friend, the captain. When his brother announces Stockmann's dismissal saying, "We regret this decision but, frankly, we didn't dare do otherwise. Out of respect for public opinion, you understand," his contempt is complete. At one point he expresses his estimate of these people in a very graphic and visual way (remember, this is meant to be seen on stage) by forcing these swine out of his house with an umbrella. At one point we see him thinking of escaping to the far West. The far West does not mean the far west of Norway; it means the United States, where he could live on the frontier (and it still was the frontier, this was before California was settled by the Republicans) in solitude. But he changes his mind about that because he is not going to concede his hometown to the enemy. So his inevitable decision is to stay alone and start over.

At the end of the play, he is starting over; he is going to build the right society, exactly in the way that Ibsen thought his whole life mission was to start over and build the right society.

We have to answer this question: is the fact that Stockmann ends up alone with his few supporters and family starting over a failure or a success for him? Is this a happy ending or a tragic ending? It is a happy ending. He is a success because he is happy, and he is happy because he has discovered that the right man is the metaphysically efficacious man, the man with the power to cope with reality and achieve his goals. That is what he calls the "strong man"; what Ibsen in other plays calls the creative, selfish individual. Stockmann has the power to start life anew, so there is no doubt that Ibsen regarded this as a happy ending.

We are always concerned with the logic of the ending. Must a play have the kind of end that it does? If it is a good play, yes it does. It is not just the caprice of the author. Why does this play end happily? Why must it? Why couldn't it have had the same situation but end up the way Socrates did in real life? He has to drink hemlock. Why couldn't it end up with Tomas Stockmann being alone, hated, crushed, and a suicide? It would have been the same situation, the same development, but the ending would have taken a dramatically malevolent turn.

There are two main reasons why it could not have ended this way. I stress to you: an author's creative freedom does not give him the freedom to have whatever ending he wants. If he has a logical situation and characters drawn a certain way, the ending has to write itself. If he wants a certain ending, then he has to start with that ending and write the entire play to bring him to that ending. The idea people have that you can change any play to make it happy or sad is fantastic. It means they have no idea that a play is like a work of geometry; that once the axioms are laid down, the theorem is inevitable. The test of the skill of the playwright is to do the inevitable while letting you think, "Oh, my God, I never expected that. I never expected it, but I see it could not have been otherwise." This is the same way a great murder mystery has to be. It startles you but then you say, "Yes, this suspect had to be the murderer." So an ending is something to be explained, not wished away.

There are two main reasons why this play has to have a happy ending. One comes from the theme, which we will discuss later, but I think you can easily see that whatever travails he goes through, Stockmann is never really threatened. He is so independent that they cannot hurt him. He creates his own well-being, his own success, his own projects, his own happiness—and therefore he is so impervious to whatever they do to him that they obviously cannot crush him.

The theme demands that ending. It would be analogous to *The Fountainhead* being as it was, but at the very end Roark says, "I just can't take Keating anymore," and commits suicide. It would be fantastic; it would destroy the entire book because of the utter illogic of it.

A secondary reason why it would be particularly ludicrous for this play not to have a happy ending is because this play by genre is—are you ready for this?—a comedy. This is not a tragic comedy, either. It is a real comedy. In other words Ibsen intends to evoke laughter all the way through, which Corneille did not. There is plenty of humor and satire here. There is even slapstick and clowning around, involving the hero himself. For example, when he tries on the mayor's hat or when he beats those people down with an umbrella. There is a crazy drunkard that is put in there to evoke laughs. So there are lots of jokes and fun and laughter; yet at the same time a heroic character with a serious struggle and a happy ending.

This was a new phenomenon in drama; this combination of laughter, seriousness and heroism all the way through and a happy ending. There was no name for it when Ibsen wrote it. Ibsen himself wrote his publisher the following: "I am still uncertain as to whether I should call it a comedy or a straight drama. It has many of the traits of comedy, but it is also based on a serious idea." Absolutely true; qua comedy it has to have a happy ending. One commentator formulates this eloquent phrase: "as one would expect, this is Ibsen's most militant play."

An Enemy of the People and *The Fountainhead* are very similar in theme, essential characters, development, etc. It is hardly an accident that Miss Rand admired Ibsen. In regard to the ending, which we usually do discuss when we get to the resolution of a play, I want you now to observe that there is a certain similarity and difference to the ending of *The Fountainhead*. Both Stockmann and Roark are individuals who successfully defy society. But Roark wins in the present. He sees the reality of his ideal in this world in his lifetime—as against in future generations. Stockmann's situation, on the other hand, would be more like *The Fountainhead* ending with Roark having his blueprints for the ideal building ready and a class of young architectural students taking notes with the idea that someday someone would hire them and they would build accordingly.

Another way to put it would be: Tomas Stockmann ends up the way I will, not the way Roark did. In other words, he has his theory, he has his hope, he is undefeated but the full reality of the change he wants in the world will take place well after he dies.

There is something to be said about this kind of deferred benevolence. One night I told my eight-year-old daughter, Kira, the story of this play because she always wants a bedtime story. After I saw how well it went over with her, I decided to present *An Enemy of the People* to her Grade Two class. Her teacher has asked me once a year to go to her school and lecture on philosophy. The preceding year I did Plato and Aristotle for them in Grade One. The teacher said that the class would be able to concentrate for maybe ten minutes. It turned out that they sat for forty minutes, absolutely motionless. They were so enchanted with the play that they demanded by popular sentiment that the class stage the play, using the original, adult text. The teacher found an excerpted version (basically Acts Four and Five) with enough exposition so you could follow it. That class put on the whole thing with props, scenery, etc. The principal and the other teachers said that it was inconceivable that a Grade Two class could perform Ibsen. And yet, they did.

I told her the story just as it happened, about the baths and the poison and the fight, etc., and that Stockmann was going to start over. Then I said, "That's it, time for bed."

She looked at me and said, "Is that all?"

And I said, "What else did you want?"

She said, "Well, what happened when they came to the baths?" In other words, she was caught up in the existential story, and she was not prepared to drop it and hear it in the next generation. She wanted the end of the story. Although Ibsen didn't really discuss this, I had to tell her the people came and dropped like flies. The word got around and the mayor was kicked out. I had to make up a whole afterstory. Then she was happy to go to sleep. What is significant is that the actual, existential concrete which provoked the issue is dropped by Ibsen when the higher moral issues are reached. He, in effect, defers the plot-line to future generations and that, understandably, bothered my daughter.

An Ayn Rand novel, by contrast, always answers the concrete question of the story. It doesn't just jump off to resolutions in the future. In that sense, I think her novels are more benevolent; they have a more perfect integration of mind and body than in this play. They do not defer the reality of their theoretical resolution to another era. Even *Atlas*

Shrugged, which she originally conceived as going along three generations (because when she first thought of it, she never thought she could make it plausible as taking place in only one generation) was something she couldn't live with. So she ended it with: we are going back to the world *now*! We have won and the world is ours *today*!—as against it belongs to my son or my grandson.

4. Characterization

Which characters are essential? Obviously, Tomas Stockmann but several others are essential because society is too broad a generality and needs to be personified. There have been playwrights who were prepared to have society represented on stage by an undifferentiated mob. I think of Gerhart Hauptmann, a German playwright of the late nineteenth–early twentieth century, whose idea of the proletariat was just a mass of workers thrown onstage. You couldn't tell one from the other, and none of them had a bigger part than any other.

Ibsen is a thorough individualist so, even in the dramatization of the collective, he wants some strong, eloquent individual to speak for them. Thus we have the mayor, Peter Stockmann, Tomas's brother. The fact that they are brothers only heightens the contrast; to say, in effect, they had the same upbringing, but look how opposite they are. It is not a hidden code.

Peter is the obvious antagonist, but if it were only him, it would be a pretty thin play. We would have to make real that the mayor does speak for everybody. If the rest of the society never appears on stage, we would end up, in effect, with a two-character conflict. It would be Tomas versus Peter, like Antigone versus Creon. Since it is of the essence that the enemy here is the mob, the group, the majority, it is very logical that Ibsen has to give society other voices of its own. You want to see different classes, different political parties represented, so that what emerges is the sense of the whole society.

Ibsen basically selected three main groups. The liberals, who are allegedly revolutionaries, Marxists who want true socialism and fight for the workers. They are, in effect, the left intellectuals and labor. They are symbolized by the editor.

The petty bourgeois are the small businessman class. They are presented as what they are: middle-of-the-roaders, trying to appease everybody. Aslaksen, the printer, is the spokesman for them.

The aristocratic establishment are the rich who are deliberately drawn by Ibsen into two branches. One of them is now outdated but it was not in the nineteenth century. That branch is Kiil who represents the feudal mentality, the pre-modern mentality, the traditional pre-scientific aristocracy before the Industrial Revolution. We don't have that any more, except among Hollywood movie stars. In other words, he doesn't even believe in science. He thinks the whole thing is a joke by Tomas Stockmann; that it is just a sheer intrigue. He is an attempt to grasp a segment of society that has now perished, thankfully. So he is the most dated of the characters. The other branch of the aristocracy is the mayor, which represents just the old aristocracy in a modernized version.

A great playwright does not just multiply characters at random. You should try to figure out what he is getting at by this character, what is the point of including that one, and how every character earns his inclusion in the play. Not just because it is intrinsically interesting, but because it is an essential, in some form, to the action or the meaning of the action. This is true of any great play. You can take any character and show why he was put in.

For instance, it is a fascinating exercise to go through *Saint Joan*, which has a very large cast, and show exactly what Shaw has in mind with every sub-character. He does have something in mind. If you read commentaries, you'll see that none of them is thrown in at random.

I do not maintain that every one of these lesser characters in *An Enemy of the People* is absolutely indispensable. It depends on what the complexity of the play will carry, how long it takes to develop these characters, and so on. You could even legitimately say that the cost of scenery and costumes is a factor for a small company. At a minimum, I think we could agree that the mayor has to be there as the outspoken representative of the establishment; and the editor has to be there as the spokesman for the liberal intellectuals. These two, at least, are essential. We have to see the fight within society, and then the fact that their fight is meaningless when compared to their agreement against the true individual.

There is a smaller group of characters that is also essential to the play; that being Tomas Stockmann's allies and friends, basically his wife, children and Captain Horster. Why are these characters necessary? One, they heighten suspense because they raise the stakes of the conflict. They help dramatize in action all the consequences that are going to flow from Stockmann's challenge to society. They make you care even more, because you see what is going to happen to his friends and associates as a result.

It is also very important, I think, for purposes of objectivity. If you are going to show a man standing against everyone one hundred percent, there is always going to be an unspoken implication, however perfectly you present him, that there is something eccentric about him. Therefore what you want is to take some perfectly ordinary, obviously healthy, decent people in however small a role and show that they admire and are friendly with him. That takes away the curse of being some kind of psychotic or weirdo.

For instance, Mike in *The Fountainhead* serves that purpose. The very fact that Mike, a blue-collar worker, is friendly with Roark automatically gives Roark an objectivity; that he is a real human being; that a decent, uneducated man would enjoy being friendly with him. The same is true of Ismene with regard to Antigone. If you saw only Antigone, without her sister and her lover, the question would be raised: is she dangerously high-strung or emotionally unbalanced? You see what I mean?

There is a third reason for the inclusion of intimates and friends of Stockmann. Ibsen wants to pave the ground for a happy ending; he wants to leave Tomas Stockmann a future. If he is utterly alone, he simply cannot build that future. He needs a younger generation that is sympathetic to his ideas who he can then shape and mold.

You see how well-integrated this play is. As early as Act One, before we know anything about what is going to happen, Petra the daughter announces the need for a school of her own where the children aren't taught lies. That idea is planted as just part of the character development. That is what you call a great playwright and a well-made play: a minor line turns out to be the whole thing that you need, only you don't know it at the time.

I think it was Chekov that Miss Rand was quoting once. She said you can tell the difference between a good play and a bad play by the fact that in a good play if there is a gun on the mantelpiece in Act One, it goes off in Act Three. There is nothing that isn't cashed in on.

Petra and Horster represent the younger generation. Ibsen insists in his stage notes that Horster, the sea captain, has to be a young man. The two have to become strongly attracted to one another, and then there is the promise of a happy resolution.

Tomas Stockmann has been likened by commentators both to Socrates and to Jesus. In the sense that he is a rebel against the world, there are some similarities. But he is a unique character in several ways. He is not a loner; he is not a grim ascetic; he is certainly not an otherworldly type. He is not even a man who knows and expects his fate the way Antigone knew what was coming. Socrates expected a clash on philosophic grounds; he knew the world around him. Antigone knew what to expect of Creon, and Jesus was omniscient. But Tomas Stockmann simply didn't expect any trouble. He is presented as a unique kind of rebel: warm, gregarious, patriotic, amiable, convivial, fun-loving. People love him. There is nothing within him prompting him to rebel or to prepare him for the role of rebel. On the contrary, he has a lot of friends; he loves them; he is a happy man. But, as he discovers, you have to choose. Truth is even dearer to him than his friends. He never expected the conflict but when, to his naïve astonishment, it happens, he comes down on the side of truth. In a way, Ibsen dramatizes Stockmann's devotion to truth even more fully by this kind of characterization of his protagonist.

Like Socrates and Jesus, Stockmann too stands to lose all worldly assets by his stand. He is going to lose money—he will be fired. He is going to lose his reputation—he is going to become the enemy of the people. He is going to lose his friends and any power that he had. He and his family will be completely abandoned. But, unlike Socrates and Jesus, he is not completely indifferent to this. He is not indifferent to love, fame, money, influence. Ibsen makes a point that Stockmann cherishes esteem. He loves having his articles praised. He enjoys his money and the luxuries that it brings him. He does want to influence and change the world. He doesn't take the attitude that he doesn't care or that he is above what goes on. He is a thoroughly worldly rebel, a very uncommon phenomenon. At the outset, he expects to earn and deserve all these good things: money, love, influence, etc. He expects to earn them in his life by his own judgment and effort. Then gradually he sees what he is up against. He still wants worldly success, but first he sees he has to fight.

So Tomas Stockmann is a first-hander, a self-starter, a self-mover. He has a fighting spirit, a love of truth, and is highly intelligent. Also, he has an ebullient, optimistic outlook about man and the future from first to last. He is guiltless, tenacious, uncompromising. There is no conflict within himself, no self-doubts. He is certain. So he is the essence of strength.

I stress this fact that he is not a pining idealist alienated from society. He feels he is really enjoying himself, that it is a splendid time to live, and that there are great things to work and fight for. Here is Ibsen's description of Tomas Stockmann to his publisher. This quote has caused trouble in interpreting the play. "I have enjoyed writing this play. Dr. Stockmann and I got on so very well together. We agree on so many subjects. But the doctor [this is the key confusing sentence] is a more muddle-headed person than I am. And because of this and other peculiarities of his, people will stand hearing a good many things from him, which they perhaps would not have taken in good part if they had been said by me."

This has been the standard line of critics ever since. The consensus is that the flaws of Tomas Stockmann are what make the play palatable. This is from one such critic: "the fact that Dr. Stockmann is portrayed as a comedy character part, muddle-headed, as Ibsen himself says, takes the curse off his violent attacks on the mobs and the masses. People are willing to accept such things from a man at whose personal foibles and eccentricities they are invited to laugh."

Harold Clurman, in his book on Ibsen says, "The little man grows big. But as Ibsen's Stockmann he remains little and loveable. A gravely thundering or heroic Stockmann would provoke personal and intellectual skepticism. But we can embrace the Stockmann who replies to the mayor's question, 'Are you a raving lunatic?' with the answer, 'Yes, I am.'"

I regard these examples, which I could multiply at will, as disgusting examples of value-hatred. Let's just explore for a moment what the truth is about Stockmann in this respect. What are his alleged flaws? What explains Ibsen's remark about him being muddle-headed? There are a lot of factors, but I will condense to just a few, because they all follow the same pattern.

One thing often invoked here is Stockmann's naiveté, his very inability to predict that this kind of crisis is going to develop. But I say that that is pure benevolent universe, the innocence of a scientist wrapped up in his work who has nothing but good will toward others. Then there is his so-called clowning; chasing these people around with an umbrella, trying on the mayor's hat and dancing around. I think it is obvious that this is overflowing good spirits; it is not self-derogation.

I will concede one thing only: Tomas Stockmann does not have the heroic resonance that Antigone or Le Cid or Saint Joan does. I think that is simply because it is a comedy; it is not because he is a flawed character within that comedy.

He has also been criticized for the fact that he seeks and needs praise when he writes a paper. I think that is unfair as a criticism because anyone who writes something good wants other people to enjoy it. The question is, do you earn the praise that you want or not? It happens to be the case that Ibsen coveted medals from foreign governments, which he thoroughly earned. So Stockmann is like Ibsen in that respect. I do not regard that as a weakness.

Of course, there is the fact that he is an intemperate extremist which all the critics see as his basic weakness. I think that is the essence of his virtue—and so does Ibsen. Stockmann in that way is exactly like Dominique or vice versa. In his play *Brand,* Ibsen has a character say, "All or nothing." He does not believe in the middle of the road or the golden mean or moderation. To Ibsen that is anathema—and I find that tremendously refreshing.

As far as his "muddle-headed" term goes, you have to remember that Ibsen applied the comment to himself as well as to Dr. Stockmann. I do not take that as a serious comment by Ibsen. It is a tongue-in-cheek, playful comment. I think it is more about Ibsen than it is about the character. Its meaning really is that Tomas Stockmann is even more innocent and hopeful, less corrupted by the world. So it is like an admiring remark with an edge of sardonic wit.

It is very rare to have an unbreached hero who evokes laughter. Nevertheless, I think that is what you have here. The message is not that he has feet of clay because the laughter has to be with him, not at him. It has to be the laughter of delight, not of ridicule. Of course, the modern critics can't conceive of such a thing. Their idea of laughter is Ellsworth Toohey's; to tear down.

Let's turn to Peter Stockmann. He is allegedly motivated by money, power and social standing which are the conventional values. However, the point is that he wants all those things out of context; short-range, regardless of justice, just because he wants them. So he is primarily a whim-worshipper. He is uninterested in thought or ideas. Interestingly, he denounces intellectual innovation explicitly. He is the real second-hander.

You can see how deep Ibsen is and how well thought-out this play is by the contrast between Tomas and Peter, which is presented from every aspect of the play. Look at the overall development of the play. Where does it start? What is the first issue? A material, physical question: are the baths poisoned? And it evolves into the very same issue on the spiritual level: is our spiritual life poisoned? Is our spiritual life corrupted by undetectable, but real, toxins? One commentator makes this point really beautifully. He says Stockmann begins by detecting the microbes within physical reality, in the baths, that are undetectable by ordinary seeing—and then proceeds to discover the polluted sources of our spiritual life that are undetectable by ordinary thinking. This movement or development is symbolized by Ibsen in the setting, which shows you how carefully this was thought out. In what room does the play begin? In the dining room, with people relishing a good meal. In what room does it end? In the study, with people discussing the proper education of the soul.

How many missed that in reading? Oh, you have to pick up on those things. If they start in the dining room, they are eating for a reason. With a great playwright, it will probably be a thematic reason, and you will see the development from there. Nothing is accidental in a great work of art. Ibsen doesn't have them sit down because he couldn't figure out where to start, and there happened to be a leg of lamb in his house so he figured he would start there. Everything is calculated. Remember what I quoted from Ayn Rand in my book on Objectivism in the part on esthetics: in a great work of art nothing is accidental, and that includes the setting.

Ibsen's point is—you'll see how deliberate it is—that on both levels, material and spiritual, Tomas Stockmann is the life-endorsing champion. He relishes material pleasures and intellectual pleasures. He is a champion, in effect, of hot meat and hot ideas.

Peter, by contrast, is the enemy on both levels. Notice he has poor digestion—that is deliberate. He is an ascetic in regard to food, a puritan. In the same way we could say he is intellectually a puritan—he abstains from thought, although he is shrewd and manipulative. It is a deliberate, decisive contrast across the board; a complete integration of mind and body in both characters. It is interesting that as part of this integration of mind and body, Peter is portrayed as having a split between theory and practice, which Tomas doesn't have. Peter says, "My brother has had plenty of ideas in his time . . . ; but it takes a very different kind of man to work them out." Meaning: Oh, yes, my brother has ideas, but I am the practical one. So, in other words, he is a self-admitted un-thinker; he doesn't care about truth or abstract values. What he prides himself on is his ability to connive and manipulate people. That is the only way he knows to achieve his goal.

Both of these characters are selfish, just in the way that Keating and Roark are both selfish in some sense. Peter Stockmann wants to grab the unearned and sacrifice others, while protesting that he is doing it for the welfare of mankind. Tomas Stockmann, on the other hand, talks about the welfare of the people. But, when you come down to it, he places his own judgment and his own ideals as supreme, and as much more important than the survival of the country as a whole, which he says repeatedly. Ibsen himself sometimes describes his own viewpoint as the defense of creative selfishness.

Observe the choice of names. Did you think "Peter" and "Tomas" were accidental? Who is Tomas? Doubting Thomas, the skeptic. And what is Peter? It is Greek for "rock"—you know, when you petrify something, you turn it to rock. He is the unshakable rock of the community. But—another little touch of genius—observe that these names at a deeper level are easily reversed. Who is the real rock on which mankind depends, the real absolutist? Tomas, the doubter. And who is the real doubter, torn by uncertainly and self-doubt? The rock, Peter. So it's a perfect little contrast.

We won't go into the lesser negative characters, but you should just observe that Ibsen was famous for his capacity to satirize hypocrisy. This is most obvious in this play with regard to Hovstad, the alleged revolutionary liberal, who preaches self-reliance and liberating the masses, and then crumbles the moment he encounters real opposition. Even better is Ibsen's famous irony in regard to Aslaksen, the coward whose motto and goal repeatedly is moderation, which Ibsen, to his great credit, hated. He has this wonderful little point about Aslaksen being timid in regard to the local authorities and outspoken in criticism of the national government, about which he feels free to talk boldly. Aslaksen offers this rationalization. He doesn't want to say anything about the local government because he might be affected by his words and make things still worse; whereas the national government won't listen to him anyway, so he can speak. Obviously, the point that Ibsen is suggesting is that, for this character floating abstractions of defiance are okay, because they don't threaten anybody or provoke any reprisals. Whereas addressing yourself to concrete reality can provoke reaction and retaliation, and so you should shut up. This is just perfect as an analysis of moderation, and it is a delightfully enjoyable satire.

5. Theme

The theme, in a word, is: individualism. The individual comes above the group. He is the source of truth, the discoverer of truth, and the unit of value. And the individual is to be contrasted with the mob, the masses, the authorities, the majority. In places Ibsen actually says the majority is always wrong. His famous statement of the theme is the second last line of the play: "the strongest man in the world is the man who stands alone." The strongest man is the one who thinks by and for himself, who places his private convictions and conscience above any external authority, including society and its rules; the man who places truth or reality above all other concerns.

By contrast, says Ibsen in the play, the majority never has right on its side, only might because the majority is stupid; the majority are the fools. The intelligent, the innovators, the revolutionaries are always ahead of the dolts. The process of history, as Ibsen saw it, is: just as the dolts start to catch up, they are still wrong because the innovators have leaped to the next discovery, the next higher truth. So the majority is always supporting old, dying truths.

Of course, if we are talking about material products, this is all okay: the horse and buggy being replaced by the car, by the airplane, by the spaceship. Each step being greeted with dismay by the mob, and by the time they accept it, the next one is here. But it doesn't work that way on the intellectual level. It's not as though individual rights, A is A, and individualism are evolving the same way that material products evolve. A is A doesn't die and get replaced by a new and better truth, as the advocates of polylogism say.

Ibsen is in a big inconsistency here. He bases his formal defense of individualism on this idea of the evolution of truth. And yet his actual defense of individualism commits him to absolutism. So there is a definite problem here. He has to hold his truth as an absolute against the masses, and yet he is committed in this play to evolution as a justification of every truth, and therefore that nothing is really an absolute.

It is too bad that he got sucked into the evolution trap, because in fact he is a thorough absolutist. He detests compromises and halfway measures. I already quoted "All or nothing" from *Brand*, but let me quote you a bit more from that play. Brand is a religious fanatic, so he is hardly what you call a secular or, to this audience, a sympathetic character. But nevertheless, Brand says to a hedonist, who is his antipode in the play: "Enjoy life if you will. But be consistent, do it all the time, not one thing one day and another the next. Be wholly what you are, not half and half. Everyone now is a little of everything: a little sin, a little virtue, a little good, a little evil. The one destroys the other, and every man is nothing." This is an excellent speech in itself and gives Ibsen's view of the evil of compromise and how most people destroy their own lives and character.

You see that by tying in his ideas to evolutionism, Ibsen unfortunately opened himself to charges like: the day of individualism is gone, and you yourself said that truth evolves; now we are in World War Two, etc., etc. The trouble is that Ibsen was not a philosopher, and therefore he did not distinguish abstract principles from concretes. There, he was just the child of his age: Hegel and Darwin and the general optimism just sunk him intellectually on this point.

Another formulation of the theme is: the minority is always right. There he is trying to say that the intellectual vanguard is always moving to the next level of truth, which the majority has not yet discovered. He does not literally mean that any minority on any question is always right. The speculation is that one of the reasons he included the drunk in the climax—because that was a guy who was completely alone, but was the opposite of being strong and right—was to try to acknowledge that not every minority is right.

Thematically, what Ibsen opposes is collectivism. And thus in Act One he gives this speech to his arch-villain in the play, Peter Stockmann, (although he's hardly an arch-villain in relation to Iago) who says to Tomas: "You have an incorrigible tendency to take things into your own hands. . . . The individual must subordinate himself to Society as a whole; or, more precisely, to those authorities responsible for the well-being of that Society." For Ibsen that is the evil: any subordination of the individual—his rights, his freedom of thought—to the group.

6. Philosophy

The first thing I want you to notice is that Ibsen writes as a moralist—not a cynic, a nihilist, or a pessimist. Individualism for him is an objective moral responsibility. It is a necessity of a man to develop himself and reach fulfillment. He does not believe that everything is subjective, anything goes, you do whatever you feel like, or that collectivism is good for Peter and individualism is good for Tomas. Absolutely not. He has all the convictions of an absolutist in regard to individualism. He is not a cynic: he does not believe that virtue is impossible, so let the rats do whatever they feel like. He is an optimist about the future. He believes in heroes who have pride, self-esteem and objective strength of character.

The fact that he ascribed this strength to a combination of eu-
genics and culture in this play we can just conveniently leave aside.
He does believe in free will, but he has no clear explanation of how
to integrate free will with biology and the role of the environment.
There are still so many wonderful little touches in his philosophy
that come out even in this play. He believes strongly that you must
love your work. Do you remember that exchange between his two
sons, who are astounded that the school doesn't think that you
should enjoy your work? He believes that you are obligated to pass
objective judgment, both in science and in morality. You are obligated to think, to develop, to grow. In that sense he is the opposite
of a libertarian who says, "Do whatever you feel. There is no ethics,
there is no truth, etc."

He is an advocate of selfishness, which, of course, would be necessitated by individualism. If you are unselfish, you have to sacrifice
your most precious attributes—and that means your individuality,
your own ideas and values—for others. In that broad way Objectivism
agrees with him. There is a very interesting quote from Ibsen on his
view of selfishness. The context is a letter he received from a friend
of his, who was complaining that he was alone. Ibsen replied, "When
one stands as you do [and by implication as he did] in so intensely
personal a relationship to one's life work, one cannot really expect
to keep one's friends. Friends are an expensive luxury, and when one
invests one's capital in a calling or mission in this life, one cannot
afford to have friends." That is perhaps a hyperbolic statement, but it
certainly captures the idea that this is not a man who is socially oriented as a primary.

Ibsen continues in another letter, "Most criticism boils down to a
reproach to the writer for being himself. The vital thing is to protect
one's essential self, to keep it pure and free from all intrusive elements." So you see here his stress on the primacy of self-development,
self-fulfillment, self-determination and independence from others. It
will have beneficial consequences on others, but that is not the goal.
And, of course, if there is to be any clash between your ideas and
friends and society, you know what direction you have to take.

So Ibsen was a real champion of selfishness. He did not have a
philosophic definition of selfishness really. He did not have a system of philosophy, of which selfishness was an ingredient. So there
were many unanswerable questions about what selfishness means in
this situation and that situation. The best I can say is that he had a

free-wheeling but genuine view of selfishness. He had the emphasis on thought, work and personal fulfillment, but it was still too generalized to become a historical moving force. Nevertheless, he did hold very strongly the idea that no group can expect you to put your sacred convictions second. Your convictions have to come before any external considerations, including the interests of the group or of any factions within it.

You get in *An Enemy of the People* lines from Tomas such as: "All those old fogies must be kicked out of office, no matter what positions they may hold. . . . What we need, my friends, is young and vital leaders—new captains at the outposts" as against Peter, the true altruist declaring, "As a member of the staff you have no right to personal convictions." I mean, this is as clear as clear could be.

Since his view of selfishness was largely free-floating, you probably won't be surprised (although you will be disappointed) to learn that politically Ibsen was a self-proclaimed anarchist. That was part of his general iconoclasm. He uttered statements such as: abolish the concept of the state and you establish the principle of free will.

So he was anti-everything. He was anti-capitalist because he took Peter Stockmann and the short-range businessman as an example of it. He was anti-labor. He was anti-socialist and he was anti-Communist. At times he sounded like he was a Communist, but not for long; remember, this was in the 1880s. He was anti-liberals, anti-conservatives. When he was asked if he was for royalty or for republicanism, he said, "I'm against both."

He was avowedly against democracy on two grounds. One, he said, intelligence always belongs to the minority. So democracy is doomed by the fact that it elevates stupidity to a ruling position. Secondly, he said it is ridiculous to talk about a right to your opinion; most people are not entitled to hold opinions. This is true epistemologically, if not politically, but he is denounced as an elitist or an aristocrat. He is some funny combination of rule by aristocracy plus anarchism which means he doesn't really know what he stands for politically. He is against everything. He couldn't figure out a theory of social relations that really protected and preserved the individual.

That also diluted his influence and made it possible for the weirdest groups of people to come out in favor of Ibsen, because he fitted in with anything, it seemed. If you hated something in the establishment, you could seize on Ibsen because he said it was bad, too.

As far as his deeper philosophy, metaphysics and epistemology, he had one, and it is in his plays, but it is just more brief than we are accustomed to from some of the other playwrights in this course. But note, for instance, the man who represents the grasper of truth in this play is not a blind seer. It is a medical doctor, a scientist, using the technology of the microscope. So implicitly he is for reason, the senses, this world, logic, secularism and the scientific method.

Ibsen himself had a later mystical slant in life, but he had essentially a secular and rational philosophy, and was an avowed atheist. Even his mysticism was a kind of free-wheeling, non-creedal one, not based in any organized religion. Christianity, he said, demoralizes and inhibits both men and women. On the other hand, in some ways he respected religion; he would never joke about religion nor let you make a joke about religion in his presence. To him religion pertained to sacred values, and he still had enough residual respect for it that he would not laugh at it, even though he didn't believe it.

He is not a systematic philosopher or thinker. In that sense, he is completely different from Schiller, who could give you chapter and verse of his views and stick them right into his plays. But he does have a broad overall philosophic trend, in contrast to Maeterlinck, who doesn't even have views on some of these questions. Ibsen has a definite view of science, worldliness and individualism.

Against this background, you can consider the typical contemporary interpretations of *An Enemy of the People*. You will not be surprised to know that it is a favorite of the modern liberals. Arthur Miller came out with a ghastly adaptation of it. Environmentalists and ecologists have used this play to support their side, because Ibsen is against pollution and so are they. From the arms race to Watergate, anytime there is a leftist minority that disagrees with the majority sentiment in the country, they come out, perform Ibsen and say, "You see? We are the only ones who know the truth. The masses are stupid and ignorant, etc."

In a way Ibsen opens himself up to this, because he doesn't always stress the need of objectivity in your self-assertion. He too often leaves the idea that the individual is always right and the majority is always crazy, without explaining context and reason. However, if you do take a broad picture of Ibsen's plays and Ibsen's philosophy, he would be all for technology over ecology, and self-defense over appeasement. So all of these modern adoptions of Ibsen are bizarre misinterpretations.

I want to conclude our discussion of Ibsen with one comment that comes under the general heading of style to explain why he has been called the Father of Modern Drama. There are many reasons, but this is one. He has heroic characters who are not nobility, aristocracy or royalty. In the plays to date in this course, the heroes are a princess and lords. Even Othello has a royal lineage that we find out about. Here we have commoners, plain middle-class heroes: workers, scientists, doctors, etc. In other words, they are people who gain their stature exclusively from their character, not from their birth or their title. Until the time of Ibsen, these ordinary characters always appeared in farce and demeaning comedies. They took pratfalls; the laughter was at their expense. They were portrayed as cowardly or, as in Molière, as miserly or hypochondriacal or whatever. Ibsen extends dignity, seriousness and complexity to human beings based solely on their character, not their status.

And that is his so-called Realism. He has middle class protagonists; the modern man in the modern world, not the heroes of antique legend or the kings of history. Ibsen started this approach which we now take for granted in a major way.

Observe that at the same time he was able to do this, he was not a Naturalist. His dialogue is essentialized. He is not someone depicting how people speak, but how they ought to speak. He is a Romanticist in his use of language and in his whole approach to art—universal themes, heroic characters and exciting, well-made plots hinging on the free choices of his characters. Since he takes real characters as they live in today's world and presents them from a romantic, idealized perspective, a really good name for his esthetic orientation would be Romantic Realism. And he knew it. Ibsen disliked being called a Realist because he knew people took it to mean Zola. He has this marvelous quote, contrasting him and Zola. "Zola goes down into the sewer to take a bath; I, in order to cleanse it." That is exactly the difference between them.

People often told him that he mustn't be so moralistic, that he should record the times. In one of his plays, *Love's Comedy*, he gave the perfect answer to that and I'd like to end with it. He said, "A man must live in his own times, but he can try to make the times worth living in."

Q & A

Q: You said that his twelve prose plays make up a cycle. Would you discuss that?

A: I really can't. I don't know the cycle well enough. I will tell you only this much about it. Some Hegelians saw the cycle as a development within the dialectic process and worked out the plays as being thesis, antithesis and synthesis. Then they worked those three against the next. They give it a kind of horrific plausibility, if you get into that rationalist role. For example, the play right after *An Enemy of the People* seems to preach the opposite; that is, conformity and that the person who stands alone is no good. And then the next play is supposedly a synthesis of it. But I am just not enough of an Ibsen specialist to be able to make an intelligent comment.

All I basically did was skim through a few plays that I really like and convinced myself that this would be the play for an Objectivist audience. Maybe in another year I will know a lot more and could answer you.

Q: Would you retell a story about the little girl at Kira's school who misinterpreted the theme?

A: This is apropos of Ibsen's theme. This actually happened after I gave the lecture on Ibsen to my daughter's class. The teacher phoned me ten days later and said, "You know, you really got me into trouble about Ibsen." And I said, "What do you mean?"

She told me that about a week after the play, two girls got into a fight—not over the play but about something else—and one of the girls started to really hit and kick the other girl. She sent the girl to the principal and went along with several of the students who witnessed what went on. The principal called them in and asked what happened. Everybody gave their account of what they had seen. The principal looked at the culprit and said, "What do you have to say for yourself?"

And this little girl stood up and said, "The majority is not always right."

The teacher apparently was absolutely dumbfounded. The principal didn't know what to say and sent them back to the class. Now that is a misuse of Ibsen. But, you see, he leaves himself open to that. It is very important to be exact.

You see how powerful these plays are and the message that can get through to kids. They were seven and eight, and were asked to write a one-page letter to me afterwards, summarizing what they got out of the play in their own words. It was uncanny. There was not one out of thirty kids who didn't state that the thing that struck them was that people aren't always right and you have to think on your own. At seven they got it. And they got it without pain and without preaching.

I, myself, think that if literature were properly taught, you wouldn't have to teach philosophy; you wouldn't have to teach art. You could do such a tremendous job because the stories and characters are so wonderful. They don't even have to be simplified if they are properly taught to a class.

The only thing I did to make the story more interesting was to throw in a few perceptual touches. I told the class that when Stockmann tested the water to see if it was poisoned, they put a litmus paper in: it turned red if it was poisoned, and not if it wasn't. And guess what? It turned red. That was the only kind of detail I made up to make it a little more visual and perceptual for seven- and eight-year-olds. But other than that, I just told the straight story and they ate it up; they were simply enthralled.

One of the things in the question period was: who was going to be the next mayor? They don't have a really clear sense between fiction and reality. And one of them asked me if I would agree to be the next mayor.

I counsel you that when people tell you that six- and seven-year-olds cannot read or appreciate Shakespeare or Ibsen, it is just not true. The class now is clamoring to do *Antigone*. It is just not true that they need Dick and Jane and all this trash that is taught in American schools. You can start them with major classics right off the bat, and they eat it up. But you have to know how to teach it. You can't be Carl Van Doren; you have to strip it down to essentials.

Q: If I understood you correctly, you said that Ibsen was a conscious advocate of selfishness, but he was not a philosopher. How is that possible, given the fact that philosophy during the nineteenth century advocated altruism?

A: It is possible because there is such a thing as being an iconoclast. An iconoclast is someone who smashes idols. Ibsen had enough of an understanding to realize that what everybody preached was wrong. You can tell that something is wrong without knowing the truth or even the full answer, or how to relate the truth to everything else. An honest man can tell that if everyone says "obey and listen and agree," you have to think on your own. That doesn't mean that he is a philosopher who is able to provide a full definition or a fully integrated system.

You can't put mankind in so abject a position that only philosophers can think or only philosophers can have philosophic ideas. That is completely untrue. You can have a philosophic idea, even a radical one, if you are intelligent. The problem is that it will not go anywhere historically. You will not be able to do very much with it, if you don't make it part of a whole system. But you must not regard philosophy as somehow exempting a man from the otherwise lobotomized state which is our natural endowment. That is not true.

Q: What can we do to guard against making errors in thinking that the characters opposing Dr. Stockmann made?

A: In one word, what Objectivist virtue do you have to practice? Independence. Read *The Fountainhead*. It is the best thing you can do. The whole idea of it is how to focus on reality rather than on other people. It is the primacy of existence versus the primacy of people. It is looking at reality versus looking at others. Putting it in deepest terms, it is grasping the metaphysical versus the man-made, and realizing that the metaphysical has to be your guide and that you can accept the man-made only if it is based on reality.

It is very significant here that Ibsen himself grasped this point. I do believe he intended to dramatize the distinction between the metaphysical and the man-made as part of the theme here. That shows you the penetration of Ibsen's thought. He goes down to the epistemological root of the distinction between Peter and Tomas, down to the basic relationship between the character's consciousness and reality. He did not know Objectivist terminology, of course, but just listen to this little exchange when Peter and Tomas are arguing.

Peter Stockmann says, "The present water-system is an established fact, and must, of course, be treated as such." That to me is a tremendously fascinating formulation. It is an "established fact." What is he doing by calling it that? He is making it a metaphysical reality that you have to bow to, even though it is established only because people refuse to challenge it and accept the real truth.

Peter Stockmann asks Tomas how he could be so stubborn; that this is a fact. And Tomas Stockmann says, "Are you mad? Do you want the town to grow rich by selling filth and poison? Must its prosperity be founded on a lie?" And Peter Stockmann says: "We will expect you to make a public statement expressing your faith in the management's integrity." *It's all just in your imagination. Just join us and don't be an enemy of the community, and everything will be well.*

This is as close as you could come to saying that one of these men gave his allegiance to the metaphysical and the other to the manmade. The play itself gives you the answer of what to do to avoid it. What is interesting is that each of them looks at the other as though they are mad; as though they are simply insane. Peter Stockmann can't grasp why Tomas would raise all this trouble; it's a fact, why would you go against it? And of course Tomas Stockmann, being reality-oriented, cannot grasp this; it is a blatant lie; everyone is going to die; how can you ignore that? This is a real feat of characterization. It goes to the very core of the two different epistemologies.

Another thing that Ibsen is celebrated for is the depth of his characterization. And this is certainly a classic example. He is going all the way to the relationship of consciousness to existence—and you can't beat that.

Q: I have in my notes here that in some way Dr. Stockmann does not have a heroic resonance. Another way of saying that is that he is not a larger-than-life hero.

A: Yes, I agree.

Q: Doesn't that present some kind of a problem in relation to the others?

A: I agree with your observation so far. But what is the problem? Ibsen was not a hero-worshipper in the way that the good playwrights that we have so far studied were. One of the things they wanted to do was to create total heroes. The best example is Corneille who got tremendous pleasure from creating a giant of stature. Ibsen wants to present the middle-class, the ordinary man as a fount of strength. But that is not exactly the same as a larger-than-life hero.

In that way you could make a good distinction between Ibsen and Ayn Rand. She took the Ibsen technique of taking the middle-class man, but she made him a larger-than-life hero that you could worship. She gave the middle-class man the stature of the Cornelian hero, which Ibsen himself did not do.

That is a very interesting question that you raised. It is relevant to the fact that several women in the audience have complained that the question I raised about which character you would like to sleep with, is not fair to women because there are many more heroic women for the men to sleep with than vice versa. They are universally telling me that they do not want to sleep with Dr. Stockmann. I can sympathize with that because, although he is an unbreached admirable character, he is not presented as a romantic hero. He would not be like the Robert Redford type, if you cast him in the movies. He would be a character-actor type. He is kind of happy with his wife in a kind of settled marriage which is not romantic bliss. He is simply not presented as that type of hero.

Is this a flaw in Ibsen? I do not know any law that says that you have to present heroes with a hundred milligrams of stature, rather than ninety or ninety-five. I don't think it's a flaw. You can prefer the other, but I think as far as Ibsen went, he did remarkably well. Do you think it's a flaw?

Q: I guess as I am thinking, it lacks a certain power.

A: It lacks a certain power, but on the other hand, it has a delicious humor. You can't have everything. It's like your eyes see straight ahead but, by that very fact, you can't see what's behind you and you can't see the periphery. Everything is limited. You choose a form, you get some virtues, but you have certain delimitations. And if you treasure, as I do, the excoriating of a character like Aslaksen, then you want a raucous humor as your leitmotif. At the same time, you can't have a solemn romantic hero that the women want to go to bed with. You cannot have everything in one play.

Q: In light of the establishment of film and movies, how do you see the long-term prospects for the continuation of stage drama?

A: Do I think the theater will continue as an art form in the light of the movies? Absolutely. I don't see a problem with that. Theater can do things that film cannot. It is completely untrue to say that film can do everything that drama can do, but better. That is absolutely untrue, because there is a live quality to drama on stage that no movie will ever capture. The actual reality of a character in front of you taking action before your eyes will never be captured in the same way on film. In film the elaborate sets and camera tricks cannot deliver what the stage can. Stage is an essentialized medium. You are given the essence.

I would say that stage is to movies what sculpture is to painting. It is a highly essentialized, simplified, dramatized version, with many fewer attributes. For that very reason it has its own charm, emphasis and style. I am not mandating this as an Objectivist virtue, but I happen to like sculpture better than painting. I would rather see five statues that I partly like than five masterpieces of painting. I happen to like the stylization of sculpture. A statue captures my eye right away. And the same is true with drama. I would go to a mediocre play over a great movie any day of the week. It is not that I don't like movies. They just do not project the power or the charge that an evening in the theater does, if it is half-decently done. I have very rarely seen a movie that I feel is a life experience; that my life has improved for having seen it. There are movies that I enjoy, but they do not reach for me the level of feeling that they are events in life that make life worth living. But I often feel that in the theater if it is a great play, even just moderately well-produced.

So I don't for a moment believe that movies would wipe out plays. On the contrary, in my more pessimistic moments when I think we are headed to a future of the Dark Ages, where there is going to be no more electricity and no more movies, I also think that there is going to be a long, long stretch where there are only plays because all you have to do is stand up and talk. If I had to pick which is the most long-lived of the two, I would definitely vote for the theater.

CHAPTER SIX

Saint Joan

George Bernard Shaw

1. Introduction

George Bernard Shaw (1856 to 1950) is our subject. We have finally reached a playwright of this century, who was alive at the same time as I. He died at ninety-four when I was a teenager so we are not exactly contemporaries.

A multi-talented man; a critic, a reviewer, author of five novels, a historian and a lifetime political polemicist. He was a founder of the Fabians and a crusading socialist all his life. He was a great wit, a brilliant man, sometimes a buffoon, always an iconoclast. And above everything else, a dramatist. I never did get a final tally of his plays but it was something well in excess of thirty major plays.

A new adjective was coined to describe him and his characteristics; namely, Shavian. To call something Shavian is approximately saying that it is brilliant, witty, and acerbic; there is an edge to it. I had compiled at one point a whole list of these Shavian modes, which are delightful if you agree with him. And here is one which has nothing to do with our play, but just gives you an idea of the quality of this man's ability to wisecrack. "Do not do unto others as you would that they should do unto you. Their tastes may not be the same."

Shaw's plays are chock-full of memorable lines of this kind, so you are always in stitches, always laughing at simply the Shavian quality of it. That, in and of itself, is sufficient to read one of his plays. On stage the slightest and most disorganized of them is thoroughly enjoyable because of this quality.

Shaw himself describes how he transformed the English theater. He began, of course, in the 1870s and '80s to produce plays. "When I began, the London stage was crowded with French dramatization of police and divorce cases, spoiled by the translators' indifference to British prudery. Speeches of more than twenty words were considered impossible and too long. I knocked all that into a cocked hat by giving my characters religions, politics, professions, and human nature." And that is certainly true.

This man became so famous around the world that in 1934 a letter was addressed to him with only a sketchy caricature of him with his huge bushy beard and the words "London or wherever else he happens to be at the moment." And it got to him.

I picked *Saint Joan* because, although Shaw does not have a great sense of theatrical structure and does not tell a good story generally speaking, this is the closest to a good plot structure that he has. It also has many other virtues as a play. It actually opened in New York in 1923, but it is officially dated from its English opening in 1924 and won the Nobel Prize in 1926.

The story he tells in this play, according to my limited knowledge, is historically accurate, except for his glamorization of the Inquisition which he knew himself was inaccurate, but he did it for a deliberate purpose that we will discuss later. The bare facts are that Joan was born in 1412 and she was burned at the age of nineteen in 1431, which was the last gasp of the Middle Ages. The verdict was actually reversed by the Church twenty-five years later in 1456, even though she was dead. She was canonized five hundred years later in 1920 so this was a very current subject in the 1920s; the fact that the Church finally, after all these centuries and after having burned her at the stake, turned her into a saint. It was the bitterness implicit in that that made Shaw decide to write the play.

It's a perfect subject for Shaw because Joan was a misunderstood rebel defying the world, and he regarded himself as being exactly that. It is often said that this is his autobiography, spiritually speaking. Saint Joan as George Bernard Shaw. The world didn't understand him, either, and the final line of the play would certainly be something that he would feel intensely: "How long, oh Lord, how long?"

Shaw was an unprecedented mixture among playwrights, intellectually speaking. He was a religious believer and a skeptic, even an atheist of sorts. He was a real cynic and a hero-worshipper. He was a tragedian and a boisterous comic at the same time and in the same scene, and virtually in the same speech. You are going to get a mixture here that you will either find rich or poor, because of its constituent conflicting elements.

Saint Joan was a later play although not his last one and his few later ones were not too important. One critic, a religious writer, describes *Saint*

Joan as follows: "His last major play, his last tribute to human greatness. As such [this is one of the debatable ideas here], it is one of the supreme statements of religious faith in the post-Christian world, the final masterpiece of a man who was willing to hope and think and challenge his readers to the end."

2. Plot-theme

The first question we have to ask to get anywhere with this play, and this is a question we never had to ask about any other play: is this a period piece or not? The fact that a play is set in the past does not make it necessarily a historical piece. None of our plays so far have been that. The theme of *Saint Joan* is obviously universal; it is not simply historical; it deals with the fate of genius in any age. But in terms of the essential action, is it timeless or is the action necessarily located in a specific era?

I tried to say that even *Le Cid*, which seems to be set in feudal times, is timeless in its action; that the essential action could be laid in any era. You cannot, however, say that about this play. The very essence of the action, the struggle between Joan and an all-powerful Church and aristocracy would lose its distinctiveness if you set it today. It would become any rebel against the environment. The way it is actually written, the action depends on and essentially involves a medieval setting. The power of the Church, the feudal gentry, the Franco-English war, the violent debate about miracles and voices, the emergence of Protestantism, the emergence of nationalism stamp it inexorably as being placed historically.

There is still a universal theme and philosophy. But in its essential action I regard it as a historical piece and we must, therefore, approach it and define the plot-theme accordingly.

With that understood, we just plunge in at random. What is the action of this play? A young country girl in the fifteenth century saves France from the English and is martyred for it. That is basically a summary of the action. To be a little more specific, she leads the French army to victory in a war against the English invaders and crowns the Dauphin (the king-elect) at Rheims Cathedral. So she sets out to save France from the English.

What must we do to make this precise? Is it relevant that she is a teenage girl in the fifteenth century? Yes, I think it is. Her age is relevant to her utter innocence and to the fantastic nature of her feat. Even the naïve Dr. Stockmann of *An Enemy of the People* was a mature scientist. A teenage girl leading a medieval army is utterly fantastic.

A teenage girl sets out to save medieval France from the English army is insufficient for the plot-theme. There is a conflict indicated in that statement, but it is the wrong conflict. The central conflict of this play is not French versus English. If we say this is the essence of the play, we are implying that the French versus the English is the heart of the action of the play. And that is completely wrong. There are brief references in this play to the Franco-English conflict only as background or setting. You never see them fighting and, as a matter of fact, what you do see of their relations is their complete collaboration on all essentials.

The central conflict is Joan versus the Church and the feudal nobility; Joan versus the medieval establishment—and that includes the English and French nobility, the army and the Church. In other words, in the nature of her quest to save France, she is brought into conflict with the leadership of both countries. That is the core of the play and of the conflict.

In contrast to Ibsen, note that Joan gets along famously with the common man; the masses adore her. So this is not Joan versus the mob. It is Joan *and* the soldiers *and* the common people (although they are not given a part in the play) against the establishment. The situation is: she sets out to save France and finds herself at war thereby with the Church *and* the aristocracy of both countries. *Thereby* indicates that by the very fact that she sets herself at war to save the French, she finds herself at war with them, and with the English, too.

This is the pivot, and Shaw's brilliant idea for the play. What is the logical reason—developed clearly and, in fact, I think even too lengthily in the play—as to why her setting herself out to save the French brought her into conflict with Church and nobles alike? What did her attempt to save France represent to the establishment that made her a grave threat? What two emerging forces does Shaw have her symbolize? Protestantism and nationalism.

Of course, Shaw understands that this is anachronistic. This is a century before Luther, and nationalism was just a gleam in somebody's eye. He knows that just as well as anybody else. He is trying to say that the forces that subsequently became Protestantism and nationalism, which dealt body blows to the Church and the Catholic power-structure, were implicit in Joan of Arc. Shaw's genius of an idea is to show future history unfolding in what happened to her.

Let's see first what the thread is and why it is implicit in her. Why is Protestantism a threat to the Catholic Church? It is not just another church that set up shop next door. Protestantism comes from "protestation." Protestantism is individualism in regard to religion. Its founding thesis was the individual's own private communion with God; that man has access to divinity as an individual. He need not go through the authority of the Church in order to find out God's message or in order to achieve salvation.

This is an obvious threat to the Church authorities because the whole church structure was based on the idea that they were the voices of God, the representatives on earth; and that you cannot get to God bypassing the Church hierarchy. Joan claimed to get voices directly from God. She was in one-on-one communication with him. Of course, if that were possible, it is a body blow to the Church. So it is Protestantism in that way.

Luther's famous theses were not nailed to the church in Wittenberg until 1517, about a century later. But you can see why Luther did not spring like Zeus out of the ground whole and unborn. There were these preliminary stirrings. It is not implausible to see Joan of Arc as one of the first embodiments of the individualism of the modern world that is going to take shape in the form of Protestantism later.

The same Protestant spirit threatened the nobility of the time. It threatened the attitude of unquestioning obedience to the status into which you were born. Protestantism said every man had his own pipeline to God, no matter how poor, whether he was born on the land or in a feudal mansion. It did not make any difference what the Church or what your lord said. This was a big threat to the ability to organize people into obedient social strata, who would owe their allegiance temporally to the nobility.

Let us look at nationalism. Nationalism is a distinctively modern attitude. It isn't just a group of loose city-states, but a whole geographic territory becoming a powerfully united entity; and the various parts of it are merely its derivatives, the way Rhode Island is to the United States. Even if you are in Rhode Island, your primary allegiance is to the United States. The whole history of the United States has been dependent on the weakening of the states and the power of the nation.

This emergence of nationalism was an obvious threat to the nobility because the country as a whole becomes the major unit, not the local estate or province or district. And who rules the country? According to Joan and according to later nationalist doctrine, the king is the ruler of the whole country and he rules by divine right. He thereby becomes preeminent over all the gentry and aristocracy.

In the earlier Middle Ages the kings were much weaker. The local lord was master and the king was somebody who put on a traveling show. He came through and you bowed to him and so on but he did not have the power that he subsequently had under the nation state. Nationalism overrode these feudal estates and so it was a great threat to the gentry at the time.

Similarly, the emerging nationalism of the time fractured the Catholic empire. What does the word "catholic" actually mean? It means universalist. The same word was coined by Aristotle to stand for "universal" and the problem of universals in philosophy: *katholou*, according to the whole. So Catholic meant the empire of Christendom, which is one totality ruled over by the Church. Suddenly now you have emerging France versus England versus Holland, etc., which was a grave threat to the unbroken power of the Church.

Both establishments, the Church and the feudal; that is, the spiritual leadership and the temporal leadership, needed to be regarded as the only spokesmen of God, to whom the ordinary man had to pay obedience. Joan comes in, in this context and says: *I heard from God directly. No pipeline from you is necessary, no middle men are necessary. And he tells me, Mr. Bishop, that I know better than you what he wants. And he tells me, Mr. Noble, that I know who should rule; and it is somebody with a lot higher power than you who is going to take over this whole vast territory.* As Warwick, the English noble, puts it, Joan represents "the protest of the individual soul against the interference of priest or peer between the private man and his God."

The whole key to this is that Joan declares that her mission comes from God himself. That is the key to the individualism of the play. If she simply awoke with ambition to save France and did so, and when they interviewed her after and asked, "Why were you so successful?" and she said, "I took these tae kwon do lessons since I was a child," there never would have been a clash with the establishment. Essential to the plot-theme is that Joan, the individual, hears voices from God—or at least thinks she does.

So let's put it all together in the shortest sentence I can make. When you get these long plot-themes, it already means there is going to be some problem with the play because there is too much in it. So, in as short a statement as possible, the plot-theme is: *a young girl in the fif-*

teenth century, moved by voices from God, sets out to save France from the English army, and finds herself at war thereby with both the English and the French.

You see that you must have the complete statement. You cannot just have: a young girl finds herself at war with both the English and the French, because that *per se* is nothing; it's not a play. We want to know the cause. If she were at war with the French and the English, and she said, "Well, the reason is I just read *Atlas Shrugged* and I have a terrific ideological disagreement with them," it's either no play or a completely different play. The whole essence of the play and Shaw's brilliance is the irony of the fact that she is committed to fighting against the very people she is intent on saving. The brilliant plot idea was: her goal is to save the country, and that requires her to destroy its leadership, and therefore, in their eyes, to *destroy* the country. That is a good conflict. It is an original idea, a truly original idea with Shaw, as far as I know.

3. Plot Development

The plot structure falls into three parts, but it is not a traditional or "proper" structure. It is not a well-made play. Shaw only establishes the plot-theme situation fully—that is, that Joan finds herself at war both with the English and the French—by Scene Four. It is the climactic scene because it is the one in which both the English and the French make the pact to do away with her. They realize that she is a threat to both of them. Consequently, there is no rise in intensity from the point of the establishment of the situation.

There is a rise of sorts as she ascends the French establishment to the point where she leads them on the battlefield. But all that rise is incidental to establishing the basic situation, and in the moment it is established you know how it will come out. As soon as you see that she is going to have to take on the establishment, in that moment you know that she is lost at the hands of the establishment. You find out as they swear a pact to destroy her, against which she obviously has no power.

Consequently Shaw forfeits one of the crucial elements of structure, the rise to a climax from an established situation. Even so, I may say, it is still a better structure than Shaw usually has. Let me tell you how Shaw defines the structure of the play. He says it has three parts: a romance, followed by a tragedy, followed by a comedy.

The romance is the happy rise and triumph. Joan gets her first start from Baudricourt, reaches the court of the Dauphin and achieves her height in the play when she is put in charge of the army at Orleans and has that nice scene with young Dunois.

And, by the way, strictly as an aside, if you are female in this course looking for a romantic partner, you should certainly consider him. He is one of the more attractive men in all of these plays: young, honest, able, courageous, good-looking, strong. He is not a major character but you should certainly take him over Iago and a few others I could mention.

In any event, there are three scenes to this romance. Each is essential. Joan has to penetrate the establishment. She has to rise to meet the king. Finally, she has to show her prowess on the battlefield. Note that there is a pronounced, almost raucous comic element throughout which is the insignia of Shaw. It starts right off the bat. She performs a miracle; a hilarious, farcical miracle. The hens will not lay anymore. The cows stop giving milk. Of course, they laugh at this because it is so ludicrous. The whole style of Shaw is the continuous injection of farce, seemingly directly integrated to the most serious, tragic or intellectual elements. You have these farcical figures at court. Even in the moments of tragedy, they are making wisecracks or doing the equivalent of intellectually slipping on a banana peel. I will comment on that later. You either find that a great asset or it rubs you the wrong way. People love him or hate him.

There is such a thing as a serious play which has comedic elements, such as *An Enemy of the People*. But *Saint Joan* is an out and out, devastating tragedy where the heroine is burned at the stake and there is not even a hope of redemption in the future. In the midst of all that, it is slapstick all the way through. If you knew only that much, it could only have been George Bernard Shaw who wrote it. So what does that mean? Shaw, himself, was aware of this combination of feats and I'll read you what he had to say about it at the end of the lecture.

After the romance comes the tragedy of her fall—Scenes Four, Five and Six. Scene Four is the essential ideology of the play, the discussion of Protestantism and nationalism, leading to an alliance between the Church and the nobility including the representative of the French, Cauchon, and the English. From that point, you could tell that it is going to have to end tragically, even if you didn't know the history. As Stogumber puts it in Scene Four: "It is expedient that one woman die for the people." If the Church and the nobility are the leader and hope of the entire country, and she is going to subvert all of them, then it is a case of one woman versus the people. To them it is self-evident that she has to go. Since they have every variant of power—foreign and domestic, secular and transcendent—she has no hope of survival here.

The climax, as I have said, comes in the very moment that you grasp what is going to happen. This is a problem with this play because it does not milk the excitement the way it would if only Shaw would discipline himself to a more well-made play structure.

Nevertheless, there is a lot of suspense because we don't know how she is going to be brought down. From history you know that, but you don't know the form it is going to take in the play. The excellent touch on Shaw's part, which preserves the suspense, is the honesty of Cauchon, the French religious man, who is going to see that the Inquisition gives her a fair trial and sets himself up against their railroading her. This becomes, therefore, a powerful agent of suspense. Is he going to intervene and save her? Is he going to hold them to some standard of judicial rectitude that will prevent them from doing away with her?

Scene Five merely shows you that what happened with the English is the same thing that is going to happen with the French. The French, we see, are moved by the same essential considerations ideologically as the English: she's just a pain in the neck and a threat to them. On top of that, they feel personal resentment at how well she has been doing. Every important person on the French side feels that she has shown them up. She is more attuned to God than the bishop. She is more in touch with the welfare of France than the king. She is better at battle than the army. So she is just sowing enmity wherever she goes, because of her virtues.

Her foes, the English, were united against her in Scene Four. Her friends desert her for similar reasons in Scene Five. She is completely doomed, and it is only a question of who is going to get her. The English want to seize her as a witch because she works miracles. The French want to seize her as a heretic because she refuses to obey the instructions of the Church.

Theoretically, Shaw could have gone either way with this play, but historically, of course, she was captured by the Church. In historical fact, the English were more pragmatic; they didn't care who got her, as long as she was dead. They did not have a big passion to seek revenge. She was more of a French woman and a French problem.

The French Church, by the way, denied that she was a witch. Why? Because a witch is somebody who performs miracles. They denied outright that there was anything miraculous about her. They were out to diminish her connection to God. If she could actually perform miracles while defying the Church, she would be a power that they did not care to recognize. She would be like a self-appointed saint, so the Church denied that she was a witch and therefore could deny that she performed any miracles.

For the English this was more or less pettifogging; just kill her under some pretext. The agreement was that they would try her as a heretic because that is what she most fundamentally was. In their eyes that was her most fundamental sin; not that she performed some tricks of nature, but that she refused to submit intellectually to the demands of the Church. She exercised freedom of the intellect in defiance of authority.

In Scene Six we have, therefore, the heresy trial with some wonderful formulations of the Church's demand for obedience and Joan's assertion of individualism.

I love these plays which have one character asserting himself and making an impassioned statement against the assembled world. I can pretty much swallow anything, from *Antigone* on through *Saint Joan*, as long as somewhere or another someone stands up and says, "I have a right to express my view, and I will not submit to authority." That is one of the common denominators of most of these plays.

In the trial, Joan has one moment of doubt when she comes to grasp that they are really going to burn her. She thinks to herself, very understandably: *It is just not common sense to submit to this sentence. If they want me to recant, I had better, because this is ridiculous.* She had an element of common sense throughout, which is very unusual in someone who hears voices from God. So she exercises her common sense and says: *Okay, I recant.* They, therefore, sentence her to a lesser sentence which is perpetual jail, at which point she recants her recantation. She says: *I made a mistake. The only mistake I ever made was I thought I was wrong. I don't recant anymore; I was right all along.* She accepts her martyrdom willingly. And it is carried out right before your eyes.

You can imagine how this would be done in a movie today. It would be too horrible to watch. *Saint Joan* with Jean Seberg is done very tastefully and very effectively, primarily by showing you the faces of the spectators. You don't have blood and gore and Sigourney Weaver all over the floor. And it's much more chilling. I saw it with a class and we were all completely transfixed, and yet there are no special effects. Something is burning at the stake, it's probably a sack of potatoes or something. So you get an idea of what movies used to be before they decided that a billion dollars replaces intelligence.

The last part is the epilogue, the comedy. This really upset critics at the time the play came out. They thought it should have ended with Joan's death at the stake. Why was the epilogue necessary? Why not simply, the rise and fall of Joan of Arc? Shaw held that this epilogue was absolutely indispensable to the play. Why? He said we have to see the comedy of the ages afterwards trying to justify their actions toward her.

In other words, he wants to have his cake and eat it, too. He gives us a story which is, intrinsically, in its action, a period piece. At the same time, he wants it to come across to us as not just a historical injustice. He wants it to come across as a universal theme, not merely an act of benighted medievals. Shaw is intent on showing that Joan would have had the same fate throughout history. In other words, her fate is metaphysical by the nature of what some people call the human predicament; it is not merely historical. Tacking this awkward epilogue on to an essentially historical piece says: by the way, this is not just historical. Therefore, the meaning goes beyond just the particular grievance of the Church.

He shows us in the form of a fantasy. You could think of this as a dream. The movie handles it really well as a flashback. He shows us what actually happened in later ages. From the epilogue we get the essential truths. Twenty-five years later, which is true, the verdict of the Church court was renounced and reversed. You know why they had to do that? It is not that they underwent a change of heart about Joan in twenty-five years, but rather that she is the one who crowned Charles. If she is a heretic, it occurred to them that that raises a big cloud on the legitimacy of his monarchy. The only thing to do was retroactively wipe out her conviction for heresy and blame the Church for having been corrupt. The Church itself did this.

In the epilogue, one by one her persecutors gradually greet her. They are so happy to see her again. Each one tells her from his own perspective why she shouldn't stay alive any longer. This goes on until hundreds of years later, when it was safe and she didn't cause any trouble, she was made a saint. A modern man comes in and Shaw gets a big charge out of the way he is dressed with many witty touches and a large comic element. He has a character who gets one day off from Hell each year because he was nice to Joan at the very end. He was a no-good guy who did one nice thing: he gave her a homemade cross to hold. He tells a story about how nice life is in Hell and how many Frenchmen there are there, etc. In the midst of this joviality, the ending turns very weary, very serious. They all desert her and she is left completely alone. She says, "How long, oh Lord, how long?" And that is the end.

What is the main conflict? To follow our form of always reading the main conflict from the plot-theme, it is Joan versus the authorities; religious and temporal, English and French. That breaks down to Joan versus the Church since the authorities have to be given some identity. That, in turn, is the French and the English. So there is Cauchon. There are a lot representing the French Church because of all the different facets of the Inquisition—from the more scholarly to the more pure to the horrible pettifoggers who fight over whether there should be twenty-three or twenty-two charges, the real casuists of the Church. Cauchon represents the best of the French Church. Stogumber represents the English Church. So that is one level of the conflict.

Then there is Joan versus the nobility. The main person representing them is Charles himself, on the French side. Warwick, the cynical, villainous English gentry man, is the English counterpart.

Least of all the conflicts is Joan versus the army. Dunois is the only one who is given much play here. The army respects talent but even here only up to a point. It is not as corrupt as the nobles or the church but it is a little afraid, too. They do not want to go on to Paris. Though Joan makes it clear that it is necessary and possible to accomplish the mission, they are afraid. Joan says: *I've done so fabulously with the help of God, why won't you believe that He is going to come and save us when we take Paris?* And Dunois makes his famous remark: "Up to now she has had numbers on her side; and she has won. Some day she will go ahead when she has only ten men to do the work of a hundred. And then she will find that God is on the side of the big battalions." That is the classic line for skepticism of miracles. If that line represents Shaw, then he does not believe in miracles. This is his way of saying: she did not perform any miracles and they threw her over when she tried to do the really impossible.

4. Characterization

The essential characters are Joan plus the Dauphin. He is weak and cowardly but not an unredeemed guy, and her concrete goal is to persuade him. Others are: the Inquisitor who has a very big role in the heresy scene, Cauchon, Warwick and Dunois. Those characters are really essential.

The others all throw some light and Shaw had a definite purpose in each one. The archbishop of Rheims, for example, shows that the clergy are becoming worldly and pragmatic: after all, we are in the 1400s already. This clergyman actually says, in effect: *the Renaissance is coming* [which would be a funny thing to say at that time]. *If I had started my career a little later, I would have gone for Aristotle instead of Jesus, but it is too late for me.*

But the one characterization that's worth discussing is Joan. As portrayed by Shaw, Joan is a genius and a saint. She is a genius as a moral leader, as one with the ability to inspire men. Historically, the French were losing, not because of a deficiency of manpower or weaponry, but because of morale. Joan was supposedly, according to Shaw at least, a genius as a military strategist. She allegedly anticipated the military realism of Napoleon. She introduced, not necessarily the full armament of modern war, but the dead seriousness of modern war as against feudal wars, which were often very ritualized. They would line up and wait until the enemy had his weapons and armor ready. It was almost ceremonial, like a courtly gavotte. When they were all ready, one gentleman would do the honors by sticking his sword into the gizzard of another gentleman. It was almost choreographed. Joan wanted to win. She was supposedly a forebear of Napoleon in saying: you jump in and you smash them down. That was her prowess as a military strategist.

As to being a saint, she was for Shaw the quintessence of virtue. She was not only honest, she was naively honest. She had simply nothing in her to anticipate or believe in intrigues. She was bluntly outspoken. She knew clearly what was right and wrong. She was impatient with fools. Just like Stockmann, she expected agreement and appreciation for being right, and was shocked when she learned the truth about her fellows.

She was also a warrior. One character says she is in love with war and religion. Of course, she was in love with the first in the name of the second. She heard the word of God, and that told her to go to war. She dressed as a simple soldier. She liked the masculine life. She had no feminine wiles: she did not wear makeup, she did not wear dresses, etc., etc. Her explanation given in the play is not a Freudian repudiation or penis envy, etc., etc. (The Freudians go wild over these plays.) She says, "What can be plainer commonsense? I was a soldier living among soldiers. If I were to dress as a woman they would think of me as a woman; and then what would become of me? If I dress as a soldier they think of me as a soldier." *I am going to live in the barracks, and sleep and eat and ride with these rough men from morning to night. How can I possibly do it if I go around, in effect, with Eve Arden cologne and Helena Rubenstein stockings? It would be bizarre. I have to go about dressed as a completely plain soldier, which is my occupation.*

On top of that, she just was not interested in a love life, romance or sex. She had a passionate sense of mission which, according to Shaw, overrode all normal desires. She was really asexual. She was not antisexual; she was just not interested in it. She had an obsession, you could say, that took the place of every other human interest.

This is supposed to redound to her virtue, because we are supposed to see her as a simple soul internally, just as her dress is plain and simple externally. There is nothing hidden and devious in her. She is courageous, iron-willed, and can stand alone against the world without even feeling the heat.

So she is a pious, virginal saint. At the same time she is shrewd, good-humored and enjoys this earth. The idea of spending her time brooding in a prison is out of the question. If she can't have the fields and the flowers and the hills, burn her at the stake, she says.

She is a very interesting character. She is not your run-of-the-mill heroine, not even a typical romantic heroine. This is typical of nobody but Bernard Shaw. Jean Seberg brings it off and makes it believable in the movie. When you read this play, there is some doubt whether you can believe such a character. You'll have to decide that for yourself. Joan is ignorant of the ways of the world; she doesn't know the institutions and the establishment and she finds out to her sorrow what they are like. However, she is not a complete hillbilly. She is the daughter of a farmer who has some prestige in his local neighborhood. She is, in effect, a middle-class girl with a modest education. She is not an ignorant field hand any more than she is a princess. Shaw sums her up as "a born boss" and, if you are interested, read the Preface on pages twenty-one and twenty-two, where he gives his description of Joan. The good thing about Shaw is that he almost always writes tracts about his plays (which are longer than the plays) to explain everything. If you have any doubts, you can read his analysis of it.

Joan has some traits that are tremendously appealing to me or to an Objectivist, despite the fact that she is obviously religious. She is a saint, after all. But she does have some traits which are astounding and very impressive. For example, she is the classic example of the primacy of existence, despite the bad feeling of consciousness; that is,

God ruling the world and communicating with her. There is a perfect interchange on page 108. She is arguing with the archbishop about something and he accuses her of pride—which is the standard ploy of the Church in order to induce guilt; to make the person forget reality and to introspect "what's the matter with me?" Joan has this wonderful line where she says to the archbishop with real irritation, "Never mind whether it is pride or not; is it true? is it commonsense?" That is what you call the primacy of existence in action. Her loyalty to truth is so deep that even in the face of a declaration of a mortal sin by the church that she respects, she is annoyed that he is trying to take the subject off of reality and onto something else.

That is, in one little line, a tremendous characterizing touch. A great playwright should be able to make the whole character leap out at you in a couple of sentences. And this is one of those lines. The very fact that he could think of it shows how much Shaw understands and how brilliant he is for being able to put that into her character and raise her miles above the typical religious zealot who is just doing his duty. It is the stress on common sense and on truth that makes Joan so appealing, not simply her loyalty to God. Adolf Hitler claimed to be loyal to God, but he never said in a million years, "Is it true? Is it common sense?" The idea would just never enter his non-mind. Joan has real self-confidence, the confidence to face and deal with reality.

Despite the fact that Shaw is always ambivalent about everything, he is not about Joan. This is one of the cases where there is no contradiction or undercutting built into her character. She is purely good. She is just head and shoulders above Desdemona. Shaw, by the way, disliked Shakespeare and was very vocal about it, which was another thing that scandalized the English. He suggested very convincingly that Shakespeare was a real coward, that he was afraid of life, and that he huddled in his Olympian detachment sneering at people who were impassioned, simply because he had been defeated by life himself. What we need are characters in plays that care about something and stake everything on it. Not characters who sit back and say, "Who knows?" and "I don't know," and "What fools these mortals be," etc. Therefore Shaw never drew characters like Desdemona; only strong, impassioned characters like Joan.

A really interesting question is: is Joan as strong as, stronger than, or less strong than Antigone? I will give you a clue to my answer. It depends on your fundamental interpretation of Joan. In other words, it depends—to put it paradoxically—on whether Joan is a human being or not. By "human being" I mean a self-created, self-willed, natural organism. Or is she really a puppet of God, a manifestation of supernatural power? There are things in the play leading to either conclusion, as is typical of Shaw. To decide on her real essence and, therefore, your final estimate; whether you are enchanted or bored, whether you believe in the reality of this kind of potential or not, you have to decide on her relationship to the supernatural. And that will take you into Shaw's view of the supernatural.

It isn't really necessary to go through the other characters. Some are obviously more sympathetic than others. Some are deliberately surprising, like Stogumber: you notice how he goes through a conversion from being, in effect, a fiend to a pathetic, guilt-ridden heap. I think he was Shaw's attempt to dramatize what we would call a perceptual-level mentality. In other words, as long as her burning was an abstraction, he was all for it. But when he was actually confronted with the fumes and saw the ashes, he was transfixed. He was supposed to indicate the level of person who could speak in floating abstractions but nothing is real to him until it reaches the perceptual level.

There are all these juicy little things on the side in characterization. The important point about all the characters is that according to Shaw there are no villains in this play, Cauchon and the Inquisitor emphatically included.

The paragraph on page forty-four of the Preface, in which he explains his reasons (a mixture of very good and very bad), starts with "There are no villains in the piece." I want to simply give you his motive for insisting on this. He is eager to present the trial of Joan as fair. He wants to have the best, most honest Inquisitor imaginable. He wants to insist that her trial was far fairer than what we today take as a fair trial. It's a decision strictly according to their law, and she would be even worse off today. Therefore, he says, he wants to head off at the pass people who dismiss what happened as typical medieval rubbish. He wants you to feel very strongly that his theme is universal; that it is relevant today; that it is not merely a matter of corrupt personalities. One commentator says, "The reason Shaw enters so sympathetically into the mentality of the Inquisition is not to exonerate them but to make his point that the most nefarious institutions always seem perfectly justified in their own eyes and in the eyes of onlookers. Shaw forces us to look at the trial with the eyes of the fifteenth century, not because he thinks the Inquisition was right, but because the fifteenth century regarded its procedures as perfectly respectable and was just as comfortable about them as we are about our own law courts."

I can agree entirely with this intention on the part of Shaw and would be happy to give you a list, at random, of the institutions and laws that are commonly accepted or praised without a qualm today, that later centuries will look at with equal or greater horror than we look at the Inquisition. I don't even know where to start, but just taking it on a purely legal basis, what about the insanity defense in our courts? What about the malpractice situation against the doctors? What about the antitrust laws against businessmen? Or, going a little wider, what about the abolition of free speech in the name of political correctness at the universities? Or even such a fantastic depravity as the abolition of public toilets in New York City in the name of egalitarianism, because the handicapped have difficulty wheeling into them?

Anybody who wants to throw stones at the fifteenth century on the grounds that they had institutionalized unreason had better first of all realize the glass house he is living in, in this century. According to Shaw—and, of course, I agree with him entirely—the evils that Joan suffer come not from her time, but from what Shaw expresses thusly: "A saint's strongest and most dangerous opposition [here "saint" means the noble person] comes from the most high-minded and best members of society." Ayn Rand had the same idea when she had Dominique say to Keating, "You're not our worst, Peter, you're our best. That's what makes it so horrifying."

Putting it another way, I agree with Shaw that the cause of history is not plain criminals or hypocrites. Shaw believed that the cause of history is what people believe, their ideas, and in that I agree with him. From that point of view, the really sincere people are the source of evil; those who are sincere about ideas which are fundamentally irrational; the ones who mean their poisons and who are the engines of spreading it. They are infinitely more dangerous than the Al Capones or the club women who mouth one thing and do another. John Galt's greatest opposition comes from Jesus or Kant. In that sense Shaw is right. The greatest opposition is from the most high-minded, even "best intentioned": that is, from those who put their cards on the table and say where they stand ideologically and what they are after. That is what moves history. So Shaw is giving a sympathetic portrait of the Inquisition to show that they are motivated by certain principles and that the evil comes, not from corrupt personalities but from the kind of ideas which, in one form or another, are still around today.

He knows perfectly well that this is a glamorized portrait of the Inquisition. But it is exactly the reason that Ayn Rand gives a glamorized portrait of Andrei Taganov in *We the Living*. She knows that there are no Communists like him, but she wants to show: what does this idea mean? The best way to show it is to take its most sincere exponent; that gives it a universality other than the accident of personality.

5. Theme

That brings us directly to Shaw's theme in this play. The basic clash you can read off from the plot-theme (that's the whole idea of having a plot-theme): the genius or the saint as against the entrenched institutions of society. His theme is the superiority of the genius over social authority.

He also has built into his abstract theme a tragic element. He believes that the destiny of the great individual is to be rejected, even martyred, by the collective. As one commentator puts it, "The Shavian hero is always an alien in the human realm." So it is an essentially tragic, malevolent universe theme, except that in the long-long run, five hundred years later, Saint Joan won. But it really didn't do her a lot of good during her life on earth.

The solitude of genius, the shrinking away of the world from greatness, the need of the great individual to stand alone—that is all part of his theme. Read page 112 of the play in the edition I recommended. Who does Joan sound like when she says, "I am alone on earth: I have always been alone. . . . My loneliness shall be my strength too."? Shaw was tremendously influenced by Ibsen and obviously he got this from Ibsen. Shaw even wrote a book about him.

If your theme is that the establishment demands conformity and is threatened by innovation or individualism, then the perfect model of any establishment would be the Inquisition. According to it, individualism is the sin of heresy; it is a capital offense. I want you to notice how Shaw labors to prove that the Church's need of authority is not a random evil and is not even a matter of power lust. It is an issue of moral principle. Shaw makes as persuasive a case as he can for this. He is trying to show, and has Cauchon and the Inquisitor say, that however innocently disobedience starts, disobedience will necessarily grow and lead in the end to the overthrow of the Church. Since the Church is, by all accounts including Joan's, the embodiment of morals and civilizing principles, disobedience to the Church is a mortal threat to human survival in a civilized fashion.

They look on it, you see, exactly as you would look at controls under capitalism. If you had a laissez-faire society and someone said, "Let's put price controls on oil, because they're charging too much for it," you would immediately say, "If you accept that principle, controls will necessarily grow and you will end up subverting and destroying the whole system." And you would be right.

The idealized embodiments of the Church, as presented by Shaw, look at the authority of the Church in exactly that way. Either their authority is to be accepted as a matter of principle, which means total submission, or it will be disaster, a subversion of the total system. This is true because as soon as they started to rebel and the rebellion got completely out of hand, the Church was broken, not only by the Reformation but by the fact that the rebellion is continuing to this day. It is just a long historical drawn-out collapse.

I don't mean that I am on the side of the Church, but what Shaw is trying to show is that these churchmen are admirably principled and therefore awful. They are much more admirable than the anti-ideological, pragmatic, mealy-mouthed types that, for instance, inhabit the White House today.

Shaw himself is one hundred percent opposed to the attempt of the Church to extract total submission. He has Joan give a brilliant answer. The Church says to Joan at one point: "And you, and not the Church, are to be the judge?" Joan has this terrific line, which is virtually in Galt's Speech, "What other judgment can I judge by but my own?" You can't beat that as a formulation. The Church wants her to use her judgment, but not to judge. She should judge if the Church is right, but without judging because: who is she to judge? The very formulation shows the complete bankruptcy of the Church and goes along with her primacy of existence, her true independence.

According to Shaw, what is the real motivation of the persecutors of the great man (or woman)? Principle is what they put forth and to some extent sincerely believe, but underneath it is, in his view: ordinary dullards resent greatness. They hate mental giants. In part, Joan is a reproach and so the ordinary people are jealous. In part, she is a threat because she shows up their pretenses. She is a better soldier than the head of the army; she has more leadership potential than the king, etc. Consequently, in the epilogue, each in a moment of innocence apologizes and loves her. Then, when she suggests coming back—because being a saint, she can come back to life whenever she chooses—they all say no. As Charles put it, if you did come back, we would burn you again in six months, even though we all adore you at this moment. Will this tragedy ever end or is this mankind's destiny for infinity? "How long, oh Lord?" The answer is in Shaw's broader philosophy.

6. Philosophy

Shaw's broader philosophy is not really dramatized in the play, although the tips of the iceberg are all over it. To get the iceberg you have to read his writings. He says it all in the Preface to this play; you can never accuse him of being overly terse. Shaw asks: how long will this dichotomy between genius and the masses last? What is its cause, what are the deeper roots of greatness such as Joan's, and why does it necessarily fly in the face of the establishment? He is not satisfied with "ordinary people resent greatness." He asks why. What is the deepest metaphysical reasons we could give that there are these geniuses that continuously clash with the establishment?

We had better start here with noting that there is a real miracle for Shaw, whatever other miracles are in debate. He regards the appearance of an individual like Joan and her type as being a true miracle that cannot be accounted for in natural terms. Shaw says flatly that something mystical is necessary to explain an individual so utterly unique, unswerving; so militant of will, such a genius at surmounting all obstacles. Not the traditional mysticism, but a new kind of mysticism which is not that far from the traditional.

Before we plunge into his full answer, let's take a look at the miracles and the voices in the play. That is really the key to the philosophy of the play and to your interpretation of the character of Joan. How do you interpret the voices and the miracles? What is Shaw's view of these? Does he believe in revelations and miracles? Does he dismiss them as puerile and scientifically explicable? Or is there still a third alternative?

Let's go through the possibilities. On the one hand, Shaw is an unbeliever. He is a skeptic regarding religious tradition. He says it in the Preface, and Joan even says in the play that her voices are the voice of common sense. In effect, she has a vivid imagination, she is a genius in terms of native endowment, and her subconscious instantaneously grasps the correct course in her field of interest, military strategy. Her subconscious just gives her the insight, which is perfectly reasonable, given the evidence available. Simply having a vivid imagination, she projects this outward as voices with no real supernatural or religious significance. There really is a line in the play that develops that theme and Shaw affirms it in the Preface.

Along similar lines, with regard to miracles, there is a lot to suggest that Shaw does not believe in miracles. First of all, many of them are big jokes that he chuckles over, such as the hens not laying eggs and then starting again. He makes a point of having the cynical archbishop explain in advance the miracle of Joan's recognition of the Dauphin. He gives that memorable line to Dunois, which he obviously agrees with, that God is on the side of the big battalions; that she won through military, naturalistic means and not through a miracle.

As I said, throughout you can find in Shaw this naturalistic, anti-theological, anti-mystical element. Of course, if you are inclined that way and you like Joan, you will be inclined to absorb and accept this as his view and the view of the play. And you will take the miracles and voices as a satire on the pathetic delusions of the religious.

On the other hand, however, you should know that Shaw passionately rejects nineteenth-century atheism, which was the righteous rejection of voices and miracles on the grounds that the voices were just hallucinations of a diseased mind, and that miracles were nothing but coincidences or lies read by the credulous. It held that the whole thing was a sham and an aberration and that everything could be explained naturalistically and scientifically. Voltaire wrote a work in which he made fun of Joan of Arc. In the name of reason, he made her a farcical figure and a prostitute, on the grounds that no one who claimed to have heard voices and purported to perform miracles was worthy of being taken seriously. Shaw was very hostile to Voltaire for this. His view is that there is something more to the voices than just ordinary vivid imagination. There is some mysterious, opaque aspect to the voices, which Joan and Shaw won't discuss because, as she says in the play, "You do not understand it when I tell it. . . . What more is there to tell that you could understand?"

Along with this—side by side with the joking miracles and the ones that are obviously predictable in advance by natural means—there are utterly unexplained miracles in this play, about which there are no jokes and about which Shaw is really serious, even the one about the wind changing at exactly the right moment because that could conceivably be coincidence. However, you cannot get away from the symbolic miracle that her heart could not be burned or drowned. This is not discussed, it is not joked about, and it is treated reverentially by the worst skeptics in the play. It is obviously meant to suggest something extraordinary. So what is it?

Shaw holds that the traditional religious interpretation is wrong, but nineteenth-century rationality is wrong, too. He says flat out in his Preface that she cannot be explained in purely rational terms. Something mystical is necessary, he says. So he does have a real similarity to the religionists. How does he explain the miracle of Joan herself, so utterly different from all of her fellows?

I can only give you his answer by giving it. This is why he is not put in the history of philosophy as a major thinker. There are, he says, mystical forces at work in the universe using individuals for cosmic purposes. There is an appetite at the core of the universe—if you were a German philosopher in the nineteenth century and you believed there is an appetite, a craving, a striving, you would call it the Will. These people were called Voluntarists and Shaw was one of them. Suppose we throw in that this Will develops by going through a process of evolution. We come out with the idea that reality is a cosmic will to evolve, a will that evolves.

This is obviously Voluntarism of Schopenhauer and especially of Nietzsche, because the will takes the form of periodic supermen. When Shaw says evolution, he does not mean a Darwinian evolution. We are way outside the realm of biology. He regards Darwin as far too mechanical, just ordinary science. This is evolution with a purpose of its own, a Hegelian type of evolution. There is a will that wants to live out its own career; create itself, discover itself, fulfill itself. In the process of its evolution, it continuously creates whatever it needs to reach the next stage. So if it needs hands and it doesn't have any, it grows hands. And suddenly there is something with hands. If it needs a brain, etc., etc. This is an evolution which is creative, in the sense that it creates the means of its own further development, in effect, out of thin air as it goes along. Shaw calls this his theory of Creative Evolution.

From his point of view (this was his philosophy, that is all that I can say), Joan was an expression of God, God being the more conventional name for this gigantic evolutionary will. She is a manifestation of will, she is a step in God's self-development. This appetite for evolution periodically takes shape, as Nietzsche had said, in supermen, in visionaries, in geniuses, in saints, which pull the race forward and thus pull themselves forward. The whole race—as Hegel said—is just this inner cosmic force, itself objectified out into a group of people.

People like Joan, for Shaw, are not lunatics or misguided the way Voltaire thought. Nor are they natural, mundane, scientifically explicable. They are tools of the super-personal and, indeed, of the supernatural because the will is certainly not natural. They are tools of the impersonal life force. And that, you see, is pretty close to being agents of the traditional God. In effect, they are agents of God, except Shaw's God is not perfect and motionless like Aristotle's or like the Christian God. He is imperfect and growing and evolving. This is sometimes called atheistic mysticism. But it is a lot closer to religion than, I think, the word atheism suggests, so it is much better to call it—as Ayn Rand does—neo-mysticism. It has all the essentials of traditional mysticism, but is given a fancy and pseudo-modern cast.

Within the framework of the religion of creative evolution, Saint Joan is the hagiography—the writing about the saints. Consequently there will be an eternal clash between the genius and the crowd, because the genius is the will moving to the next stage and having to pull the crowd up the evolutionary development. What this really amounts to is Platonism all over again. There is a clash between those who are in touch with God, the elite, and the mass of men. Those in touch just have to drag the rest of the world to destiny.

If you see Joan within the framework of this philosophy, I'm afraid it will have a tremendous impact on your feeling for her as a character. Shaw insists that she has free will; he is rabidly opposed to determinism, to mechanism, to materialism. She is not, he says over and over, a puppet. But the question is: how can she possibly have free will or self-responsibility or self-determination, if she is a fragment of a cosmic will pursuing its destiny and simply manifesting itself momentarily and temporarily as her? Isn't she then nothing else but a shadow or puppet expressing the deeper forces calling the tune?

If you take seriously the mystic element, I think Joan loses all credibility and, therefore, everything that makes you admire her. And the play collapses. You have to struggle to keep her a volitional, strong, self-sustaining human being. To do that you have to overlook not only the creative evolution theory—which, thankfully, is not in the play—but all of the slant toward mysticism which *is* in the play, and which is the tip of the iceberg of his basic philosophy. If Shaw presented his mysticism and his view of miracles and voices too clearly in the play, you would just say she is a cardboard figure; she has no reality.

If he doesn't present it at all, though, he doesn't get across what he wants to. He leaves utterly baffling why there is going to be an eternal dichotomy. Shaw is in the position that he has to suggest and then withdraw the suggestion. He has to get you to think that there are miracles and voices at work—and then: "isn't that ridiculous?" The combination helps to allay your critical faculty and enlist your heart on her side.

It is really sleight-of-hand here. He is drawing her strength from her individualism, while repeatedly hinting murkily that there are forces beyond her control moving and determining her. He really never connects the two. This is typical of Shaw. He is not a systematic thinker. He wants to have his cake and eat it, too.

As you know, when you compromise on fundamentals or you try to have your cake and eat it, too, you ultimately have to capitulate to the worst element. Therefore, you shouldn't be at all surprised that despite his intellectual brilliance and his extreme intellectuality, he is generally classed as a philosopher of irrationalism—and correctly so—who preaches feeling above reason.

As one commentator puts it, "Shaw favored the psychology of the romanticist which was akin to that of many earlier thinkers, such as Pascal." Here he is using "romanticist" in the sense of Fichte, Schelling and Schopenhauer, the real German irrationalists of the nineteenth century. Pascal was the real French mystic of the earlier period. "The heart has its reasons which reason knows nothing of"—that's Pascal. Shaw asserted that man is primarily a feeling, not a thinking, animal. He insisted that the driving force of human existence is an irrational will about which we can do nothing.

This quote from Shaw pretty much brings this point to a close. "Life is not the fulfillment of a moral law or of the deductions of reason, but the satisfaction of the passion within us of which we can give no account whatsoever."

I am afraid you have to conclude that Joan's heroism is essentially mystical and irrational. That is why I don't vote for her (along with her outfits, which I don't find sexually attractive) as one of the strongest heroines.

Shaw, you see, is a really interesting, unusual, but not too coherent case. If you look at this play and try to sum it up superficially, you can make a good case that he is for reason: he comes out for thought in the face of the Inquisition. He is strongly for egoism: he likes Joan's pride and self-assertion, and he has her say that her only mistake was that she mistrusted herself. He is for individualism, as against the collective or obedience to the authorities. On the face of it, this is reason, selfishness, individualism—he is a soul mate of Objectivism.

But the opposites of all these ideas are much stronger and much purer in him; the neo-mysticism and the altruism. Remember, the whole motive of this struggle is not for Joan's own happiness or ful-fillment. It is what he calls "heroic altruism." In other words, she is a tool of the higher power and she is destined to suffer, abnegate herself and die the way Jesus did on the cross for the ultimate goal, which is the complete fulfillment and moral development of the human collec-tive. That will be, in Shaw's opinion, when God has finally reached the end of the creative evolutionary process.

So Shaw is a thorough altruist. You understand now why, despite being an arch-individualist, he was a total crusading socialist, an egal-itarian, and even a totalitarian due to his contempt for the masses and his Platonic idea of the few super-individuals who have insight into the mystical truth. He was an admirer of Stalin and even Hitler.

You have to be really careful when you say somebody is an in-dividualist. A lot more is required than merely to say, "I uphold the right of the individual to think." Schiller upheld that and Schiller, on a scale of one to ten, is a nine in individualism relative to Shaw being maybe three.

I think you now get an idea of what ambivalence means, not to say outright self-contradiction. I would summarize it by saying that Shaw was a great playwright, but a terrible philosopher.

In conclusion, I am going to throw in a comment on his stylistic approach. The stylistic attribute that is unique to Shaw is the combi-nation of deadly serious intellectuality with raucous comedy. It is that distinctive union. On the one hand, he is serious about ideas; he is deep, he grants ideas an important role in history, he thinks that they have to be taken seriously. He has, in that sense, a philosophic view of history and criticizes Shakespeare for not appreciating the importance of ideas as motivating factors. He says everybody in Shakespeare acts as they do because they are angry or they are jealous or they are ambitious. You never get an idea of what their view of the universe is, what they think. And that is really what moves history.

You see that in this play. *Saint Joan* has its share of intellectual, very serious, and even very deadly moments. When she says, ". . . for I am His child, and you are not fit that I should live among you," there is no witty edge to that. But at the same time there is this comedic element pervasive in all of his plays. A sly, bantering element—wit, wisecracks, farce, satire, caricature—all the way through, not even stopping for a minute during the tragedy.

This is a unique form of what you could call tragic comedy. Corneille, at the beginning of the tragic-comic idea, meant serious issues and heroes of stature with happy endings. Shaw means serious issues, heroic stature, tragic endings—and a laugh a minute from beginning to end.

This would have been just simply inconceivable to earlier centuries. They would just have thrown their hands up. I may say, there are still a lot of people who throw their hands up because they are completely put off. But in a way it seems to me such a perfect counterpart to his style. He would give every idea a hearing and every stylistic approach a hearing. It is like he wanted to be everything and he couldn't commit himself to the limitations of an identity. But the tragic part is that he did everything so brilliantly and his wit has a great value. On stage, if it is done by a British company that can deliver lines like these and do something other than grunt, it is really enjoyable. You just laugh and laugh, you are just completely satisfied. You kind of lose sight of the fact that you are not entirely sure what the play is about, where is it going, what it means. But it is really entertaining stuff.

The question is, in a total and mature assessment: what do you do with the clown in Shaw? I am ambivalent about it because I enjoy that element in him, but I don't really think it ultimately sits well with the tragic element, not in the form he does it.

Here is a quote from Shaw himself, talking about the continual eruption of funny business in his plays. "This has prevented me from becoming a really great author. I have, unfortunately, this desperate temptation that suddenly comes on me. Just when I am really rising to the height of my power that I may become really tragic and great, some absurd joke occurs and the anticlimax is irresistible. I cannot deny that I have the tragedian and I have the clown in me, and the clown trips me up in the most dreadful way."

You don't know whether he is serious or not, or whether he was serious that day and changed his mind the next. The deeper question is: is this a liability or an asset; an extra dimension of greatness or an undercutting of his greatness? I will leave you to think about that.

I will just tell you in my modest way, without any pretensions, that I am the equivalent of Shaw. I tried to write a serious fiction scene at one point within the last couple of years. The theme of the story I was telling was that the young hero learned that he had a fatal disease and was going to die. My assignment was an exercise for a class, but it was part of a novel which I was once thinking of writing. I wrote this with what I thought were heart-strings and complete seriousness. In accordance with the rules of the class, I had to make Xerox copies so everyone could read it in advance, and they would come back with their comments. I just about fell through the floor when I learned that the consensus of the class was this was the funniest thing they had ever read. I just gasped. I didn't even know whether they read the same thing I wrote. I got all this praise for being so clever and so witty. Here I had written a scene about death and how this guy is going to die, and I was just baffled. I went home and reread it a couple of times. And then, as though from a distance, I said, "Well, you could take that as sarcasm, I guess." I hadn't been conscious of it.

At any rate, to make a long story short, within about a month I thought the thing was funny, too. Not to presume to compare myself, but I can understand having this acerbic element that just has to come out and it comes out whether you know it or not. I think this is one of the reasons why I like Shaw so much. I identify entirely with the fact that he is serious but he cannot resist bitter wisecracks. I go for that combination, even though intellectually I don't think that it is the highest of all possible forms. I stopped writing fiction when I found that out.

Q & A

Q: I think a lot of Objectivists discuss the issue of combining humor with seriousness and when humor is appropriate. Could part of the issue be a matter of whether it's a negative or the absence of a positive and whether the humor gets in the way of something that could be an intensely dramatic moment in the play?

A: I think there's something to what you say, but that's not a full exoneration. You want to laugh at the negative, not at the positive. That is certainly true. You satirize, you laugh at the fools, because the laughing means "don't take it seriously." Laughter, as Ayn Rand used to say, is a denial of reality. Humor is a way of making something unreal. It's saying: I refuse to take this as part of reality. So it is a weapon of negation, and therefore, it is very appropriate if you are against the world. One of the ways of retaining your sanity is to use humor—and I do that—to cut down the things that you are opposed to. It is a way of continually reaffirming what you believe in.

Whereas if you use humor at the expense of what you regard as the good, then you are using it as a weapon for denying the reality of the good. That is why, for instance, Ayn Rand was very witty but she would never laugh at a hero slipping on a banana peel because the idea there is to make the hero, and his heroism, unreal.

Shaw sometimes laughs indiscriminately at everything, including at his positive characters. When he does that, I have no hesitation in saying that it is a bad use of humor.

But he does not laugh at Joan. He is very reverential about her, which is one of the reasons I chose this play. It is very uncharacteristic of him that he withheld his humor from her. So that is not the problem here. It is still the case emotionally. The best example is: at the very moment when your heart is in your mouth and you are wondering what is going to happen to her, there will be a wisecrack about the French versus the British. It descends into a tinge of sarcasm. Shaw says that he can't stop putting it in. It's irrepressible, and he was too powerful for any editor to take it out.

As someone pointed out, it has the effect of muting the impact of his plays. It is as though he couldn't face the full reality of how awful what is happening to Joan is and the way to stop it is to make a joke, not at her expense but just in conjunction with the event. Therefore the idea is: don't take it too seriously, nothing is that desperate. See what I mean?

The accusation was that he was repressed; that humor was a means of keeping tragedy at a distance. If that's true, it is a very bad literary trait in a tragedian. If he's writing comedy, that's one thing. If he is writing witty satire, that's one thing. But what stops me is that here he's put humor in the heart of a tragic moment. And that, I think, is undercutting it.

Watch the movie from that point of view because Graham Greene did not keep the same degree of Shaw's raucousness, so you decide for yourself what effect it has.

Q: We see the idea of evolution being common to both Ibsen and Shaw. I was wondering if it was common to other playwrights of the period. I didn't see it in *Cyrano*, for example, which I believe was of the same period.

A: No, *Cyrano* was a little later. As far as I know, any playwrights in the nineteenth century who had a pretension to philosophy or intellectual seriousness, made an obeisance to evolution. Maeterlinck certainly did for *Monna Vanna*. It was just taken for granted; it was in the atmosphere. That does not mean that it has to come up in every play, or that every play, however great, had that somewhere at its base. But it was much more widespread than Ibsen and Shaw.

Q: My question is: could the tragic comedy aspect of Ibsen and Shaw be due to what I call the "neo-absolutism" of both; like their evolutionary aspects?

A: How would that relate to it?

Q: Well, if you're an absolutist like Rand, you would take ideas totally seriously. But if you believe you evolve, you get to a point, then it changes, you would say, "well, you got it here . . ."

A: You're saying that his humor frees him from the need to commit to intellectual absolutes?

Q: No, it's an expression of his neo-absolutism.

A: Oh, it's an expression of the fact that he's not committed to absolutes.

Q: Right, he's committed and not committed at the same time.

A: Well, first of all, I balk at Ibsen being included because, despite his few relativist statements, he was an absolutist. He was an utter extremist. But now with Shaw, you might have a better case there. He does not want to commit to an absolute, and the laughter has the effect of softening any commitment, intellectually, that he makes. The whole thing with laughter is that it has the effect of undercutting—because that's what laughter is. It's a weapon of unreality, of creating unreality.

I think you are entirely right. If Shaw were completely convinced of one unequivocal, unambivalent ideology, he could not write this way. I tried to indicate that, but you're doing it even more clearly. It's precisely because he's got a foot in a whole bunch of different camps and he doesn't want to have to stand all in one camp, that he'll laugh at the religious people and then he'll laugh at the cynics. It's like universal putting down. At the same time he wants to have hero-worship. So he wants everything.

I think laughter is an expression of that and gives him a means of achieving it, but I think that that usage is a problem. The problem is that he never commits to anything. Therefore, everything is up in the air, and even the laughter stops being funny.

However, I don't accept your view that that is inherent in the combination. Because—just speaking of my own private tastes—I've always liked those British wits like Oscar Wilde or Noel Coward. They deal with serious issues in a witty way, with an edge. They can come up with immortal epigrams. It's a typically British or English trait.

Of course, they don't write tragedies. Or if they did—like *Salome*—they don't make jokes about it. I like the humorous element in *The Fountainhead*. There's a lot of bitterness in *The Fountainhead* which I thoroughly enjoy; not in the essential theme and characterization, but in little touches, which I just treasured when I was growing up. Just little things. Like Ralston Holcombe whose hair was up in a great sweep and left dandruff on the back of his neck. Ayn Rand is full of those scathing remarks. I don't even know in what dimension the people live who say she has no sense of humor.

The thing is, she is very clear about what she is impassioned about and what the good is or what the true is. She makes fun only of the bad or the lesser. If you could retain that in a combination, then I think that humor is a terrific adjunct.

I use humor as a deliberate device of lecturing. I stumbled on it. I first started using it because classes got bored. They got bored no matter how interesting I thought the presentation was. I discovered that modern audiences simply have an antipathy to ideas from the way they are brought up: that it's going to be boring and deadly and irrelevant. And that takes over no matter how interesting they find the idea. What you have to do is periodically rescue them from the demon of serious ideas. I would just inject a little wisecrack, the audience would laugh, and I would feel that I bought myself three minutes of time. They see it's not as horrifying as they thought and they sort of smile. Then about five minutes later they drift back and the thought strikes them subconsciously, "Oh, some more of this serious stuff." So you give another wisecrack.

I built that into lecturing as a style. It was deliberately a pedagogical device, but obviously it had to grow out of an interest in humor itself on my part.

Q: Was the movie version done after Shaw's death?

A: I don't think it was done after his death because he outlived just about everything. I think it was done in the forties.

Q: Do you know how he reacted to it at all?

A: I think he approved it. Graham Greene is a very prestigious writer. I believe Shaw was consulted, and it was a great honor to have Graham Greene. You know, he was the one who did *The Heart of the Matter* and *The End of the Affair* and all kinds of famous novels. So I think he liked the movie, from what I know.

Oh, the movie was done in 1959? And he died in 1950. That refutes everything out of my mouth. Maybe I am thinking of the Estate of Shaw. I vaguely remember that *someone* connected with Shaw approved the movie. Or maybe I have megalomania and am just thinking that *I* approved the movie.

CHAPTER SEVEN

MONNA VANNA

Maurice Maeterlinck

1. Introduction

Maurice Maeterlinck was Belgian but wrote in French. His dates are 1862 to 1949, so he died at eighty-seven. He is slightly earlier than Shaw, but I wanted to end the course on his play rather than on the martyrdom of Saint Joan.

Maeterlinck wrote about sixty major works of fiction and non-fiction; essays, plays and poetry. He was raised by a conservative, rich, French-speaking family in Flanders. He went to Catholic school but he never became religious. He had a very definitely structured life, psychologically. The three phases of his life form an arc. He started with gloom and depression—that is his youth, including his marriage. Then he fell in love and a soaring, benevolent, optimistic quality took place; he was transformed psychologically. And that is the period during which he wrote *Monna Vanna*. He gradually grew depressed again and remained so until he died.

So we are analyzing one of the happiest and most romantic of his works with *Monna Vanna*. There were two women in his life: his wife and his mistress. His mistress was Georgette Leblanc, a famous singer. Their affair was new, and that is what made him blissful. She wanted a debut on the stage so he wrote *Monna Vanna* for her. It opened with her in the lead on May 7, 1902. So that's a couple of decades earlier than *Saint Joan*.

At first the play was banned in London because Queen Alexandra interpreted it as saying that virtue and fidelity are secondary to human lives. In other words, Monna Vanna should not have taken up Prinzivalle's immoral offer just to save a city; this was the destruction of all virtue, fidelity, and morality—and could not be shown in England. The English were also very upset by the fact that she was naked under her cloak. You see how things have changed.

Finally, however, *Monna Vanna* became famous in world repertory prior to World War One. World War One is the conventional date for the end of the Romantic era in Western history. Prior to World War One, Maeterlinck ranked as the greatest dramatist in Europe; he got the Nobel Prize in 1911. Unfortunately, after the war he was gradually, but inexorably, forgotten.

I went to a bookstore in New York City—one of those highly specialized bookstores that exist only in New York where you can usually find a library on anything, however esoteric. When I said that I was doing research on *Monna Vanna* by Maeterlinck, the eyes of the ancient man behind the counter lit up and he said, "I haven't heard anyone ask for that since the 1930s." He said they used to come in all the time for that, but he just hadn't heard it for over fifty years. He suggested that the only place where I would find books on Maeterlinck was the Belgian Consulate, whose mission it is to spread Belgian culture in the United States.

So I did contact them and they were exceptionally gracious to me. They gave me four or five books from a vast library on Maeterlinck. New York did live up to the fact that you can find anything there, if you know where to look. So I owe this lecture basically to their books.

I have a nice quote on old age from Maeterlinck when he was in his eighties. He said, "I try to be bored, so that the last hours of my old age may be longer for me. But they pass more quickly than those of my youth and middle life. It is very difficult to cultivate boredom when one takes to it too late." I always think that implies a nice, active, thoughtful life.

Now as regards *Monna Vanna*, the only preliminary thing we need to know is that the setting is the end of the fifteenth century. It is the High Renaissance, about a hundred and fifty years after the burning of Saint Joan.

2. Plot-theme

Again we just jump in and take a stab at it: a man wants to sleep with another man's wife. Or even: a powerful man wants to sleep with another man's wife. But that leaves us nowhere. There is no conflict; there is nothing at stake; she just says yes or no and that's it.

Let's try to bring in a third party and make a triangle out of this. A powerful man offers a value to a husband, if the wife agrees to sleep with him. This already suggests that the husband has a say in what goes on. He is in conflict, he debates whether or not he should let his wife do it. He needs to have the offer made to him. So we have the beginning of a conflict and a situation.

You will immediately, and unfortunately, recognize in this situation the movie *Indecent Proposal*, where the man offers a million dollars to the husband. It is an indecent takeoff on *Monna Vanna*. I did not see it. I tried several times and I could never actually press the Pay TV button for that movie. But, as I understand from my spies and reporters, the differences are very substantial in plot-theme (let alone everything else) to *Monna Vanna*.

In the *Monna Vanna* situation, money is not a significant value. In *Indecent Proposal*, the couple has no really desperate problem to which money would be the solution, except something about saving their house. Basically, as I gather, they have gambling losses they need to make up. If they hadn't gone to Las Vegas, they would have gone about their business and been okay. So it is a kind of chance situation.

Contrast that, for instance, with something which is not yet *Monna Vanna* but much better: a powerful man offers a million dollars to save the life of the dying husband, if the wife agrees to sleep with him. Here there is a conflict, a real motive, and a real source of temptation and struggle; it is not just a million dollars which, after Clinton, is only worth about two hundred thousand anyway.

That is still not a good enough idea for a worthwhile play, let alone a great play, because what is the motive of the man offering a million dollars? Does he have a passion ruling him? In *Indecent Proposal*, it is basically a whim; it is a stunt to see what he can get away with; a kind of cynical test of human nature. Therefore the motive is either low and evil or, at best, spur of the moment. But suppose now that the man who offers the bribe is really deeply in love with her and has been for many years—and he offers the million to save her husband's life if she will sleep with him. That is already a better situation.

It's still not good enough because it is too callous. If this man is so much in love with her, why does he subject her to this? He wouldn't do it in real life. *We the Living* is a variant on just this situation. A woman decides to sleep with a powerful man who loves her in order to save her husband's life. It is a very similar situation. But in *We the Living*, it is very clear that the other man must not know that she is doing it for the money because he loves her. The husband mustn't know because he is too proud to accept money from his mortal enemy.

How could this happen? Ayn Rand figured out that that kind of situation could happen only in a dictatorship, because in a free country the wife wouldn't be reduced to that. So she reached the idea that a woman decides to sleep with the head of the secret police in a dictatorship, a man in love with her, in order to save her husband's life. That is a great plot-theme, made even better when she actually falls in love with him.

Monna Vanna and *We the Living* have basically the same type of plot-theme. A powerful man offers an enormous value—not money. It is much too simple to offer a million dollars, or even a trillion dollars. Money is just not something that will make a play go. It has to be life or death; that is really the only thing that will make theater work.

To return to *Monna Vanna*'s plot-theme: a powerful man offers an enormous value to a husband if his wife sleeps with him. The motive of the offerer is passionate love of the wife—and the value he offers is not just the life of her husband but of her entire country, the city-state of Pisa which has about thirty thousand people, who will otherwise be annihilated. It is even harder for the husband to say no because his native land is in jeopardy. You have an idea here which really intensifies everybody's conflict. That is just leagues above the idea: "Here's a million dollars, can I sleep with you?" "Okay, my house is at risk." It is insulting to Maeterlinck to have to make a comparison to *Indecent Proposal*.

Maeterlinck had to make real to himself how one man could threaten a whole country. That's one problem he had with creating this play. Another is that he needed a context where sexual fidelity is a major issue so that excludes the twentieth century. He wrote it right around the turn of the century. There were already rather liberated attitudes in the avantgarde. Essential to his plot is the idea that these two men could not abide the idea that she just sleeps around, as against the convention on TV today. He was basically caught in a time frame from the Renaissance to the end of the nineteenth century in order to have the attitude that he wanted toward sex.

He picked the Renaissance as his setting since one man could plausibly hold the fate of an entire country in his hands because of the city-states. If he is the commander of the invading army of the city under siege, and he is in love with the heroine—then the only thing we have to throw in to get the final situation is: he is risking his own life to do so. So he has a conflict, too and all he wants is one night with her.

Monna Vanna seems doomed with the city anyway. She hears rumors about the man. Is he a wicked barbarian? Oh, no. He is an early Renaissance man: he is a highly cultured, literate man. Even her husband's own soldiers say that he is strong and admirable. Now we have a situation that is worthy of a great play.

This is how I formulate the plot-theme, now that we have discussed the factors that go into it. *The captain of a besieging army offers victory to a dying city, at the risk of his own life, if the wife of the city's commander spends one night alone with him.*

Notice all the things that we have to omit from the plot-theme because they are the story as it develops; they are not the essential action-situation. We do not include her answer, whether she goes or she refuses to go—that will come out when we tell the story. The situation is just: she is given the choice; what happens? We do not, most emphatically, include that she is lukewarm about her husband. That is something that even she doesn't realize at the beginning; it is part of the story as it develops. We do not include the fact that her husband was hostile to the offerer. All we know is that there is obviously going to be a conflict here but what his reaction is going to be, we do not know.

Wherever possible, state actions not emotions in a plot-theme. This is a plot we are talking about, an action situation. Instead of saying "a captain of a besieging army, madly in love . . ." which is an emotional statement, say, "the captain, at the risk of his own life . . . ." You leave his action to suggest that he is madly in love. There are plays in which you simply cannot state the plot-theme without an emotional word. For instance, I defy you to capture the plot-theme of *Othello* without the word "jealous." But it is better to deal with the bare essence of the action situation when possible.

From this we can immediately define, as we always do, the main characters and the essential conflict. And here it is self-evident that there are three main characters: Prinzivalle, Guido and Monna Vanna. "Monna" means "dame" or "lady" or "Ms." Her name is Vanna. Which one of the three is the protagonist?

It is not Prinzivalle. He is responsible for what is called the inciting incident. He takes the step that incites the action. But thereafter he has to wait and see what is going to happen. Guido waits throughout to see what will happen. Who is it that makes the essential decisions: to go or not to go, to love or not to love, to remain faithful to her husband or not? Obviously the plot-moving figure is Monna Vanna, so the title is a faithful indication of the protagonist.

Marco, the father, is just a go-between; a philosophic commentator. He is more or less like the Greek chorus, so not an essential character.

The basic conflict is between the two men. Guido is against it: that is why he has to be offered so incredible a price as the salvation of his whole country. Prinzivalle wants to stake his whole life for it. And, of course, everyone has conflict, as in a proper play, derivative from that basic one. Monna Vanna has a clash with Guido as soon as she decides to go. She has a clash with Prinzivalle at the beginning. Guido wants to kill Prinzivalle. They are all interplayed but it all hinges on the basic conflict over this value.

3. Plot Development

This is an eminently logical, classic plot structure: an Aristotelian beginning, which is what we call the establishment; a rise to the climax, which Aristotle called the middle; and then a suspenseful, drawn-out resolution, which Aristotle named the end. It is very neat: three parts; three acts.

Act One is the establishment of the basic situation. We get Prinzivalle's offer, and then the conflict between Vanna and Guido and the reasons they give each other for what they are going to do. Next is her decision to go, despite his raging. At the end of the act, Guido asks if she is going to come back and she says, "Yes, . . . if . . ." It is up to you to fill in the if—*if* he lets me; *if* I still love you; *if* I have something to tell you. Who knows?

To make a really good story, it is important that in this act Guido's violent feeling for Monna Vanna be established. If he is laid-back or noncommittal—if he says, "Sure, go ahead"—there is no play; no crisis. On the other hand, if he loves her with an immortal passion like Prinzivalle's, then there is no basis for her to make any decision. It becomes deuces wild; she might as well just toss a coin. So there is a very delicate balance in the writing here. Guido has to be violent, but not impassioned in love. He has to be strong enough so we feel the conflict. And yet, when we get to Prinzivalle, we can say, "That wasn't love, even though we thought it was." Similarly she has to think it is love and make the same discovery we do when we get to Act Two; that it really is not. That is very tricky writing. You are absolutely at the mercy of the actor, Guido: he can kill this part with an identical fidelity to the text if he is too sincere or too much of a cold fish: he has to be just exactly right for this to work. That is Act One, the establishment of the conflict with Monna Vanna's departure.

Act Two is the rise to the climax. Monna Vanna discovers who the mysterious enemy is. She falls in love with him or, rather, re-falls in love with him when she remembers who he is. That is the climax, when she actually falls in love with him again because we now know, given her character, given her commitment to him, where the play has to go. He leaves her untouched, precisely because he loves her so passionately. That is a point we will have to come back to. That is utterly essential to the play; that he doesn't touch her because he is so passionately in love with her (and that does not mean he is Catholic). She decides to return with him. The reason given in the play is she is going to save his life. She also wants to explain it to Guido.

The rise is the whole section where they are exploring each other. "Who are you?" "Oh, yes, I remember, and why didn't you . . . ?" "And why did you . . . ?" Finally she comes to see who he is and who she is, and falls in love.

Act Three is the resolution: she confronts Guido who refuses to listen to the truth and finally threatens Prinzivalle's life. She saves Prinzivalle by telling Guido the lie he wants to hear. And then the ending. I was astonished to hear that some people regarded it as controversial. I think it is self-evident. How's that for a dogmatic end to controversy? They are going to live a blissful life together, they are going to run off together, and it's goodbye to Guido. You cannot get more clear than her last speech: *I want the key alone, no one else. My life* "was indeed an evil dream, but a fairer one begins—ah, a fairer one begins." Curtain.

You can just see her: she has the key, she runs to the prison, and it is very clear what she plans to do at the prison, let alone after they get out of it. You are never going to see them again. They take off. It is definitely, unequivocally, a happy ending.

In essence, the structure is very logical. Act One: she goes to Prinzivalle. Act Two: she falls in love with him. Act Three: she saves his life and runs off with him. The sequence here is unavoidable. If she didn't go to him, there would be no play. When she gets to him, it is essential that she recognizes him and that she falls in love with him—but they don't make love. Why is that necessary? Why is that so crucial to the play? There are many reasons. What we have to see is the depth, the metaphysical quality of her love. It would simply not be objective if, when she is summoned coercively, she falls into bed with him right away. That smacks too much of a coerced roll in the hay. Even if she agreed after recognizing him, it would still be coerced in inception and it would be too fast for her to fall that deeply in love with him. To be convincing, you need some stage time and action.

Most important we, the audience, need to see Guido come down in our estimation. Otherwise we can never judge her character objectively. We don't know her history. If she falls in love that fast, for all we know she is a slut who falls in love with anybody. In order for us to be able to judge her, we need the same passage of time that she needs in order for her to judge him. We need time to pass and then we need to see Prinzivalle in relation to Guido, which is exactly what Monna Vanna needs to see. It is perfectly synchronized on Maeterlinck's part. What the drama needs for objectivity is exactly what she needs in order to be able to behave rationally. If they made love prematurely, it would sink her character and sink the audience's interest in the play. It would turn the whole thing into a materialistic melodrama of the lowest order.

It is not that they don't want passionately to make love. The whole thing is that they do. It is not that they have anything philosophically against making love. It is a great situation, where your hands are trembling to touch the body of the beloved, and there is a powerful reason why you can't do it now. The same situation was present in *Atlas Shrugged* with Dagny and Galt, where she knew all she had to do was get up and walk down the hall, and that was it. And she just tossed and tossed and tossed. Everyone reading it wants her to do it. But she can't. And that drives the audience mad. It is the same situation here; a fabulous situation. It just can't be overdone.

It is even better that they both think that sex is good. If they didn't; if they had a hesitation because one of them thought that sex was evil, it wouldn't be as powerful. It is precisely because they both think sex is wonderful, but they can't engage in it, that it drives you crazy.

In any event, they do the right thing: they fall in love, but they don't touch each other—and that is precisely what Guido cannot believe. That's when the audience starts to root for it to really happen. Guido can't believe a love of that dimension, of that power. He doesn't hold a view of human nature which is that exalted or that passionate. He believes that people are essentially average guys. Women, if they don't sleep around, cheat. Men are pretty much apes with a great sense of bravado and macho self-images. He has, in other words, a kind of conventional, low view of life. It is a metaphysical issue to him; it goes to the nature of man. Guido can't stand the idea that they spent the night together with her naked under her cloak, that they really love each other but they didn't touch each other. That represents a way of life that he feels is impossible.

Maybe he tolerates his own inadequate marriage by saying: there just isn't such a great passion in the world. Maybe he is using it to rationalize. The trouble for him is, if their story were true, it makes them saints—saints of passion—in a way he feels he just can't equal. To him, it is a self-esteem or a metaphysical issue.

Maeterlinck is so brilliant at presenting this that he has Guido willingly give them up. He tells them: *go and love, and I'll leave you alone, if only you tell me the truth.* It is more important to him that his view of human nature be confirmed and his life retroactively justified even if he loses her, than to discover that there is an exalted quality to life that is possible that he is betraying. He needs her to confirm his metaphysics, his view of life and of himself. She refuses to lie until he forces the issue by threatening Prinzivalle.

Then, of course, she has to go along. She poses as Prinzivalle's enemy for the sin of his lust against her. That immediately kills Guido in her eyes and in the audience's eyes. He is out now as a consideration. You would be horrified at this point if she decided to go back to him—that would be a drama of Christian renunciation, worthy of the sacrifice of Isaac to God. It would be the end of all self-assertion.

The brilliant twist on Maeterlinck's part is that Guido will not believe the truth. He demands the truth, he is doing everything to get the truth but he is too weak for it. And he will only accept a lie as the truth. Thereby, he loses the battle for his own soul and lets his hated rival win out. He demeans himself to the status of the ordinary.

4. Characterization

I am afraid in the throes of excitement I gave you some characterization out of order. But let's go to characterization in a more organized way. To grasp the theme and meaning of this play, you must understand the motivation of the characters in their key decisions; what factors they are weighing and what kind of factors decides them. There are really only four crucial decisions that make up the entire progression of the play.

First, why does Monna Vanna decide to accept Prinzivalle's offer? Why doesn't she just say, "No, I'm going to die here beside my husband?" Well, for one thing, there would be no play. But remember, you have to give an answer from the point of view of the character, not the author.

Second, why did Prinzivalle make the offer to begin with? What did he really want from Monna Vanna, given the fact that he never did sleep with her? Why did he want her naked under her cloak?

Number three, why did Monna Vanna return to Guido at all in Act Three? What does she expect from him when she returns? Does she want his blessing? Does she want to defy him? What?

And four—the very easiest one, once you know the answers to the others—why does she finally choose Prinzivalle over Guido?

I am just going to pose some issues here. Decide whether you agree with what happened in the play; not the reasons, just the facts. Did Monna Vanna do the right thing in accepting Prinzivalle's offer and going to see him? Was Prinzivalle right to make the offer in the first place? Did Monna Vanna do the right thing to return to Guido at all in the end? Do you think she did the right thing in choosing Prinzivalle over Guido? I agree with all four. If you didn't agree with at least one, it sinks the play. It is up to Maeterlinck to convince us of all four, as the play goes on.

Let's take them one at a time. First, why does Monna Vanna accept Prinzivalle's offer? The standard answer—which scandalized Queen Alexandra—is that she was willing to sacrifice her virtue for the well-being of her city. She is, in effect, a true follower of John Stuart Mill and the Hedonic Calculus. She is a real Utilitarian. There is even some evidence that Maeterlinck thinks that, but we don't have to agree with him.

Look at it this way: if a woman says, "In the name of all my compatriots who do matter something to me, I'll let him have my body for a night," is that necessarily a sacrifice for her city? If the government orders her to do it, that is obviously a sacrifice of the individual. Here the conqueror asks for a night of lovemaking. Is that so obviously a sacrifice? She could reason this way: thousands of innocents will be spared, and he is going to get me eventually when he conquers the city. It is no moral stain on me, since it was done under physical coercion. So the worst is an unenjoyable pawing, as against thousands of lives, including my own. If you look at it that way, it is a calculation of positives and negatives, so it's not a sacrifice.

However, you can't really talk it away. To the extent that she has to give her body for a night to an unknown man for the sake of saving her city, you would have to say that there is a core there that involves a sacrifice. She is giving a value by force that she would not give by persuasion or left to her own choice. She is having a value forced out of her and, to that extent, she is being made to sacrifice.

Guido, correspondingly, is a sympathetic character in Act One, to the extent that he is fighting for individual rights against the idea of sacrifice. This is a perfect setup to trap an Objectivist audience because he makes convincing speeches for individual rights and denounces the idea of sacrifice to the collective. It is true that he seems to focus mainly on his right to his property—which is his wife—rather than on her right to *her* life and pursuit of happiness. But this is, after all, the Renaissance and prior to Women's Lib.

All in all, however, I do not think Monna Vanna's decision is a sacrifice; not to her and really not to Maeterlinck. I don't think it is insignificant that the man wants to sleep with her, which is implicitly a compliment. Just imagine if it were you, ladies. You are home one day and you get a call from an unknown admirer who is prepared to save the entire neighborhood from the plague if you will come over for the night. You might start to inquire about him and you find out that he is heroic, literate, strong, romantic. I mean, at a certain point, this is a real fun sacrifice.

The other important thing, which we learn later, but she implicitly, subconsciously knows now, is that she is not really in love with her husband—not in the deepest, most passionate way. She has a yearning for a dynamite kind of love; the kind that would come in just this sort of way—as against the security of a boring, conventional love. So her motives are quite mixed in Act One. The reason is that she does not really know herself yet; she doesn't know what she craves. She doesn't know that she is frustrated in love. She doesn't know fully that she settled for second best in her marriage. In a sense, on the surface, she is doing her "duty" for the country, but it is her duty insofar as she is unawakened to her true nature. It is her duty while she is in a dream world—or in a rut.

It's really a very different situation from what would be an unequivocal sacrifice; namely, if she were passionate for Guido and disgusted by Prinzivalle. That would be a sacrifice. But the reverse is hinted at very strongly: that she is not so hot for Guido and this other man sounds really intriguing.

Act Three is the further proof that she is not a self-sacrificing type. She has a real chance to sacrifice—to give up her true love for the sake of her husband, who is kind and conventionally decent. She has a chance to sacrifice and live the rest of her life with Guido. How many seconds does she consider that option? Zero. She is not a sacrificial type. In fact, she sacrifices precisely only when she is not clear on the values involved and therefore has no passionate course of her own to pursue; or when the situation is mixed which is the way it stands in the beginning.

In regard to her development as a character, she goes through what is called a true character arc. She grows before your eyes, reaches a certain height, and then acts on it. In Act One she is unclear about her true values, even though from the very beginning she is adventurous, strong, and relentless once she has made a decision. Her decision is a mixed bag: it has partly to do with saving her city and partly because she wants, in an inchoate way, something more out of life. Then she proceeds to discover her true values—not only Prinzivalle, but the kind of love that he represents. Then, you see the very same strong relentlessness that she had in making the decision in Act One. Now she is going to secure and enjoy the value which that opened up to her. It's a beautiful paradox of the kind that Maeterlinck loved to create: she discovers the necessity of total selfishness by a seemingly selfless act. The seemingly selfless act—giving her body for her country— opens her to find her true values and turns her into an apostle of total selfishness. That is the kind of paradox playwrights like to find. That is why she accepted his offer.

The second of the four questions: why did Prinzivalle make the offer? What did he expect of the encounter? Did he want to sleep with her; was he moved by a lust of the body? Perhaps, in part, but their actions make clear that his is first a spiritual love. It's a spiritual and physical love but first he wants to see if she remembers, if she reciprocates. Is she happily in love with Guido? Is there still a chance for him? He does not want her body out of context. He wants her to love him, and then he wants to sleep with her. Remember, he was twelve the last time he talked to her. He wants to find out if she is as great as he remembers.

At the outset he has no definite plans. I will not say that it is a "fishing expedition" but it is an enraptured hope and a chance to see what is going on. He is going to play it by ear, according to how things work out.

One commentator in one of the Belgian books has the effrontery to say that Prinzivalle's motive is that he is testing her purity, and that his secret hope is that she will reject his offer and go back to Guido, proving that she is still the virtuous girl he remembered. Then he can go off and pine for her until death, and she can stay with Guido and suffer till death, and everyone will embody Christian virtue. My comment to that, which I wrote in the margin, is "BS." It is a very helpful comment, because there is nothing calmer that you can say. This is actually the way many people interpreted it in 1905 and 1910. They were actually trying to defend Maeterlinck against the incredible charge that he was for selfishness and sex, and all those bad things.

The third question, what is Monna Vanna's intention in coming back with Prinzivalle to Guido in Act Three? Why don't they just run away? Is it only to rescue Prinzivalle? I don't think so. That is a conveniently created and pretty transparent setup by Maeterlinck, and it is obvious that she would still go back even if she had another way to save Prinzivalle. Why, then, does she go back?

Part of it is that she needs to see the two together, to test Guido's love and compare the two. Suppose she was completely decided in her own mind. Imagine that you had lived with somebody for many years and it was, on the face of it, a happy marriage. Then you went away and fell passionately in love. Would you think it was right just to take off? Would you send him a postcard and write, "Florence is great. Glad you're not here."? Morally, she owes him an explanation. She is not the kind of woman who could just vanish forever. They are not a hostile couple. She has found a greater love; she expects Guido to understand and accept that. She wants him to know the truth, and she fully believes that he will believe her story, which is the truth, including her love for Prinzivalle. She wants him, in effect, to bless them in their new life. This is the hero she married, she thought, and this is what she expects. It is a matter of elementary justice and objectivity on her part. She is not going to treat him like dirt because she does not regard him as dirt.

In fact, if he had come through the way she expected, she would have been in a terrible conflict. He would then, in understanding this love, have proved that he was the type who was capable of a love of that dimension. He would have been as metaphysically profound in his approach to love as Prinzivalle; and by the very act of setting her free out of his very love for her, she would have had a horrible time choosing. In my opinion, if he had done this, I think the best ending would have had to be some version of *ménage à trois*, or something like alternate custody.

I am quite serious in saying that in that situation, under these circumstances, I would vote for that as philosophically absolutely justified. But it would make a different play. That would have required some remarkable character change on his part, because from the outset he is presented as a conventional man; basically good, a good commander, even a man with a grasp of principle but possessive in a bad sense. She is his wife, like a piece of property. He is also presented as very social. Remember, in theater every sentence counts. If the author lets him say, "What will everybody think?" he is already a social type. Given that type, it is a setup for him to react the way he does. If Maeterlinck wanted to make her life hell, he would have had to make Guido so good at the beginning that she is constantly torn. It would end up, in effect, the indecision of Monna Vanna. She just never knows which man she wants—and then you would have a different theme, different characters, and a whole different play. It wouldn't be this play.

As it is, Guido condemns himself to the status of non-valuer by the very fact that he will not accept her truthful story, and thereby frees her to live with Prinzivalle. The eloquent fact is that she has to lie for him to recognize and feel at home with what she is saying. He has to feel that they are all on the same "human level," which exalts them and frees her morally and emotionally from him.

The answer to question four—why does she leave Guido?—is that now she is really in love with a worthy man. Why should she go with the man she loves? Because one must always act on what one really loves, not what people expect—no matter whether they are your husband, the city, society, whatever. And that, of course, takes us right into the theme.

5. Theme

The theme of *Monna Vanna* is the importance of love. Not just sexual love, but romantic love as the expression of soul and body; love as a response to fundamental values. In Monna Vanna's case, it is a response to the kind of man, the actions he takes and the life he lives. The importance of love really means the importance of values in life; the importance of personal values and of action to achieve these. That's what counts in life: values are achievable. So this play is thoroughly benevolent universe. These values depend on man's choice.

How do we know that Maeterlinck believes in free will and man's choice of values? It is exactly the same way we know from Corneille. They agonize, "Should I do *this*? I've got *these* reasons. Should I do *this*? No, I've got *these* reasons." Back and forth. You see the process of thought, of debate, of discussion, of trying to figure out what to do—and then their decision. So his theme is the importance of man's or woman's strength in their commitment to their values and to life. Marco actually puts it in this sentence: "And life is right." I think the meaning of that is that the pursuit of values is right as against duty or obligation to husband, family, society, etc.

We could say that the theme is: life demands and goes to the passionate valuer. Guido fails the test: he doesn't know what valuing is. Prinzivalle and Monna Vanna know: they refuse to sacrifice their values.

Prinzivalle tried to sacrifice for her by thinking that she would have a happier life without him with her wealthy husband, and thereby almost lost her. The really interesting thing in connection with this aspect of the theme is Monna Vanna's anger, her indignation at Prinzivalle, for having dreamt of sacrificing; for not going after and seizing what he wanted in life; for hanging back all those years, watching and waiting, and thinking he's not good enough.

This is a truly brilliant twist on Maeterlinck's part. In a play like this, by all precedent from traditional plays, in Act One the villain makes a demand: "I want your body, I want to sleep with you." In Act Two she is supposed to come back and say, in essence, "How dare you?" The absolutely brilliant thing in this play is that she comes back in Act Two and says, "What kept you?" That is really brilliant. Maeterlinck transcends his entire generation with it. She denounces Prinzivalle for being a coward, for not knowing what love is. He expects he is going to be denounced for asserting himself and suddenly he finds he is on the defensive for being too humble and self-sacrificial.

It is a wonderful twist and it brings out Maeterlinck's idea that Monna Vanna is so selfish that she simply expected selfishness on the part of someone she loved. She was just indignant; she equated love with selfishness. In other words, if you want something, you want to possess it. Prinzivalle had to really work to dig himself out of that hole.

So that makes the theme clearer than any other thing. It is the primacy of personal love over duty of any kind; the primacy and achievability of selfish values, to put it more abstractly.

It has also been worded in some of the books I read as: "the power of love to triumph over obstacles and to illuminate the essence of life" or as one commentator put it: "love can elude destiny." When Maeterlinck was younger in his depressed phase, he thought love was doomed and that destiny would crush us all but here he has broken through to the idea that if you love passionately, you can break any deterministic bounds.

This ode to love is in tremendous contrast to Shakespeare, who thinks that love sinks you like a stone if you love too well. It is even in contrast to Sophocles, who has an ode or two to the effect that: you had better be careful around love because it smashes everything; it is wanton, and who knows where it is going to lead. Now, here we have love as liberating, so it is a very historically distinctive theme.

The message of this whole play is really: the need to discover your personal values, which is what Monna Vanna had to do, and then act on them—against everybody if necessary.

This is a play purely on the moral level. Maeterlinck himself has nothing much to say about social ethics. By now, you are probably inured to the fact that all of these playwrights have said things that make you roll your eyes. I doubt if you are surprised that in other works Maeterlinck is capable of abundant altruism, praise of sacrifice, and even of socialism. Somehow, despite all of this, he has a conviction, at least in his optimistic phase of life, of the supremacy of personal values. He let the logic of this conviction lead him to write a play such as *Monna Vanna*. You really have to say that the theme of this play is the same as the theme of *The Fountainhead* in essence. He doesn't distinguish the second-hander versus the first-hander, or the consciousness that accompanies them. But he has the idea of connecting selfishness with nobility and the highest aspiration of man, with the soul of the morally elite as against the petty desires of the masses or the ordinary people, who care for very little and who are busy making sacrifices and expecting to receive them. That is absolutely *The Fountainhead* and so it should be no surprise to you that Ayn Rand loved this play and I hope no surprise to you that Maeterlinck loved *The Fountainhead*.

It was a mutual admiration society between the two of them for a while, despite the fact that there was a tremendous gulf between them on many philosophic issues. I do not know if Ayn Rand met him personally but she did correspond with his wife. And he did, through his wife and through his editors, retell to her stories about his discovery of *The Fountainhead* in the palaces of European nobility, which he frequented. Needless to say, she got a lot of pleasure out of that. Ayn Rand tried to get a movie made of this for years but just could not get the studios to come near it. The closest they ever came is *Indecent Proposal*.

6. Philosophy

Maeterlinck does not have a deeper philosophy. All you can ascribe to him with any meaning is the essence of Romanticism: free will, choice of values, the need of strength, the importance of selfishness, the possibility of the good. All of that he is very aware of, including the issue of free will, although he was a determinist earlier in life. Remember that Monna Vanna says it is never too late. There is still time, no matter how many years we lost. The idea is that it is within our choice; definitely man is a being of self-made soul. There is no more to be found philosophically in this play and, in that respect, it is beneath all the other plays in this course. There is no metaphysics or epistemology of any kind expressed in the play. And every other play, in some form or another, has those elements.

If you want to scrounge for implications, you could say that it is not too religious a play. The theme is the importance of your own life on earth and of sexual love as a tremendous value. Maeterlinck was not a religious type but, on the other hand, he was a real free-wheeling, wild mystic. At the same time, he was a strong valuer and not a skeptic who says, "Who can know anything?" You could try to argue that he is really an Aristotelian, pro-earthly, pro-reason. If he was, he sure didn't know it. I do not think it is accurate or profitable to ascribe metaphysics or epistemology to authors who have no explicit idea in their play about these subjects or who, in other plays, have diametrically opposite ideas when they do discuss philosophy. For instance, Schiller is full of explicit ideas as is Shaw. Corneille has metaphysics and epistemology right next to the surface of the play; the idea of a feudal intrinsicist code gives you his fundamental, philosophic approach.

This is the only unphilosophical play in the course. It has a theme pertaining to morality but that is it. It has a great sense of life but I debated whether to include it. Because this is "Seven Great Plays as Literature and as Philosophy," I have to explain why I regard it as essential to greatness in a play to have philosophy in some form. This is going to be the most controversial thing I say but, since I say it, I have a little doubt about this play being included. On the other hand, it has such a terrific sense of life and it has so many wonderful things in it that for this one case, happiness outweighs philosophy.

If you want to see where Maeterlinck actually stands on philosophic issues, I'll give you a brief glimpse of his philosophic development, so you can see where *Monna Vanna* comes in his works. He was brought up in Catholic schools, but it never really took. He had a precarious faith for a while, but it withered. He was eventually put, believe it or not, on the Index. He was open to anything: science, extrasensory perception, whatever came by.

In his early years he was influenced by Schopenhauer and the malevolent universe. He felt there was no use in having any emotions because you are doomed to defeat so he took as the champion of repression, the Roman stoic Marcus Aurelius. Because he lived in the nineteenth century, you have to throw Darwin in. Those were the three figures that most influenced him.

He was also depressed; he thought that life was hell. Part of it was that his parents forced him to become a lawyer. He held explicitly that man is helpless. In fact, in his early plays the actors have strings attached to them which is supposed to show that they are merely marionettes dancing on strings who have no will of their own. He had Death with a capital D as one of the characters in the play, and Death would always wipe out all the others. He was a real pessimist. This is the same man who wrote *Monna Vanna*.

Then comes the revolution, Georgette Leblanc. He fell in love, and it had a tremendous effect on him. This quote from Prinzivalle to Monna Vanna is supposed to be pure autobiography on Maeterlinck's part: [When I fell in love] "me thought that men were somehow changing—that I had been deceived in their true nature until this day. Above all, I thought that I myself was other than of old; that I emerged at last from a long imprisonment; the doors were parted, flowers and green leaves took the place of iron bars, the sky stooped and drew up to it all the heavy stones that had shut me in, and the pure air of morning penetrated at last into my heart and bathed my love in its fresh fragrance." So there is a huge changeover philosophically to the benevolent universe, the power of man, love as able to overcome all obstacles, etc.

Did he have any distinctive or definitive ideas philosophically in this period? He was a dabbler. He just pontificated; he came up with observations out of the blue. Here is a typical Maurice Maeterlinck idea from this phase: he was writing on bees and it came to him that maybe it would be profitable to compare man to the bees. I quote from a nonfiction essay of his: "Man's goal, the aim of life, like that of the insect, may be no more than its own initial impetus. Yet just as the destiny of the honeybee is to produce honey, man's may be that of creating the strange fluid known as thought. We know not where this activity will lead. But the bee knows not why it secretes nectar, nor who will profit from this spiritual substance in the world, but the process must continue. The final principle—God, providence, nature, chance, fatality—may be good or evil, but the life process must be lived." So that is the message of the more optimistic Maeterlinck. In effect, it comes down to: live, think, love—who knows what it all means or what is behind it.

That is the reason why I consider him far less philosophical than any of the other authors. He is just not a philosophic thinker, period. It is hardly surprising, therefore, that after his affair with Mademoiselle Leblanc was over, he fell again into darkness and pessimism. The tragedy is that he had such a soaring moment in his life, and then in his old age he ends with this confession: "I shall leave this life having sought to know all and having learned nothing." That shows the power of philosophy. That shows that a sense of life—even one so brilliantly articulated that could lead to a play like this—is just not sufficient equipment. If you need any more propaganda, he ended up anti-Communist, anti-Christian, vaguely mystical, pro-individualist and, all in all, defeated. So if you rush out to get his other plays, are you going to be surprised!

I want to close with two stylistic observations about Maeterlinck. He has a fine sense of drama, which is something you cannot find anymore. As an example, consider the deliberate twist of the ending. Think how much more dramatic it is that Monna Vanna wins by a lie rather than by the truth. We have discussed the meaning, but from the point of view of drama: it is a paradox, a twist, an O. Henry-type of ending. If she had said, "I love him," and Guido had said, "Okay" it would have been dramatically flat. The idea here is that the lie wins because, although he is after the truth, he can't take it. The lie is like an incredibly dramatic slap in the face. It is not just communication of information. Monna Vanna is telling him implicitly: *You are too pitiful to face reality. You are a nothing.* It is decisive, judgmental and passionate in a way that no mere communication of ideas could be.

The fabulous double meanings in the final pages of this play are also stylistically noteworthy, similar to those in *Othello*. There is a wonderful speech by Monna Vanna to Guido on page ninety-nine, allegedly about Prinzivalle, but actually about Guido to his face. It is wonderful drama, precisely because we know her meaning and Guido doesn't. She has the brass and the courage to tell him in this way: "Ah, what fools men are. It is just to deceive them, since they worship falsehood." She is saying this bitterly to Guido about him, but allegedly about Prinzivalle—it is fabulous double meaning. "When one shows them life, they take it for death. When one offers them death, they grasp at it for life. He thought to master me, and I have mastered him!" She is saying this to his face. "Behold him already in his tomb, and I shall put the seals upon it." She is telling him to his face: in three seconds I am going to be in bed with this guy. "I brought him hither, decking him with kisses as a lamb with garlands, and he is in my hands that shall never loose their hold."

She turns to him and she says, "Ah, my fair lover Prinzivalle, we shall have kisses such as none have ever known." It is just chilling because Guido thinks she is being really sarcastic. She goes so far as to go up to Prinzivalle and give him a so-called ardent kiss and says, "Gianello, I love you. Kiss me again. These are the kisses that avail." Of course, Guido is supposed to think she is just torturing Prinzivalle, showing him that this is what you are never going to have. And, of course, she is showing him: this is what you are going to have right away.

You cannot beat that for drama. Properly acted, that is completely enthralling on the stage. It just sends shudders through you as you watch the different characters. If it is well done, it is a fabulous, life-altering experience; just that quality of drama, in and of itself.

Despite Maeterlinck's deeper ignorance of philosophy, when he was liberated from depression, he did have a joyous and highly dramatic sense of life. With that and with his talent, he wrote a truly great play. I hope you liked it as much as Miss Rand and, thanks to her, I did.

I have an anecdote that I thought you may be interested in. This is from a 1951 book by Patrick Mahoney called *The Magic of Maeterlinck* that I got at the Belgian Consulate. He comments: "This play is made to order for a film production and was actually done in Italy about 1913." If anybody has connections to Italian silent movies, I would be fascinated to see it. Nineteen thirteen would be just about right; that is still before World War One. If it has survived, it could be a real treasure.

Mahoney goes on to say:

Monna Vanna was the subject of conversations between myself and a major Hollywood studio during Maeterlinck's exile in America. The speeches are a little long for presentation to the current American taste [He's saying this in 1951, so you can imagine it now.] but I think the technical skill which Maeterlinck shows in unfolding the plot is self-evident. There are the three distinct elements which I believe are the ingredients of a successful film treatment: Monna Vanna's sacrifice [that is Act One], the awakening of her soul, and the triumph of her love over destiny. The film deal fell through because the studio wanted to turn the story into a musical comedy for one of their more famous lightweight actresses to play the lead. Maeterlinck refused, and wisely I think. In this connection I couldn't resist telling him the story about the Irish playwright who was asked to submit something for a certain Hollywood studio. [This is undoubtedly Shaw, because he would be the famous Irish playwright at the time.] The script was found unsuitable, and there was a polite note accompanying the rejection from the studio, which said that the studio hoped that he might make other submissions. The reason for the rejection was that the story of the play did not contain the essential ingredients of a successful film. For his information the studio recounted these elements: religious sentiment, dramatic surprise, sex appeal, brevity, and human interest. The Irish playwright wrote back a charming letter saying that he had pondered their formula and had come to the conclusion that the best film story could be written in one sentence: "My God," cried the duchess, "let go my leg!" for that has the entire mixture.

And now you know why, in 1993, they didn't want to make a movie of *Atlas Shrugged* that was true to the novel.

Q & A

Q: I was a little thrown off by a couple of things in *Monna Vanna* that had me confused at the end. She was weak when she left the tent of Prinzivalle and he had to help her get back to Guido. Then in her final speech, when she was being very strong, I remember she leaned against a pole as though she were going to pass out. I feared the worst: that she was actually dying of her wound because of this underlying idea that I couldn't get out of my mind about her weakness. Do you know what his intention was?

A: I don't know, but I can guess certain things. I think first and foremost, the weakness is the power of emotion: she is overcome by the intensity of the scene. I think Maeterlinck wanted to invoke a certain additional suspense. At the turn of the century and before, women died very frequently, especially on stage. They got a chill, they coughed, and that was it. I think he is basically cheating there a bit: he is using a conventional formula to eke out a little bit of fear on the part of the audience. I do not think that is inherent in the characterization. I think she is the opposite of the kind that would go weak with too much emotion.

To me, the issue of her being wounded when she gets cut just above the breast as she is entering the tent is really extraneous. Maeterlinck uses that in the third act to prove that she really underwent a threat at the hands of Prinzivalle, but it was completely gratuitous. I think that the reason he had her wounded was for a symbolic, not an actual, reason. He was a Symbolist, with a capital S. A symbolist is somebody who sees symbols everywhere. I think from his early training he liked the idea: here are two lovers, separated, yearning, bleeding from the wounds of life—and they are both bleeding in fact from their bodies.

I think part of the reason he gave a wound to each is so you would have the symbol of their souls bleeding. Then they staunch their wounds, put their arms around each other, and transcend the situation. I do not believe that it is a plot indication at all; that her life was ever for a moment in jeopardy. If he threw you off, that is a flaw on his part.

Q: Do you think there are any moral rules that apply to the question: should a man start a courtship of another man's wife? And if so, did Prinzivalle follow any of those moral principles?

A: Well, the only moral rule that I could think of is that one man should not abet a dishonesty on the part of the wife. Inviting her out for the night is certainly suggestive of something, but it was done openly. He didn't send her a secret message. He gave the ultimatum directly to Guido. In fact, he thought the decision was Guido's so it was completely out in the open. It was tantamount to saying to Guido: you decide. If her fidelity is that important, you make the decision; you keep her.

I do not think that Prinzivalle did anything covert or hidden. In fact, he had the honor not to touch her for the reasons I have mentioned, even when he could have. The only point at which he did anything that could be considered as starting a sexual relationship with her is when he was seized by guards, thrown into jail, and taken prisoner. At that point, he is under force; Guido is the enemy; he owes him nothing. I do not think there was a *moment* of immorality.

It is a much broader question. If you know that a wife is unhappy, it is not your obligation to call her husband and say, "I think I'm going

to move in." It is her obligation. On the other hand, you could be legitimately uncomfortable but you basically have to take the attitude: it's
hers to live with; it's not mine—as long as you can see a reason why
she is remaining faithful, even if you think it is wrong.

Now why did Dagny have an affair with Rearden, knowing he
was married? She was not immoral. On the contrary, she said, "If
that's what you want." He did not conceal that he was married. She
knew that he was married to somebody not worthy of him, but he
did not fully know that yet. She was prepared to live with that, and
I think that was completely moral on her part. It was even moral
on his part, because he was absolutely torn. He owed his loyalty
to Lillian, he thought. On the other hand, everything in him rebelled against that because he was a hero. He thought it would be a
dishonor to breach his marriage vows. He couldn't live with them
or without them, so he had a terrible conflict. He was utterly mis-
taken, but it was not a reflection on his morality or on Dagny's. In
this case it was a reflection on Lillian; that she was such a witch and
could conceal it.

So, I don't have a moment's hesitancy in giving Prinzivalle A+
for morality.

Q: Can you comment on the characters' contexts in judging them? I
was discussing this play with someone and telling him how much I
admired Prinzivalle, and he was horror-struck. He said, "Well, he
initiated force."

A: How did he initiate force? You mean the war?

Q: Yeah, I think that's what he was saying.

A: We are not told anything in this play by which we would be able to
judge whether you should be on the side of Pisa or Florence. You
are just told that they were at war. That's all that is required. The
Florentines say the Pisans slaughtered somebody, and the Pisans
say the Florentines constantly go around killing. This is now not a
play but international diplomacy.

It's important that you know where you begin judging the play
and where you don't. You can't trace the backstory back forever.
What you do is plunge in with what is given, and then you judge the
moral issues within that framework.

It is exactly analogous to Sophocles. We are not given the basis to decide which of the two brothers—Eteocles or Polyneices—is the best or whether one is better than the other. All we knew was that they were on opposite sides, and that set up the situation.

The same thing is true here. It wouldn't make any difference if they both honestly believed in self-defense, or one country was wicked and the other wasn't. That is not the story. The story is that they are Renaissance city-states that go to war on a regular basis. It is like Republicans and Democrats. They are gentlemen and scholars; they fight each other; and they always have grievances. The Florentine council is corrupt, but undoubtedly the Pisan elders are corrupt. All of that is completely beside the point. To judge Prinzivalle on that basis is just to make a mockery of moral judgment and to create an entirely different play out of whole cloth, out of sheer dogmatism. Saying "whoever uses force is wrong" is absurd. Guido has been using force all the way through. There is no use telling me which city attacked which first because that is not an issue in the play.

An artist creates his own universe and, within certain limits, you have to accept his universe. In other words, he doesn't tell you who started this war because it is irrelevant. On the other hand, you cannot go beyond certain limits. There are certain historical facts which are so indelible and so monstrous, that if an author said, "I'm ignoring those facts," you would have to say, "I can't go along with it."

For instance, suppose somebody has a story in a concentration camp, and says "I'm discounting the guards; let's forget that there were Nazis in charge here." What should you do? You have to say, "I can't read this, this is depraved"—because the author is omitting a major fact of history which cannot be put aside.

We are centuries away from this. These are all decorous gentlemen here; I mean, they are playing cricket here. The idea of judging Prinzivalle as an exponent of force is just ludicrous. It's tragic to spend time discussing it.

Q: Among the plays we have read, *Monna Vanna* seems peculiar in that the protagonist is not in the main conflict; the main conflict being between Guido and Prinzivalle.

A: But she is . . . oh, I see what you mean. No, the main conflict revolves in relation to her and she is really deeply involved in making the decisions. If you want to reword it to include the protagonist, you would have to say: the main conflict is Monna Vanna versus Guido, and Monna Vanna versus Prinzivalle because she is fighting both men. She fights Guido to get to Prinzivalle. She fights herself and fights Prinzivalle. In fact, she is mad at him because she doesn't know what to think of him.

The reason I identified the conflict as between Guido and Prinzivalle is because that is the naked, unequivocal conflict that goes from beginning to end. Monna Vanna switches, and a defining, essential conflict has to run throughout in a united play. The antagonism between the two men is from open to close over her.

So it is not so paradoxical, because it is a conflict over the protagonist that the protagonist has to decide. They are still the ones at war over it and trying to influence her decision.

Q: This is a true story. I personally know a woman who was in love with a man. She was married and the other man turned out to be the best friend of her husband, to make it more complicated. She came to him and told him that she was in love with this other man, and she wanted his blessing, in essence similar to the play. He, in fact, loved her so much that he did give her his blessing; he said I want you to be happy; this is your choice. As a consequence of that action on his part, she was so torn that she could not leave her husband and stayed with him.

A: So she rejected the lover? Was she able to feel happily fulfilled by that choice through the course of time?

Q: Well, in the course of time the romantic relationship did disintegrate.

A: Oh [disappointed sigh]. You mean she went through all that and then, nothing. Did she go back to the original lover?

Q: No, she never did that.

A: If you are in love, you should be in love for fifty years without wavering, unless you change your mind. The idea that she gave him up, and then found out that he was really the one, so all she had to do was watch TV instead . . . The unhappy ending part would be similar to this, but she would be in terrible agony over the fact that the husband did come up with a magnanimous answer.

Q: That part was true. Can I ask my question now? I hope it is not misunderstood. I am thinking about Ayn Rand's life and the fact that she had such passionate values when she was very young, and she gradually formed an explicit philosophy of Objectivism. I wonder if you can answer this question. Is the main function of an objective philosophy to lead us to find values worth living for or is it to teach us how to objectify, integrate, defend and achieve rational values which we already have discovered and have possessed?

A: Well, what is the main function of nutrition—to discover food or to eat it? What is more important? Obviously it is a false alternative. You have to find out that you need food. You have to find out what kind of food is good for you. You have to find out how to grow, cultivate, or provide it. And then you have to eat it and find out how much to eat in a given setting, what to do if you don't digest it, etc. There is an entire complicated process which nutrition has to study. You can't take one element of it against another element and say, "Which is it really trying to do?"

What philosophy does with values is everything. It tells you what kind of universe you are valuing in—which will govern what kind of values are even possible. How do you know that those values are any good? How do you know anything, which is your epistemological basis? What kind of a being is man and what does he need values for? Then, what are values? And what are the right values? And what are the options within those values? And how can you achieve those values and what kind of actions should you take? How do you know when you're right and how do you know when you're wrong? Will you win; will you gain success or not? What are the implications of your values for art and politics? All of that is philosophy. It is one continuous subject matter and its main function cannot be broken into either/ors.

The main function of philosophy is to establish the correct relation between man and the universe. It is to connect man to reality properly. That involves first connecting his consciousness to reality, and then connecting his course of action to reality. The main function doesn't even mention the term "values." Values are involved in your course of action.

There is a way in which everything you said is part of the main function of philosophy. And there is a way in which nothing you said is part of the main function of philosophy. I don't know now if I have helped you or made it worse. Do you want to ask a follow-up?

Q: Which came first for Ayn Rand, her values or her philosophy?

A: In Ayn Rand's life there was no dichotomy between her values and her philosophy. In discovering her values, she was making the first steps to discovering her philosophy. If she found that she admired the hero of a child's story, that did not mean to her, "Well, this is an interesting story, and someday I will think about philosophy and what it means." In the same moment it was man the hero, free will, the struggle against evil, the need of action to achieve—all of that was what she was responding to and identifying; all of that was at the same time her value and the start of her philosophy.

You put it as though she had an impossible alternative. Either she starts without values, comes up with a philosophy, and says, "Well, now, by deduction, by all this philosophy, I have to hold this set of values; A, B and C." Nobody could do that, because where would all this philosophy come from? On the other hand, you could not say, "I have just a bunch of mindless, unintellectualized values, and one day I am going to abstract away and find what they all have in common." That would be too gigantic a feat. You would end up as an unconscious repository of whatever your subconscious conclusions were.

The actual way that a philosophic mind develops—I mean, on the positive type of philosophy—is having strong values, which you identify contextually as you go. So there is no possible way of saying at any moment, "the values preceded the philosophy" or "the philosophy preceded the values." The values are the means to the philosophy, or the philosophy is the means to the values. It is exactly simultaneous. It is like the mind and the action aspect of exactly the same process of mental growth and interaction with reality. So there seems to me something really rationalistic about your question.

Q: Could you explain why you say that Monna Vanna made her decision to stay with Prinzivalle in Act Two?

A: To be exact, I say that she fell in love with Prinzivalle in Act Two. That is the climax. That is not exactly the same as making her decision. As a climax, it led to her final decision. We have every reason to expect from her falling in love, given her character and the situation, what she is going to decide. She doesn't actually make the decision to stay with him until Guido falls in her eyes at the end. That is when she says: *All right, to hell with you.* Remember, she says she will come back "if . . ."—and she does come back partly to give him the explanation (that's what threw you off; I said that she came back to explain it to him). But she also returns partly—and importantly—to re-evaluate Guido through the eyes of what she has now learned about Prinzivalle and to see if he is the man that she had thought.

In that sense, I do not think she makes her final decision airtight until she announces it to Guido himself.

Q: Did Prinzivalle know that she was going back just to get Guido's acceptance?

A: No, I believe that Prinzivalle's motivation was supposed to be provided by Maeterlinck as: he went back for his own safety. He wouldn't have an interest in saying, "Good bye, Guido, it has been nice and I hope you understand." So I don't think that was his motivation.

Q: You compared *Monna Vanna* to *We the Living*. I saw tremendous similarity to *Ideal*. It is the metaphysical soul, the great person, trying to find a soul mate. Two unusual spirits who are alone find each other through a series of encounters. So I saw the spirit of *Ideal* there. Would you comment?

A: I think that is a very good point, the parallel to *Ideal*. The only difference is that the heroine of *Ideal* is more formed from the very outset: she knows what she wants and she is embittered by the world whereas Monna Vanna is presented as more confused, with less self-knowledge at the beginning. She is not outward looking; life is okay. Then from the outside she is struck with the discovery that there is something much better and she comes alive. So there is that difference.

I think it is very understandable, knowing Ayn Rand and the life she lived. She was very alone in life. Growing up she was like the heroine in *Ideal*. She was highly conscious that she could not find what she wanted from the world or from boys at that age. I think she would sympathize with the heroine of *Ideal* and with

Monna Vanna and with Kira. They are all stories that center around a woman. And that is like the early Ayn Rand.

At a certain point she became man-centered, and then her concern was that she looked at the world through the eyes of Roark or Galt. But in her early days, this would have been a natural. I think you are right to point out a similarity to *Ideal*. There was definitely a community between her and Maeterlinck but she took that as just a starting point and then developed an entire philosophy. He reached that point as the culmination of his optimism and then sank back. So he never went anywhere with it.

Q: I just want to make three short points and then a comment. The first one is an aspect of the play that you didn't mention at all, and that is the aspect that the Florentines were planning Prinzivalle's demise. In other words, he was on the threat of death.

A: Let me just take that as we go. I tried to imply that, by saying that he needed to save his life; to get away from them. I didn't think that was important enough: that's just the mechanics of the play. I don't try to cover every aspect of a play. If I covered every aspect of a play, you know what I would do? I would do it like this. "Good morning, ladies and gentlemen. Now Act One, Scene One, begins in a hall in a palace of Guido Colonna. We see Guido and his lieutenants, Borso and Torello, near an open window from which a view is gained of the country about Pisa. Now I happen to have a slide here, which is just . . ." That is not the way I cover plays. I venture to say that if that is the way you cover plays, you don't get the essentials. Next?

Q: I couldn't agree more, and the point I'm looking for is motivation for his actions. I don't mind being the butt of humor; let 'er rip.

A: I'm glad you don't. I don't think that his motivation at that point is key to what happens in the play. I do think that Maeterlinck tried to provide him with the need for safety as a plausible motivation, but I don't think that's a strong point in the play, so having mentioned it I'll let it go. It's not a thematic point to the play.

Q: Point two was that he did offer Monna Vanna an impossible choice. You did make several points to that effect in the analysis. The main one to me was that if the city was sacked, in all probability she would lose her life. In that sense, there really wasn't a lot of choice.

A: No, there wasn't a whole lot of choice. And yet she still had the choice, if you want to put it that way, of staying and being raped or going and being raped.

Q: The third point is coming out of the previous question where the gentleman was asking about the morality of approaching another man's wife if you happened to be in love with her. You mentioned that if she was unhappy, the situation changes but he certainly had no knowledge of whether she was unhappy. I just feel that, with those three points, it makes it a little implausible to give this man an A+ for morality.

A: I don't want to repeat what I have said about all of those points again. I don't feel I have anything really substantial to add to what I have previously said. So we will simply acknowledge that you don't like some of his actions. But I don't believe that you can use Objectivism as a standard to criticize him. Let's just have our impasse stop at that point.

Q: When Prinzivalle makes this offer to Monna Vanna, doesn't he then treat her, an honorable woman, as a prostitute?

A: Does he treat her as a prostitute? No, I don't think so. I gather there is a fair sentiment against Prinzivalle. Many of you are dubious of or antagonistic to Prinzivalle for having made this offer. I don't think you have a leg to stand on. I will try one last time. Is she a prostitute? That is an absurd equivocation on language. A prostitute is a woman who has no values and sells her body for money. This is a woman who has very intense values and is torn by the question of whether she should sleep with him in order to save the lives of thirty thousand people, including her own. That is a pretty stretched definition of prostitution. I wouldn't even dignify it by debating it.

Q: I saw Guido as a concretization of second-hander values, and the characters of Prinzivalle, Monna Vanna, and Marco as characters of independent values. Wouldn't this explain some of the character motivation in the plot development?

A: I agree with that entirely. It is a different way of putting it, but you are right. Guido is a second-hander—that's what I tried to suggest by calling him a conventional man. But by calling him a second-hander, you are ascribing to Maeterlinck a degree of psychological profundity that he doesn't have. "Second-hander versus first-hander" was a concept introduced by Miss Rand about the way your consciousness works: whether you look first to other people as your psycho-epistemological frame of reference, or first to reality and to facts. It is certainly true that Guido was a second-hander and the others are first-handers. Marco is a little debatable: in some of his moods he is a first-hander; in some he is a real compromiser; and in others he is nothing, just a Greek chorus. So he is not a clearly developed character.

The reason I didn't use that language is that I was trying to present Maeterlinck's characters, and he didn't rise to the point of stressing or making those analyses. If you wanted to go all the way with it, you could say that Guido, by implication, is not pro-life and the others are. It is just not presented in those terms. You couldn't say Guido was the equivalent of Jim Taggart; he is just not presented in those terms or on that level. I was trying to keep the characterization within terms that the playwright would recognize, which is the only reason I did not use that terminology. I do agree with you, as an Objectivist looking at this play, that in fact that is what they represent. Here again I am trying to keep separate what an Objectivist would say and what is in the play for anybody to see, whether he is an Objectivist or not.

Q: I agree with you totally that Monna Vanna is not a prostitute. My question last time was: does not Prinzivalle treat her as one?

A: No, he doesn't treat her as a prostitute any more than she is one. He knows that he is in love with her and that his motive is not to get a cheap titillation. He knows that she is not the kind of person who would engage in love for money. He knows that he has no plans to sleep with her even if she comes. You cannot drop all of that context. I have already been accused of being improperly antagonistic toward questioners so I would like to humbly suggest that you go back to the play and try to read it without the rule that a marriage is necessarily sacrosanct, and also without the rule that anytime a character does something to achieve a value, it is tantamount to selling your body for money. If you drop those two, you might find that Prinzivalle is a better guy than he looks right now.

Q: We seem to have given *Monna Vanna* a philosophical mercy grade by including it in a list of great plays, yet the reference to the Ayn Rand quote about it being one of the greatest plays leads me to wonder what different standard she was applying.

A: I would include it as a great play but I do that with a certain hesitancy. It depends in what context you are thinking. There are many plays that I would classify as great plays but that I would not necessarily print in a catalog and deliver to an audience. When you say "this is a great play" or even write it in a letter to someone, your context could be wide-ranging: you could be thinking of a brilliant plot-theme; you could be thinking of character development and elevated dialogue; double meanings; twists; benevolence; sense of life. There are a hundred different reasons why you would say: "judged by these standards, this is one of the top plays in world literature, in world history."

I had a very definite context in mind. I had the title "Seven Great Plays as Literature and as Philosophy" and that is not an empty title. What I am trying to indicate are plays that qualify for greatness in both their literary *and* philosophic dimensions. This is a higher rank than just a play which qualifies on one scale. And, because I'm using that and I'm making a formal address which is going to last beyond my lifetime, I have to be able to justify. I cannot just say it's a great play and toss it into a list of great plays. I have to know what exact criterion I am using. There are thousands of plays that in one way or another you could legitimately say are great.

I do not have any reason to believe that Miss Rand had the same context. She was not preparing a course and making a formal selection from the ages. She might very well have disagreed with certain points I make because they do not come *ex cathedra*.

CHAPTER EIGHT

ESTHETIC EVALUATION

This is judgment day; specifically objective esthetic judgment. That means, not your opinion versus my opinion or our opinion versus their opinion, but the correct opinion as objectively provable. The first eleven questions take us into the preliminary material that we have to judge; those components which we have to decide in order to ultimately reach the last four which are the overall final judgments. So on the analogy of the Tonys, we are first giving all the technical and supporting cast type of awards, and then we will get into Best Drama, Best Artistic Development, etc.

1. Who is the strongest heroine in all these plays? Who is the most admirable hero? Who is the worst villain?

2. Which character has the strongest motivation, i.e., the most intense passion and the most inflexible will?

3. Which character would you most like to sleep with?

4. Which character do you most *like*?

5. Which play has the most ingenious plot-theme?

6. Which play has the strongest conflict?

7. Which conflict has the most gripping climax? Which has the most dramatic ending?

8. Which *story* do you most like?

9. Which play presents the most complex or intriguing theme?

10. With which play do you most strongly agree? With which do you most strongly disagree?

11. Which play most admirably *integrates* theme and plot?

12. Speaking purely esthetically, which is objectively the best play?

13. Speaking purely philosophically, which is objectively the best play?

14. Taking both art and philosophy into account, which is objectively the best play?

15. Which of the dramas is your *personal* favorite?

The purpose of this analysis is really a small-scale example of evaluation in real life. The point I want to make is that evaluation entails comparison. If you ask a simple question about a man such as "is he hardworking?" (which, other things being equal, is a virtue), you have to know what is meant by hardworking; i.e., hardworking in relation to what standard? Does he work harder than Roark? Does he work about like Eddie Willers? Does he work like I did last year, only two days a week? Esthetic evaluation, similarly, requires for clarity an implicit comparison among different artworks within the same genre.

For example, if you want to judge "does this play have a good climax?" your ability to answer depends on your concretizing: what is a mediocre climax? what is a poor climax? what is a truly great climax? In other words, you have to have implicitly in your mind a continuum, of better or worse on which you can then locate a given climax.

So this is not an artificial, academic exercise in which we are comparing great plays. Rather, this should give you some guidance for esthetic evaluation throughout life.

Another introductory note: we are judging these plays within the context of the exact title of this course. I purposely chose every word that was in the title. We are evaluating these plays as philosophy and as literature. Putting it negatively, we are not evaluating them as dramatic spectacles; in other words, not as theater, not as plays enacted on the stage or screen.

The theatrical form of art uses a different medium. The medium of theater is actually human bodies moving on stage and speaking. It is not the printed play script, which is simply concepts or language; in other words, literature. A theatrical performance is an event which involves a whole new category of issues and judgment that I don't purport to know a great deal about. But you would have to take into account numerous factors that are not purely literary. For instance, the visual spectacle of the stage, the costuming, the time compression, pace, movement, color, physical transitions, smoothness. There are all kinds of things that go into making a great dramatic spectacle that are just not part of the discussion, if what we are talking about is: plays as literature that you read—in other words, essentially as novels but with only dialogue and no exposition or comment by the author.

This is not irrelevant to judging great plays, because you would have to judge the play as literature in order to know how good the performance actually could be when it is enacted. This is really just a stage in a more complicated undertaking and, thankfully, this is enough for us now.

I have created a fallacy, which I call the Modernocentric Predicament. This fallacy occurred to me when my preliminary seminar on this topic was given a list of questions and, lo and behold, every play that was the best—whether philosophically, esthetically, as a whole, or personally—was always *Saint Joan, An Enemy of the People* or, more commonly, *Monna Vanna. Always.* And I thought this was really suspicious. There are four old plays and three modern plays. And isn't it a funny coincidence that everyone loved the three modern plays?

Frankly, this disappointed me because my goal in teaching this course is to broaden your receptivity. I think it is a terrible and needless constriction to confine yourself to the last hundred or so years of a declining civilization which has lasted for two and a half thousand years, with its greatest genius before our time. So if your estimates come out predominantly endorsing plays from Ibsen on, then I feel safe in saying you have this problem. You are trapped in the modern perspective; the ease of getting into a modern play. Probably the two factors that trap you are your age and your education. Age is a factor because, as you get old enough, you finally reach a state of thorough disappointment with most contemporary stuff, and you are willing to put in the time and effort necessary to open up the great classics of the past. Education comes in because one of the purposes of education should be to make great literature from the past accessible. Today the opposite is true: schools either keep you in ignorance of great literature or else it is presented in such a way that you run for your life from it forever.

I want to repeat one propagandistic point that I mentioned earlier. If your modernocentric attitude were sustained, it would mean that three thousand years from now people would be justified in saying, "Oh, I don't want to read Ayn Rand; all that archaic stuff about telephones—what's a telephone?—and having to read footnotes at the bottom of the page and talk about railroads and constantly reading explanatory texts in the back. Why can't I just plunge into something good and racy from my own time?" You would, by this method, actually never get to read Ayn Rand: the language would be archaic. And yet what a tremendous value you would have lost. I think that this parallel is true right now. If you cannot get what Greek literature or Renaissance literature has to offer, you are missing an immortal value.

Be aware of your answers. Any given answer is fine but if you are completely skewed on the side of the last three plays in this course, you are already committing this fallacy.

Take out your crow summaries of the seven plays, so you have them right beside you. *Antigone*, *Othello*, *Le Cid*, *Don Carlos*, *An Enemy of the People*, *Saint Joan* and *Monna Vanna*. With each you have the characters, the plot-theme, the climax, the theme and the overall philosophy. Generally speaking, I am going to give you my thoughts on these first and then I am happy, within the limits of time, to take your comments. It would be more fun to elicit all kinds of different views from you *first*, but it would be unlikely that we would even get a start on the evaluation. So let's plunge in with Number One.

1. Who is the strongest heroine in all these plays?

The strongest heroine, in my judgment, is Antigone. (I'm not going to keep adding "in my judgment" all the time because that is implied.) I don't think there is a second that is equally strong. And I gave my reasons for that in discussing her. She is the one most like Ayn Rand, and to me that is a self-evident proof of strength.

For second, I have Joan and Chimène tied, for different reasons. Joan has a lot of good qualities: a stressed idealism, youthful self-confidence. She is actually more of an initiator than Antigone. Antigone waits for the order and then reacts to it. Joan comes out of the blue with her own plan. She has a wider scale of achievement which, as you'll see, counts for a great deal in these things. She takes on an entire world, leads armies, and so on. As I've reiterated in discussing her, the problem with Joan is: can you believe in her fully? There is this Shavian ambiguity of Joan as a human being with all the virtues, and Joan as a super-personal manifestation of a cosmic power that manifests itself in miracles and the mystical. That edge takes her out of the category of being the strongest to me. It's an active abstraction; you have to look away and just imagine what she would be if she were more fully of this world.

Similarly, but for completely different reasons, I would put Chimène as less strong than Antigone. It's not that there is any ambiguity in her character, but we do not have a really full presentation of Chimène. Largely her character is presented as love-oriented. There is a significant element of Chimène facing reality—facing the king, facing the court, arguing down the Infanta—but dominantly it is the love of Rodrigo that is the focus. What we want in a strong character is, above all, a character facing reality and, therefore, implying an enormous potency of being able to do whatever he or she sets out to do. By somewhat delimiting the scope and development of Chimène—a requirement of the play—Corneille doesn't make her the full heroine that Antigone is, who takes on all comers and who you see fully flourishing in action. So Chimène has tremendous power but I put her second, for a different reason than Joan.

Monna Vanna I put third here, as last of the good females, specifically because she is not metaphysically developed at all in action except by implication. She is entirely love-oriented. The whole question in her mind is: this man or that man? However, there is no doubt that a great strength is implied: she is willing to take on the city. But the problem with Monna Vanna in this regard is the full-blown version of what we have partially with Chimène. For a full depiction of strength, she is far too much of a romance-oriented rather than a reality-oriented character which includes romance as one part of it, the way Antigone does.

To me there is no question that objectively the strongest heroine in all these plays is Antigone.

Who is the most admirable hero?

Here I have no doubt in saying that it is Le Cid, Rodrigo. This man has strength, independence and achievement on a larger-than-life scale. He is a truly glamorous, romanticized figure. He's a colorful hero, he savors every moment of his life. I think—this is kind of a good test—it would be a pleasure to be friends with him.

To compare him to his closest rival, I think Tomas Stockmann would be next in order as the most admirable hero. Rodrigo is a more unique character than Tomas Stockmann. He is morally innocent, like Stockmann, but he is not so naïve as Tomas Stockmann. Also, there is no element of him being a martyr to a world that doesn't understand him. He is a conqueror, not only in intention but in fact, despite the fact that he perhaps offers his life one time too many to Chimène.

Tomas Stockmann has all the same virtues and the same strength, in essence, as Le Cid. But he is somewhat reduced in stature by the comedic overtones of the play.

Both Corneille and Ibsen project an enjoyment of life. But the *joie de vivre* of Corneille is not undercut or reduced in any way by silly touches or clowning around. It is more of a sheer, exalted exuberance. That is not matched by Ibsen in his play and for that reason the hero I would most look up to would be Le Cid.

Who is the worst villain?

I don't think there is even a debate that, without a doubt, by forty lengths, Iago is the most villainous. We have already discussed why: this is the hater of everything that is good, the destroyer of everything that is good. I would not put even Schiller's Grand Inquisitor, who is decidedly wicked, in the same league. The Grand Inquisitor is not a nihilist: he has definite views. He has a whole coherent philosophy. And in some sense, on some level, he believes it and he lives by it. And that is miles above Iago, whose attitude would be modern nihilism. He doesn't want ideas; he thinks ideas are just a ruse to trap the unwary, just a game. So the Grand Inquisitor has a certain stature; Iago is at the very bottom of the pit.

For these reasons I arrive at Antigone, Le Cid and Iago. I think that those are the three most memorable characters in the plays. When time goes by, you forget the lesser characters, the mixed characters, the undeveloped characters, the ordinary ones. These three portraits have a force for good or evil that will be like someone you will know for the rest of your life. And that is a very important issue in a play.

2. Which character has the strongest motivation, i.e., the most intense passion and the most inflexible will?

Which character displays the most intense passion and the most inflexible will? Here we are talking about a specific aspect, not just who is the strongest or the most admirable, but who is the most intense and inflexible in pursuing his goal? For practical purposes, since you can't really measure these, I would list three as pretty much tied on this count: Antigone, Le Cid and Dr. Stockmann. Stockmann may be downsized by the comedic element, but he is certainly inflexible and he certainly has an intense passion. So these three, I think, are unequivocal.

Chimène is, in a sense, even stronger than Le Cid so you can include her if you want. The reason I don't is that she is not fully developed in the play so we don't get to see as much of her motivation. Le Cid conquers Arabs, he conquers the world; this is a truly metaphysical character. Chimène conquers him which, in its own way, is definitely a feat but she is not as integral to world-scale actions. We don't have as full a display of her passion to judge it.

Where do I put Joan here? She is absolutely in the running. Count her number one—if you can abstract away from the ambiguities; if it is really her passion and her will, and not just the cosmic will of German philosophy.

What about Monna Vanna? She certainly implies full-scale heroism and intensity of passion but, again, we do not see it. We see only her romantic intensity; not world-scale passion or will.

I want to make a theoretical point here that I think is of some importance. What counts in evaluating heroism broadly, and in evaluating intensity, passion and will more specifically? It's not only the passion and force of the inner dedication—but the objective, external scale of the conflict or the achievement. After all, what is the purpose of holding value judgments and inflexibly clinging to them? It is to achieve something in action, to do something. Aristotle said—and Ayn Rand agreed—that nothing is more important than what the characters do. Granted, in a great play they all do something (except Don Carlos who does virtually nothing and is a wimp for that reason). But the way that you judge—in conjunction with the rest of the context—is the scale of what they do.

Let me give you just a common sense analogy here. Without meaning to be unduly self-effacing, let's say you regard me as heroic for learning Objectivism, and Ayn Rand as heroic for creating Objectivism. I put to you two cases as an objective test: who comes out as the strongest? The student who struggles sincerely for decades to master a philosophy and finally does so? Or the master who created the philosophy, perhaps much faster and with less sustained agony of inner chaos? You measure that by saying: look, when the chips are down, she thought of it. She did it. Not to take away from what a student has done but the scale, the sheer breathtaking dimensions of the action, are most relevant to strength or passion.

I want to bring in here the broader theory. Art is perceptual. Therefore, a world-scale achievement, the huge scope of the characters' actions brings the metaphysical perspective that we seek from art directly to the perceptual level. You see the hero fighting the world and, if it's a benevolent play, beating the world as opposed to merely beating a rival.

This is the primary reason why I require a play to be philosophical in order to be great—because a philosophical play most obviously fulfills this need of art. It concretizes the metaphysical, and thereby condenses an entire view of life to your percepts. It reveals the full potentiality of human passion, the full scope of its operation facing the entire world of society. And this is why a philosophical quality gives a play and a character, in my opinion, greater power to either uplift you profoundly or depress you utterly. If a play and a character are on a world scale, they thereby bring to the perceptual level the profoundest character values.

Of course, I hasten to say that all art is implicitly metaphysical. I don't deny that. But a philosophical play is special in this regard because it conveys the added power of the explicit over the implicit.

Let me stress this. *I do not mean* that a play has to be like *Atlas Shrugged* and have a lengthy speech synopsizing its view of metaphysics, epistemology, ethics and so on. Let's say that there is a continuum. At one extreme is *Atlas Shrugged* or *The Fountainhead*, which both have avowed philosophic revolutions and summarize their philosophies as part of the work. On the other extreme would be what I call one-note or one-theme plays. For example, *Monna Vanna* with the theme "you should be selfish" or *The Miracle Worker* with "the importance of the senses." On the way to that extreme would be the standard detective stories and comedies which also have an implicit metaphysics, but no particular abstract theme except "let the good triumph."

Now in the middle (I hate to use that word, but I don't know any other way to put it) between philosophic texts on the one hand and one-note plays on the other, are most of the plays in our course. That is, Shakespeare, Corneille, etc. Those are not filled with philosophic speeches which express their viewpoint, the way *Atlas* does. But they have much more than simple one-note themes. They actually present to you—in the course of the action, the dialogue, etc.—a total philosophy in its bare-bones essence.

And what I'm talking about when I say that I attach so much importance to a philosophical play, is in the sense that six of our seven plays were philosophical plays, even though none of them were philosophical the way *Atlas Shrugged* is. They are all much more philosophical than, for instance, *Who Killed Roger Ackroyd?* or *The Miracle Worker*.

All right, this is by way of still explaining why I give the strongest motivation to a world-scale conflict or a world-scale action. In regard to passionate motivation there are three characters that I would not allow anywhere near the top rung. So if you chose them, I think you're wrong. Number one, Iago. Iago has an urge to destroy, and when he sees that his course is doomed, he just quits. He simply turns off and says, to hell with it, I'll never speak again. This is not a man of passion. Nihilism is not a passion. And I think if you knew Iago, you'd find him a very emotionless, cold fish. The great Iagos on stage do not twirl their mustaches and slaver saliva. They are repressed, quiet. The whole idea is that Othello has to take him as honest Iago, he has to be mild. And they are that way in real life. You should be only so lucky that depraved people come across the way they really are. They may be seething with revenge down in their soul, but what you see and what they primarily feel is boredom. And they get a little flicker of glee when they stick the knife in someone. So if we're talking in serious terms about an intense passion and an inflexible will, Iago is simply out of the picture.

The same is true for Othello. Any character whose action contradicts his passion loses, if the contest is "who is the most passionate?" We judge passion in large part by action. You can say, "I love her till the cows come home," but if you can nevertheless smother her when she's sleeping, that is a really grave indictment of the passion of your passion. So anybody who contradicts his passion in action, is not of the stature that you thought.

And this happens to be a very true and important point in life. You never have to have the problem of: "this person loved the good or loved Objectivism so passionately. I can't figure out why he went and joined the New Socialists." And the answer is that you were wrong in thinking that he was that passionate to begin with. Words are cheap. It is very easy to put on an act of excitement. But it is the course of your action, especially across decades, that is the deciding factor. This was what made Aristotle, who went a little too far with this point, decide that you can't say that a man is happy until he dies, because you never know what's going to happen in the next week. I wouldn't go that far, but certainly a couple of decades of fidelity is very helpful.

For the same reason, Posa absolutely is out as far as having the most intense passion. However inflexibly committed he seems, he permits his neurotic self-image as a big-shot leader to eclipse his passion for freedom and tempt him to becoming a dictator in regard to

Don Carlos. And that is so grave a lapse, even if it's a momentary one, that he is just out of the running as far as a passionate character is concerned.

3. Which character would you most like to sleep with?

We have pretty much exhausted the character mine here. Questions Three and Four are really results of your answers to Questions One and Two. I have to answer, as a man, the one I would most like to sleep with is Antigone. No doubt in the world. She is the strongest. She has the strongest motivation. Second to her, I would put Chimène. Now Monna Vanna I would not be interested in. She is not a three-dimensional character to me. She is too definitely a romantic heroine. So I feel I know her in relation to the man she loves, but I don't know her. I don't know her soul in relation to the world. It's suggested, but it's not explicit enough. Joan is just too drab for me. I certainly understand her reason for not dressing like a woman but I just do not go for an androgynous character.

The answer to this question for a woman was fairly unanimous in the seminar. The number one choice was Prinzivalle. Well, let me see if you are the same as the people in the seminar. How many of the women in this class—just by a show of hands—chose as their number one choice Prinzivalle? Yeah, well, that's pretty decisive. Did anybody choose Dr. Stockmann? [Laughter.] He's not a romantic hero, I grant you. Did anybody choose Haimon? Now this is obviously a completely free question; you don't get any points off for this.

Did anybody choose Dunois from Shaw? Not one taker for this gallant military commander? So who else did you choose if you are a woman? Oh, I forgot about Le Cid completely. How many of you chose Le Cid? Well, let me ask you another question: why did you choose Prinzivalle over Le Cid? What did you say? "He's sexier." Why?

Prinzivalle is sexier in the sense that the action of the play revolves around his desire to sleep with this woman. He wants her to come naked under her cloak, etc., etc. Whereas Le Cid is really oriented around the Arabs and riding off on his horse, etc. But that's just a glimpse of two portraits. We could just as well have taken Prinzivalle, who is a professional soldier and caught him in the middle of a war and so on or followed Le Cid, if the rules of Classicism had allowed it, into the boudoir and heard him making love. Would that have changed your mind? How many of you are more at home with Prinzivalle because you're afraid that Le Cid would talk poetry to you? That is an acceptable point. If you think that Chimène comes across as stronger than Le Cid, you want the strongest possible. However, I think that—without wanting to debate this point—you would have your work cut out to say that Haimon is stronger than Le Cid as an objective proposition. Because one of the usual comments on this play is that Haimon is not strong enough for Antigone and that she would devour him in real life. I don't think we have to beat this one into the ground.

4. Which character do you most *like*?

Here it is Antigone or Le Cid; I could not choose between them. I thought they were the two most memorable of the positive characters. It would be literally impossible for me to tell. A close second in terms of a character I like is Dr. Stockmann, for his many good qualities and the fact that he has such good ideas. But I do definitely put him as a second, because he is not a character of the standing and the stature of the other two.

This is really a consequence or summation of your previous judgments. But it is very important to your final evaluation of a play: what about the characterization? Does it create the kind of character that sears itself on your consciousness, for good or evil? If it does, that's a monumental esthetic (*not* philosophic) achievement. Within a literary form that has characters, if you can create a character with the resonance and the power to fill your consciousness as unique and strong, or as unique and monstrous, and still be credible—that, in itself, is a tremendous achievement. Nothing can be a great play completely if it doesn't approach this.

I think in all of our plays we have some characters that conceivably qualify. But the ones I would pick out as the obvious great characterizations are Antigone and Le Cid on the positive and Iago on the negative.

Q & A Characterization

Q: As to the characters with whom I would like to sleep . . . As to the best couple, I picked Vanna and Prinzivalle. And the reason I picked them is because in my psyche I do see the sexual attractiveness of the dominant/submissive mode, and I see it very strongly between them.

A: Well, that's a good point, it's a good point. The dominant/submissive mode is essential to sexuality. Le Cid is a little too submissive to Chimène. And there are not many other couples that have that quality in our plays. The other thing is that that play is about sleeping together. The whole thing in that play orients you to an erotic message, and the very last line is: *Okay, I'm off to the cell. Lie down and get ready.* That, in effect eroticizes the whole play.

5. Which play has the most ingenious plot-theme?

Here I could not choose between two plays and, as much as I tried to avoid the modernocentric predicament in order to give you an object lesson, I had to say that the two best plot-themes were *Le Cid* and *Monna Vanna*.

Of those two, I would say *Monna Vanna* is a little lesser, because it is more conventional. It's the kind of thing you could see Hollywood ripping off. But I do say Maeterlinck presented it so well that the situation itself is tremendously suspenseful. I give the edge to *Le Cid*. What these two plays have in common—I want to stress this—is an artificial situation. A good plot-theme is not a natural, everyday-type occurrence. *Artificial* is a compliment in esthetic judgment, not an insult. Remember in *We the Living* when talking about scenery, Lydia looks at the stage and says, "Oh, how beautiful, it's almost real" and Kira looks at it and says, "Oh, how beautiful, it's almost artificial." Ayn Rand was trying to make the point that art has to be artificial.

What does "artificial" mean in this context? Every aspect is deliberately chosen to achieve the purpose of the artist. They are not just taken from life but are stylized and slanted and selected so the force of a human mind and human purpose is controlling it. It is made by art—artificial—as opposed to just happening.

These two plays have artificial situations. I repeat that I don't mean unbelievable. These situations are deliberately constructed for passionate, unusual conflicts. The other plays, for whatever their genius, as sheer plot-themes are basically stories of a man or woman who asserts himself against a hostile world. But here we have worked-out situations of conflict which are complex. They are entirely credible but not common—ingenious, that is the word. They are not common in the sense that "I rebel against people" is common.

Le Cid is the best because it is pure ingenuity and sets up a conflict far beyond the conventional. In *Monna Vanna*, a man wants to sleep with another man's wife. It's a good conflict but it's not yet a great conflict. For him to have to kill her father in order to deserve sleeping with her would be even better.

Here you can compare *Atlas Shrugged*, where the plot is very much like *Le Cid*, not in concretes but on the level we are talking about. If Dagny were merely torn between Rearden and Galt, that would be a conflict of a woman having to choose between two men. But if she's torn between her railroad and Galt, it is a much more unique and unconventional conflict, especially if her railroad is what her lover is destroying. On top of that, the railroad is her supreme value which she needs in order to feel that she is worthy of his love. He is ruining the very thing that she needs and what she wants in life, and yet she wants to sleep with him. So Dagny is put through hell. *Le Cid* is like a feudal version of that same plot-theme. I hope Ayn Rand doesn't rise from the grave and strike me dead.

I do think *Le Cid* has by far the best and most ingenious plot-theme of all seven plays. And that is a really major consideration. Ayn Rand was asked in an interview once to name the three most important things about a literary work. Do you know what her answer was? "Plot, plot and plot." And, of course, plot-theme is your key to plot.

In relation to *Le Cid*, *An Enemy of the People* is not ingenious. I am not putting it down in any way. The plot-theme is: a man gets mad at society and takes a stand against it. *Antigone* is not an ingenious plot. I'm not blaming Sophocles: the Greeks had just barely got the idea of telling a story, let alone a complicated, artificial plot where every step puts you in conflict with somebody else. *Othello* is certainly not a complex plot. Besides, Shakespeare disdained plot. He took whatever tales he could find and then embellished them with poetry and character. The plot-theme of *Othello* is simply: a man gets jealous.

Don Carlos is just too long and over-complicated to qualify. A great plot must be ingenious but also simple, essentialized, so that even a child can grasp it—as long as a child knows what love is. If a child doesn't know what love or lovemaking is, they don't have access to the world's great literature. They don't have to know the mechanics of intercourse but they have to know that there is such a thing as love that is really, really important to people. If you are explaining it to your child, you can say, "It's like bubble gum"—or anything that they can translate into their own terms.

What about Shaw? Shaw is very ingenious in his ability to interweave historical ideologies, like nationalism and Protestantism, into the story. But the story as such is just pure history. There is no ingenuity in the plot situation. Joan hates what is going on and she is martyred. So *per se*, it's a straightforward story.

6. Which play has the strongest conflict?

I have stressed over and over again that a play stands or falls with the depth of its conflict. And, of course, that will reflect both the type of plot-situation, the type of conflict that is possible, and the type of characters. Here there are two different conflicts that qualify as best, and it is not surprising that both derive from the best plot-themes. Rodrigo versus Chimène or Guido versus Prinzivalle. The reason I choose these two is that neither party in these two cases bends, breaks or gives up right to the bitter end. Nothing stops them, even when the play is over. They are still at war.

But of these two, I take Le Cid versus Chimène as the best conflict in the seven plays on two grounds. One: it is the only conflict between purely good characters, as against one character being good and the other being evil or weak or very ordinary, as Guido is. Here the principle is the impotence of evil: the strongest clash is always between the most heroic characters. We have already discussed how in both *Atlas Shrugged* and *The Fountainhead*, Miss Rand centers her conflicts on the positive characters.

The other reason I take Le Cid versus Chimène as the strongest conflict is that the strongest external conflict; in other words, the strongest conflict with the outside world is the one which can withstand and endure in the face of the characters' inner conflicts. If a man has an inner crisis tearing him apart and he still remains inflexible in action, then that shows how completely passionate his outer commitment is. That is what makes the conflict between Rodrigo and Chimène so intense. They are completely torn by conflict. They love each other and part of the time just throw aside the feudal requirements and go to bed with each other. And yet they are utterly adamant about their course. This makes the passion of their conflict truly awesome.

Guido and Prinzivalle have much less inner conflict. Basically speaking, Prinzivalle is unconflicted. And Guido has some doubt, but not much. Their dedication is less dramatized; they have less of an inner obstacle or hurdle, and therefore their interaction is less awe-inspiring.

There are other possibilities which, I think, are not as good as conflicts although certainly all these, I reiterate, are great plays. Therefore they must have a great conflict somewhere. It is a question of degrees on a scale.

Dr. Stockmann versus the mob. The only problem with that conflict is that the mob is too collective to be an entity. Conflict is always strongest between separate individuals that you get to know, rather than one individual against a mob which doesn't have as clear and firm an identity in your mind.

Antigone versus Creon. This is an excellent conflict, but the problem is that he is too weak. Not too weak for a great play, but too weak for an ideally powerful conflict. He capitulates suddenly and then grovels.

Iago versus Othello. Again, Othello is too weak; he is taken over too easily. If we could allow such a conflict as Iago versus the good, that would be a great conflict. But in that formulation, the good would then be a floating abstraction and there is no character in the play that represents the good.

As far as *Don Carlos*, I don't believe that any of the positive characters in the play are heroic enough to qualify here. Don Carlos himself is a whim-worshipper and Posa, as I already indicated, has a major weakness that just takes him out of the league.

7. Which conflict has the most gripping climax? Which has the most dramatic ending?

These are two different questions. Climax pertains to when the strands come together and you finally reach the culminating event which decides who is going to win or lose. The ending is the resolution; that is where you see the winning or the losing worked out in detail. It can have a whole life and tremendous suspense of its own. So this is not the same question.

I reached the best climax by elimination here because that was the only way I could do it. It is definitely not *Saint Joan* because the climax is much too theoretical and a play is action. The climax is Scene Four, the agreement between the clergy and the nobility which is a purely intellectual event and pertains to minor characters. Of course, Shaw never attempted to write a well-made play, but unfortunately he succeeded and, therefore, I have to judge him accordingly.

I don't think the climax in *Antigone* qualifies because it's just barely a climax. The climax is her resolve not to give in and that is just a final reaffirmation or statement. It is not a new event, a specific event, a visually gripping event.

The climax of *Le Cid* is the king elevating Rodrigo to the title of Le Cid. That is more ceremonial than an action or a visual occurrence. As it comes across in reading, it is more talk than action. I leave open the idea that a director could stage this coronation with such excitement and solemnity and music, everyone bowing into the dust, radiance, etc., that it is an event. You say, "Oh, my God, I can see him elevated to king of the universe." But in reading, it goes right by. "You're Le Cid, great, on to the next." As climax, it doesn't come across in reading.

Monna Vanna? Too predictable. If a climax is one hundred percent predictable, it is disqualified as a gripping climax. We know from the moment that the play starts that if she doesn't fall in love with Prinzivalle in Act Two, there is no play.

So the three best climaxes by elimination are: *Don Carlos*; the death of Posa is a gripping and unexpected event, but perfectly logical within the structure of the play. Next *An Enemy of the People* has an excellent climax, the confrontation with the mob. But in my judgment the most gripping climax is *Othello*'s. Here I think you see the true genius of Shakespeare, his power of visualization. I remind you that, according to Objectivism, art reduces concepts to the perceptual level. It is a visual re-creation of a sense of life.

The climax is not just that Iago wins over Othello in the temptation scene because that would be merely an internal character change. The brilliance—the really magnificent brilliance—of this climax is the two characters kneeling side by side in a religious ceremony, dedicating themselves solemnly to the death of Desdemona. This is an eloquent action, externalized, visualized—yet much more subtle than obvious events such as a death or a mob scene. It is a climax that could work only in the hands of a master artist, but in his hands it is more gripping than the more conventional action climaxes.

As to the most dramatic ending, I don't think there is a choice in the world. Hands down to *Don Carlos*. Nothing tops those last two scenes; the Grand Inquisitor, followed immediately by the king saying to Don Carlos, "It is your last [deceit]!" And finally to the Grand Inquisitor, "Now I have done my part. See you do yours!" Curtain. Nothing in world literature that I know tops that as the ending of a play. That is why I included the play. If drama means a clash that is both unpredictable, inevitable, devastating, profound; and we throw in that it is philosophically all-encompassing and takes place with the speed of a telegram or a single sword-stroke, then I can't conceive what could surpass the ending of *Don Carlos*.

Antigone has a very powerful ending. For me, it is the most tragic ending because I care more about her. It has a soul-searing ending and the only one at which I regularly cry. But it is not dramatic in an unpredictable and yet devastating way. You know from the outset what is going to happen, and it is simplified.

The epilogue of *Saint Joan* has too much farce and undercuts real, sustained drama. It is a powerful situation, but it is Shaw clowning around and I think it does hurt the power of his ending.

Monna Vanna has a very dramatic ending, but not on the world scale of Schiller's play. It is the same issue as the most admirable character or the intensity of motivation: scale or scope is a crucial factor.

Le Cid, which I really like as a play, does not have a dramatic ending, and that is a flaw. It is too inexplicit, as we've discussed. It is undoubtedly positive, but it is not entirely clear what is happening.

An Enemy of the People's ending is too futuristic to be dramatic. Stockmann just sits down and says: *In the generations to come things will get better.* But it's not like someone just dropped an atom bomb and closed the curtain.

The trouble with *Othello*'s ending is that it is completely predictable in terms of the sequence of events. Not the poetry. Not the style. But in terms of what actually happens—he gets jealous, he kills her, he finds out the truth, he kills himself—and it moves kind of leisurely. It doesn't have the electric force, I think, of *Don Carlos*.

8. Which *story* do you most like?

Because this question is a summation, your answer is going to be heavily influenced by the quality of the plot-theme. A story is a beginning, a middle and an end. Obviously, you have to get into it, it has to intrigue you, it has to grip you, wring you out, and leave you washed out or exalted at the end. I think—for the reasons that I've mentioned—that the two best stories are *Le Cid* or *Monna Vanna*, with the edge going to *Le Cid*.

The others as stories, however expertly told, are comparatively simple. Antigone defies a dictator. Othello gets mad at his wife. Dr. Stockmann defies society. Joan defies the establishment. Et cetera. On the other side, *Don Carlos* isn't simple enough; and he is constantly changing his mind about who he wants to be in love with, so it is not focused enough.

9. Which play presents the most complex or intriguing theme?

I would say *Othello* and *Don Carlos* because the other themes reduce to simply "the importance of X," whatever X happens to be. *Antigone*: the importance of the individual or of individual moral judgment. *Le Cid*: the importance of honor. *An Enemy of the People*: the importance of truth. *Saint Joan*: the importance of greatness. *Monna Vanna*: the importance of personal love. These are all excellent themes, but they are simple, one-line value statements. *Don Carlos*, however, is not merely about the importance of freedom as against dictatorship, which would be a conventional theme on the order of the others. What makes it so intriguing is that it is the importance of freedom as against selfishness, making this an unusual, very philosophical, and horrible theme but nevertheless certainly complex and intriguing.

Othello has an even more complex theme because it is the irrelevance of virtue and vice to life, the self-destructiveness of any intense value. This is much more difficult and complicated to dramatize fully than simply a theme on the order of the importance of X. And yet Shakespeare does it perfectly. He shows us vice and virtue, mixed major and minor characters, and integrates all of it to this relentless theme. He is expert at depicting a complicated idea.

It is interesting that the two most intriguing themes are the most corrupt. Here we see again the tragedy of the good in history having no real philosophic basis. The great artists in history who were good men, basically had no philosophic base to work with. They had to content themselves with simple affirmations of a value, whereas the evil or corrupt had profound philosophic systems behind them, and they could venture dazzling complicated ideas. They are at home intellectually with philosophy and ideas in a way that the better playwrights are not.

10. With which play do you most strongly agree? With which do you most strongly disagree?

Speaking as an Objectivist and to an Objectivist audience, this is cut and dried. The play we most strongly agree with thematically is *An Enemy of the People*. And the play we most strongly disagree with is *Othello*.

The three worst playwrights philosophically are Shakespeare, Schiller (who was a reincarnation of Kant) and Shaw, although Shaw's philosophy, Creative Evolution, is not clearly explicit in *Saint Joan*. The two best playwrights philosophically are Ibsen and Maeterlinck, given the selections that I chose, especially Ibsen because Maeterlinck's play is not philosophical. Then we have two mixed playwrights. By "mixed" I mean they have substantial elements of truth and of error. Those would be Sophocles and Corneille; *Antigone* and *Le Cid*.

Why do I disagree with Shakespeare the most? Schiller at least purports to value reason and freedom, whereas Shakespeare anathematizes all values. Why do I agree with Ibsen the most? Aside from relatively minor errors, as when he gets trapped in evolution, his play could have come straight out of Objectivism. Maeterlinck doesn't reach definition as a total philosophy, either in *Monna Vanna* or anywhere else.

11. Which play most admirably *integrates* plot and theme?

I realize the word "admirably" is shorthand, but we have to get the questions on one page. I'm trying to suggest that integration, as it is being viewed in this question, is a feat, a unique esthetic virtue that implies complexity. Of course, theme and plot—meaning and action—have to be integrated in any proper work of art. A simple value-judgment reflected in a single event or a simple straight-line story may be perfectly integrated but it is not a feat of integration. For instance, suppose my theme is the value of persistence. And my story is: a student sits at his desk studying and refuses telephone offers to go to the movies. He is persistent and then he gets an A in the course. That is certainly integration of theme and story. We are not in the big leagues esthetically here, because the theme and plot are just too easy and one-line.

Othello qualifies here as an admirable integration of plot and theme because of the complexity of the theme and, therefore, the sheer intellectual, artistic difficulty of integrating that theme to the plot-line. We saw how Shakespeare does it brilliantly on both the positive and the negative sides across the spectrum of characters.

Le Cid also qualifies here as an admirable integration because Corneille has a more ingenious, twisted plot-theme. He has a less complex theme so his integration of plot and theme is somewhat easier than that of *Othello* because his abstract theme is easier. Nevertheless, he does his integration through a complicated storyline with supreme skill. In all the twists of the raging conflicts—Chimène and Rodrigo, the two fathers, the king and the Infanta; all the characters major and minor—the theme is what breathes life and motivates the action.

I don't think the other plays have as admirable an integration simply because they're not as complex either in plot or in theme. *An Enemy of the People* has too simple a theme and story to be in the very top rank of integration. The same applies to Shaw. He has, of course, complex, intellectual disquisitions, but that does not mean a complex theme. His theme is the importance of greatness. Both *Antigone* and *Don Carlos* have weaknesses in the actual telling of the story, which take away from focused integration. *Antigone*, as you know, switches from Antigone to Creon as the focal point which tends to give it a diffuse or a not-fully-integrated air. *Don Carlos* has the switch in the middle of the play from one triangle to the second which is really harmful from the point of view of integration.

Integration means everything belongs to one. Aristotle gives an analogy to a living organism. You couldn't take any organ or element or tissue away without the thing dying. A play that has total integration has to be that way. From any one part you should be able, in theory, to reconstruct the whole, once you see the genius that presented it.

I think third on the level of integration of plot and theme, after *Othello* and *Le Cid,* would be *Monna Vanna,* because it has an ingenious plot. But, again, it is a less complex work: fewer characters, fewer ideas, and less depth and richness.

12. Speaking purely esthetically, which is objectively the best play?

And now we reach the final awards. Here we have to review and marshal the evidence that we have already collected and throw in a few more things that we didn't. Then we will try and put it all together and see if something emerges. I am not doing this because I'm eager to push a certain play down your throat as dogma but so that you get an idea about how to approach these types of questions.

Let's look at characters first. I just want to remind you that the three best characterizations are Antigone, Le Cid and Iago. I think these three have the strongest, most powerful impact; they are completely real; they have the force of a locomotive. That is a very important esthetic achievement when compared to more mixed or more ordinary characters, such as Don Carlos or Posa, or those characters of enormous stature who have a comedic or farcical overtone or background, such as Dr. Stockmann or Joan, or less developed characters, who are delimited to a more conventional situation like Monna Vanna. The three I mentioned are the three great character portraits in our plays, and to that extent qualify their play as in the running for the top greatness, esthetically.

Another consideration is plot-theme. I think *Le Cid* or *Monna Vanna* wins on that front.

Best climax is a very eloquent indication of dramatic power and the level of artistry. The climax is to a play what it is to sex. There is foreplay and afterplay, but there is the moment. It is really a powerful contributor to the assessment. Here I think *Othello* takes the prize for the reasons I have already stated.

I would nominate *Othello* or *Don Carlos* as most complex or intriguing theme.

Unfortunately, I have to consider another factor, which we haven't discussed. Which is the greatest in style? That's the big unknown, not only because we have never worked out canons of style in a systematized way, but also because it can't be judged in translation. And basically five—or six, if you count Shakespeare—of our plays are read only in translation. I'm going to try to suggest an answer within limits, taking for granted that we are comparing all works in English.

By "style" I mean here use of language. A play is dialogue, people talking. So style really means the way people talk in the play. What I demand is a playwright who exploits the full potential of language. Not merely the use of language to communicate character and action, which goes without saying but a use of language which is pleasurable and fulfilling by its very texture and quality—a use which stretches language to show us the value and power possible to the linguistic medium. For example, take Oscar Wilde, a playwright not in this course. He uses language brilliantly in the specific form of epigrams. It is something of value over and above character and plot, although necessarily subordinate and integrated to them. It is a unique pleasure, an esthetic value in his work.

Several of our playwrights share this kind of quality. There are passages of brilliant dialogue, where one characters tops another in formulations which epigrammatically capture their view. Or they top another character by a small change in wording or syntax, and the whole thing has the force of verbal, linguistic pyrotechnics. The perfect example of that is Haimon and Creon arguing in *Antigone*. There are breathtaking interchanges there. And, of course, the Grand Inquisitor scene in the Schiller play is another fantastic example and even deeper, more philosophical.

Related to this category is intellectual wit; the ability to deal caustically and incisively with complex issues. It is a great literary stylistic value, and, of course, Shaw is a master at that. As an example, reread the archbishop's definition of "miracle."

Some of the other plays don't have these outstanding features. For instance, *Monna Vanna* has elevated, eloquent language, but no special linguistic value that I can see beyond that. It doesn't have the verbal genius of Shaw or the brilliant pyrotechnics of Schiller. *An Enemy of the People* has simple, eloquent dialogue fully appropriate to its characters, but I have no experience of relishing Ibsen's use of language, like a cat rolling in catnip. Now, of course, I don't know Norwegian. And similarly, the few fragments of Greek I know are not enough to give me a clue to judge Sophocles' use of language. But I do have some rudiments of French. And on this basis, I award the best style Tony to *Othello* and *Le Cid*, which I couldn't choose between. That's not yet the best esthetically but simply for style, which is one element of esthetics. Character and plot, etc., also come in. My criterion for picking these two is that they are the most beautiful. Not only elegant, dramatic, incisive—but beautiful in the sense of pure poetry, down to rhyme or meter, with the unique power of poetry to convey emotion. These two plays by their style have a haunting power; an ability to create mood and impact purely from language that I think is unmatched by the others. Perhaps *Antigone* in the original Greek has this power. I doubt that any of the others does even in the original.

I am not saying all great plays must be poetry. But I do say this much and I venture out on a limb to this extent: If everything else is equal, then a play which is immortal poetry fully integrated with the work—not extraneously introduced—offers a unique esthetic bonus that has to be taken into account in judging the work's esthetic and emotional value.

Of course, if you are in the modernocentric predicament, you have been brought up to believe that poetry is "artificial," which it is, just exactly the way everything good in art is artificial. You have been told that poetry is unreal, that it is not the way people speak, that it's boring, etc., etc. If you think this, you have been brainwashed by a bad culture and bad schooling. You may not like a given poem, but if you are turned off to poetry as such, you just do not know what is out there and what power language can have directly on emotions. Poetry is a supreme form—not necessarily *the*, but *a* supreme form—of exploiting the full resources of the literary medium.

So with this brief, fairly dogmatic excursion, I conclude that stylistically—which is one of several esthetic counts—Shakespeare and Corneille come out as pretty much tied. And Sophocles is a real possibility; I just don't know enough to know.

It's interesting, too, that Frenchmen hate Shakespeare because they don't know English that well and Englishmen don't like Corneille because they don't know French that well. And so to come to a purely objective judgment, you would have to be completely fluent in both. But I had had the experience of hearing sections of *Le Cid* read by a seventeenth-century French expert—I mean following the text in French—and it is thrilling, poetically speaking.

We're now closing in for the kill on the question of which is the best play esthetically. Art is an integration of all the elements and details. It is not merely the consideration of theme and plot, but the best total integration and thus the most unified work. And here I refer you to my book *Objectivism: The Philosophy of Ayn Rand*, in which I discuss the criterion of integration. Let's do it by elimination. By the standard of integration, the storyline changes too much in *Antigone*. *Don Carlos* is two plays, and therefore, out of focus. Also, the Grand Inquisitor is not integrated into the plot situation. Shaw has an uneasy union of tragedy and farce, and, therefore, is not fully unified. It is not like a lens; it is only a single reality.

Monna Vanna and *An Enemy of the People* have no objective flaws in integration, but they are comparatively simpler works, like *Antigone*. They have simpler stories or themes, fewer developed characters, and fewer stylistic values. In other words, there is less to integrate.

Therefore, in the sense of integration as an admirable feat uniting a rich complexity into a unity, the two best plays are *Othello* and *Le Cid*. They are unbroken and unbreached in their integration of every detail, and they have a complex wealth to integrate on every level.

You see, I'm resting here as a conclusion on our earlier analysis. Which play has the best features, and which integrates them best? And therefore my conclusion is that the best—taking into account all the esthetic elements and only esthetic elements—is *Othello* and *Le Cid*. These two plays represent mastery of every aspect of the art form. In other words, the greatest mastery of the means in order to create the most focused and unified end. Question 12 amounts to: which artist best uses all the elements of drama to portray and make real his type of universe? Which is the most potent and inescapable re-creation of reality from the author's perspective? By definition, all of the plays in this course are great, but these two are utterly flawless and fully matured. They are explicitly metaphysical in scope, with a complete exploitation of the medium to create a total universe—not just to suggest a universe, à la Maeterlinck, by concretizing one element—for you to step into. In these two plays we actually perceive and walk into a full reality, which is the task of great art.

If I had to look at the other end of the spectrum and say which of our plays is the least good esthetically, I would say all are great, but then either *Saint Joan* or *Don Carlos* has been noticeably less than perfect; *Saint Joan* because of the multiple inconsistencies of Shaw and *Don Carlos* because of its major failure of integration, and excessive length. (Schiller is better in other plays, although none of them has that magnificent ending.)

Antigone is potentially superlative, but the theatrical form had not yet developed enough for complex plots and multiple characterizations. And *An Enemy of the People*, as I have said repeatedly, is a great play but not as demanding and complex a work.

If you put a gun to my head and made me choose between *Le Cid* and *Othello* on purely esthetic grounds; if I had to speak at the price of death, I would choose Shakespeare. But I can't do it really, because I don't know French as well as I know English, so it's natural that I would be biased in favor of Shakespeare.

13. Speaking purely philosophically, which is objectively the best play?

I did not mean: which is the most or the least philosophical play. If I had meant that, Schiller is the most philosophical; Maeterlinck is the least. What I meant by the question is: which play is philosophically closest to the truth? So it is really the same as an earlier question. The answer is

An Enemy of the People. Philosophically, it is the best. And, judging by Objectivism, without a doubt *Othello* is the least true.

Of all of our playwrights, if I could summon them down from heaven where they undoubtedly are (if they go anywhere, all seven of these men went to heaven), there are only three that I would want to talk philosophy with. Who would you want to talk philosophy with? Sophocles, Corneille, and Ibsen. All three I would expect to be open, intelligent and interested. Shakespeare and Schiller I project as being closed to argument. You couldn't pin Maeterlinck down; he would jump all over the place. And Shaw would be like Bertrand Russell. I think it reflects this fact that the best works philosophically are the works of the three that you would most want to talk to, with Ibsen's play being the least contradicted by wrong ideas.

14. Taking both art and philosophy into account, which is objectively the best play?

This is a really difficult question. How do you integrate both of those into an objective assessment, since they are basically independent factors? A playwright can be great on one factor and lousy on the other. Obviously, to be the best play as a total, each element—art and philosophy—must reach a certain minimum level and then we can see what we have.

First of all, we have to give philosophy its proper due when we are evaluating both art and philosophy. We know you can't equate philosophy with art. And that's why *Othello* can be greater esthetically than *An Enemy of the People*. But you cannot ignore the fact that philosophy counts toward the verdict on the total. And here I remind you of Ayn Rand's point that art is a composite of means and ends or, as I put it in my book, of mastery and truth. Or another way of saying it: of esthetic standards and philosophic validity.

So if we are talking about the best as a total, there are some works you can eliminate objectively simply on the grounds that the philosophy in them is utterly corrupt, without a redeeming note. And in such a case, however expert the work is in terms of its means, it is debarred from the status of best work as a total. A brilliant means to portray utter falsehood disqualifies the work in this competition. It can still be great, great as a total. And I think that all seven that I chose are great. But it can't be the very top; it can't be the greatest as a total, if the heart of its meaning is corrupt.

And for these reasons I disqualify two playwrights out of hand as having the best as a total—and they are Shakespeare and Schiller. They are just too awful intellectually to put them on the top, most exalted rank.

On somewhat different grounds we can eliminate Shaw. His philosophy in the play is not nearly as bad as Shakespeare's or Schiller's who just beat you mercilessly over the head with corruption. Shaw has some valid elements in his philosophy, but the problems are multiple with Shaw on strictly philosophic grounds. His ideas are pretty shaky—this voluntarist German-type metaphysics. His ideas, worse, are inherently ambivalent and contradictory, which is really bad for a work which is supposed to concretize and make real your ideas. On top of that, his broader philosophy is not fully integrated to or even presented in his play; just the tip of the iceberg. You have to read his Preface to really get what he is after. As a further expression of his ambivalence, he oscillates from farce to tragedy and back. So if we are talking about the greatest as a total work, Shaw is disqualified; not for having a thoroughly corrupt philosophy but for having a philosophy inadequately defined and integrated into his work.

Monna Vanna is out here because it is simply not philosophical enough for the present league.

That leaves us with three plays which still can qualify as objectively the best after the philosophic test has been passed: *Antigone, Le Cid* and *An Enemy of the People*. Each has a focused, definite view of the universe, expertly integrated to the concretes of its artistic re-creation. The choice among these is not self-evident. You can't say, "Well, *An Enemy of the People* is truer, whereas *Antigone* and *Le Cid* have only elements of truth; therefore *An Enemy of the People* is the best." You would be considering purely on philosophic grounds. Because we are trying to judge the best play as a total, we have to add the esthetic element.

Let's go back. Which of these three is better purely esthetically? *Antigone* has the best characterization, in my opinion, even better than *Le Cid*. I would never forget Antigone. *Le Cid* has a more complex and ingenious plot situation than *Antigone*. Those are the two crucial elements to get us under the wire.

An Enemy of the People drops out here as a contender, because it doesn't reach the level of colossal characterization or ingenious plot situation. In this company it is just simply a little too "naturalistic" in terms of people and events, although I would definitely rank it as third from the top as objectively the best play. Number one and two are, in some order, *Antigone* and *Le Cid.*

The way I reason here is: *Antigone* is drama at its earliest stage, before the development of the complexities of a sophisticated plot. Because I understand French somewhat, I understand Corneille's style more than I can ever hope to understand Sophocles' style. Leaving that aside, *Othello* and *Le Cid* are the best esthetically. So now we have to choose between *Antigone* and *Le Cid,* which are about on a par intellectually. Both are a mixture of heroic philosophy undercut by the same error; namely, intrinsicism in some form.

This is the situation we have. *Le Cid* is tied for the best intellectually within the final competitors. And it is tied for the best esthetically. It is the only finalist in both categories. (This is a lot more than they give you at the Tonys.) I, therefore, conclude that, as a total, *Le Cid* is the best play, taking both art and philosophy into account.

You can see that I picked three different plays for three different questions. *Othello* is the best esthetically; *An Enemy of the People* is the best philosophically; *Le Cid* is the best as a total. This should concretize for you that these are not the same question and give you an idea how to approach objective judgment; how to first distinguish art from philosophy and then how to integrate them at the end. I hope that this does give you an indication of how to do it.

15. Which of the dramas is your *personal* favorite?

Why is there room for this? We have already analyzed everything in the work—its art, its philosophy, and their relationship. There is room for personal and cultural factors that weigh heavily in your own soul and life, even though they are not appropriate to a purely objective appraisal. As long as you know to keep them on the side, it is perfectly legitimate to feel them and express them. As long as you know it is a different category; that you are talking about an association you have, a personal experience you had, a desperate need you happen to have at this point in your life. As long as you see that you are bringing in a personal factor (which may be a perfectly legitimate factor).It is not simply inherent in looking at the art form and saying, "Is this great?"

Personally I am torn between *Le Cid* and *Antigone* as my favorites, with *An Enemy of the People* as third. I give an edge to *Antigone* as my personal favorite, even though *Le Cid* is more sophisticated and developed. And this relates to personal reasons that are involved. One is my association of Antigone with Ayn Rand; my own life was tremendously molded by a woman like Antigone. It is really difficult for me to read a play that has someone like her and say, "Oh, I really feel closer to another play." That is not obligatory and I would never venture to put that forth in an esthetic or philosophic discussion. That would mean that if I had not known her personally, my objective judgment would change. But it certainly is relevant to my personal reaction.

Another personal factor involved is that I love Greek culture over everything succeeding it. Also *Antigone* is our only pre-Christian play. I like the fact that it is so early, so pagan. It personally gives me a thrill as an onlooker observing mankind's history, to witness what no post-Christian play can do, unless it were utterly to repudiate religion which, of course, *Le Cid* does not do.

Again, that test is hardly mandatory or requisite. It just happens that in my life work the big divide is before and after Jesus, with everything being downhill since that time. Therefore the fact that *Antigone* brings back Greece *and* Ayn Rand is just too powerful. For me personally, it pushes it over the top.

I must admit that in some moods I like *Le Cid* best personally, precisely because of its greatness and also because it is so much happier than *Antigone*. It offers an enchanting picture, I think, of human life. I have to say that in some moods I like *An Enemy of the People* best, because it is right and I don't have to sigh and abstract away from falsehoods and say, "Okay, forgetting this and forgetting religion and forgetting feudalism, etc." You can just read exactly what they say without rewriting it and just give yourself fully to it. I know when I feel that way, that I have been swamped by intellectual considerations, but as long as I know it, that's okay.

Undoubtedly, many of you like *Monna Vanna* the best personally. Am I right? I don't, because it's not philosophical enough for what I personally want in a play. But if you do, I understand that perfectly and approve. *Monna Vanna* has by far the most benevolent, the most romantic sense of life, and therefore is the most sheer pleasure to experience. If you are starved for exactly that experience, who can fault you for responding to it? I certainly can't and don't.

Some of you likely picked *An Enemy of the People* as your favorite. This is the only one of our plays that is a modern play set in a modern era, so there is no question that it is the easiest play to follow. It is probably the easiest for you to identify with in concrete terms, because in your own life you presumably stand up to society regularly, whereas you don't lead armies, take on Arabs, defy kings, etc. So it is understandable if you find *An Enemy of the People* your personal favorite. I don't criticize that but I do want to stress again that if you are content to stop at that level, you are losing out on the great values ready and waiting for you in the Western Canon. If you are making easy accessibility your operative standard, you are stunting your growth. Ideally you should reach the point where you can surmount these obstacles of accessibility and pick your personal favorite with an easy grasp of all the greatness that the West has to offer—rather than because you have no time or knowledge to do anything but to pick up what is immediately familiar and identifiable.

I just want to make some concluding remarks and then I have some interesting written questions. What can you learn from objective evaluation? I think there is an analogy here in regard to judging people. It is the difference between responding blindly to some person as a package-deal, and analyzing and evaluating objectively in conscious terms. Why is it essential in dealing with people to judge objectively? You want to know who you are dealing with and what action is appropriate in the future. These same considerations apply to judging art objectively. If you analyze the elements of an artwork and evaluate them objectively, one great result is that you know what you are observing. You know what it is and what your values are. You know exactly what you want in art by the nature of your evaluations. You are, therefore, able to seek out deliberately in the future what you want and then enjoy it consciously and fully, rather than reacting blindly with no idea of what you are responding to, or where else to look for more.

Part of objective evaluation is that you see the full work with a tremendous clarity. Just as in regard to people, your analysis reveals the essence of the person and not just out-of-context aspects.

After this exercise, hopefully you will see each of these plays even more sharply and clearly than you did when we were simply just analyzing it. I hope you see them for the virtues they offer and for their limitations, if any. You should feel freer now, if you are asked out of the blue, "Is Saint Joan a great characterization?" to answer. Your mind can say something like, "Well, by comparison to, say, a bromidic heroine, like Cathy Earnshaw in *Wuthering Heights*, Saint Joan is a great characterization. But in comparison to Antigone, she is not the equal." In other words, you can relish the combination of

values that one play has to offer and you can put your finger exactly
on what inhibits your admiration of another. You can tell which of
the problems with the play is caused by your own ignorance and
how to remedy it; and which problems flow from the play and where
to look for better ones in that regard. You become your own master
in the realm of art; knowing your values, recognizing and relishing
their full expression, having the whole field at your fingertips and
in your control.

It is the same as the difference between having an implicit and
an explicit philosophy, with all the power of the explicit. Once you
know your objective evaluation of the key aspects of a play, you can
proceed to milk your pleasure systematically. You can go to the used
bookstores and, above all, the university libraries and find great plays
or poems or novels in abundance.

Q & A

Q: Several times during the lectures you have pointed out the beauty
and majesty of the language, such as the line from *Le Cid*: "Half my
life has put my other half in the grave." Could you please talk about
what epistemological principles distinguish a momentous and moving line from a run-of-the-mill one?

A: Now that is a whopper. You want not only a treatise on style, but I
should derive everything from the essence of human epistemology.
If I could do that, I would be writing that book. The best I can do is
to offer you some considerations that make a great line for me.

Originality of the thought: It does not necessarily have to be
profound. But the idea of half your life burying the other half is an
angle on something that I had never thought of looking at before. So
it's an original thought. The line has to be both content and form—
that combination is what has to get you.

Brevity and condensation: This is crucial to the crow epistemology. If she had said something like: the great value in my existence, something that I had treasured, has wrecked another great
value, something that I equally treasure; I don't know how I'll live,
and she just went on and on like that, it is dead. But if she says, "half
my life has put in the grave the other half," it's the sheer condensation. It's just a few eloquent words and it is a whole volume. It's
the simplicity in the expression of the complex that makes great art.

Use of metaphor to concretize and make something vivid: Remember, art is the reduction to the perceptual. Here you see the grave and terrific line I've mentioned before: "your daughter and Othello are now making the beast with two backs." You could never, for as long as you live, not see that, once that metaphor is expressed.

Sheer wit: Shaw's line, "Do not do unto others as you would that they should do to you. Their tastes may not be the same," is an immortal line for sheer wit. I love epigrams.

Rhythm in the right moment and in the right context: A short line can be extremely effective.

The unexpected and the double meaning: The best example in this course is a very simple line from *Don Carlos*, which on the face of it seems completely without wit and these other elements. The blind Inquisitor asks, "Are you the king?" and the king answers, "Yes." The Grand Inquisitor responds, "I could no longer tell." If this line is delivered correctly, it is like a knife in the heart of the king. It is a fabulous line, and yet it is only five words without anything except the context that gives it the powerful double meaning.

Those are some of the considerations. And, as I say, if I could give you a systematic list, I would be in business as a writer about style. Try to notice those things when you read. Every line that you can relish is that much more pleasure that you can extract from the work.

Q: I'm enjoying your analysis of the seven plays. I'd like to select another seven to ten plays on my own, read them, applying the six-step method you taught us. Without any guidance, I'd probably select another play by each of the playwrights from the course, but I'd rather read plays which you suggest. Can you suggest other *great* plays worth the time and effort? For example, were there other great plays, which nearly made it into this course but were cut for lack of time?

A: This is a really good idea. Several people that I know, in different places around the country, are forming a kind of "play of the month" club, in which they are going to read one play a month with one person responsible for doing the guided tour through the play. If you get twelve people in your group, you only have to prepare one play a year and read the others. It makes a great social evening: you can do it in an hour or two; it's stimulating; you have the fun of other people helping you out if you get stuck. If you like plays, I strongly recommend this to you just as a social activity.

You want me to list great plays that I didn't cover. I'm going to give you many here, but I don't say they're all great. And, to tell the truth, I'm not that knowledgeable in the history of the theater. I've always liked certain plays, and then I started reading more methodically in the last year, when I finally decided that I'd had enough of philosophy. But I really do not know enough. So I could give you some suggestions and you're going to have to decide. Browse through some of these suggestions. If your interest is piqued, okay; and if not, there are still lots of others.

Now, I would try one from each of the famous Greek writers. From Aeschylus, *Prometheus Bound* you have to like. It's not a full play, but it's really dramatic. From Sophocles, Aristotle thought *Oedipus* was his best. From Euripides, try *Medea*. From Aristophanes, the comedian, *The Clouds* is his famous satire of intellectuals, in which he lumps Socrates and the Sophists together.

Now, where is Bob Mayhew? What was the name of the Aristophanes one, which was a satire of Communism? *The Ecclesiazusae*. I don't know it at all, but he says it's an interesting satire of Communism.

Unfortunately, I just don't know Roman drama well enough, so I can't make suggestions here.

For a medieval play, I would recommend *Abraham and Isaac*. It has a truly awful theme but if you want to know what it was like to live as a medieval, this is the story of what Abraham goes through when he decides to kill his son for God. It's anonymous. You'll find it in any collection of medieval plays. The other famous one is *Everyman* but it is not so interesting.

As for Elizabethan plays, anything of Shakespeare, if you can take it. The one that I don't know very well, but I have advance reason to believe is probably one of his best is *King Lear*. I hate *Hamlet*. I can't stand *Macbeth*. But the theme of *King Lear* is something I can more closely identify with; rage out of control. Maybe you would enjoy that.

Also, don't overlook Christopher Marlowe, a contemporary of Shakespeare. I had a lot of fun reading *Doctor Faustus*, a badly flawed play, but a real window into the aspirations of the Renaissance man and the Christian guilt he still felt for those aspirations.

Read a lot of Corneille because it's really good. The two that I was torn about including are *Polyeucte*, about an atheist who was a Cornelian hero and *Cinna*, a fascinating play which raises moral issues, set in ancient Rome. I was set to pick *Cinna*, and then I thought, "No, they've got to have a happy ending or there's going to be mass rebellion." So I switched to *Le Cid* and I'm glad I did. But you shouldn't miss *Cinna*.

Racine and Molière, the other two French playwrights, I don't like at all. So read them at your own peril.

Switching to Germany, Goethe's *Faust* is not to be sneezed at. Schiller actually has written better plays than *Don Carlos* (because this was a youthful one of his) but nothing approaching that ending. You may find it very interesting to read *The Maid of Orleans* which is Schiller's version of Saint Joan because you could compare the same story in Shaw and Schiller. Also *Wallenstein* by Schiller is an excellent play. A lot of his plays are excellent.

Just about everything in Ibsen's final cycle is fascinating. I recommend particularly *Master Builder* and *Hedda Gabler*. I can't take *The Doll's House* simply because I always think of Gloria Steinem when I read it.

By the way, here is a play completely unknown to me, but someone said I would like it. It's by Machiavelli, in Italian, but translated: *Mandragola*.

Getting back to more modern times, I'm very strong on Oscar Wilde as an excellent playwright. I once had the honor of writing a piece of fiction which I showed Miss Rand, who thought it was very flawed, but she said to me, "You are the Oscar Wilde of Objectivism." I've read everything of his. Of serious works, *Salome* will give you an example of relishing language. The language itself is like an orgiastic experience, it's so exquisite. In terms of plot stories, I don't know which to pick. *An Ideal Husband* and *A Woman of No Importance* are wonderful. As far as his famous comedy, *The Importance of Being Ernest*, I cannot say I went for it but I do not know an Objectivist who doesn't like it, so maybe it's just a personal aberration.

Don't ignore Terence Rattigan. He wrote some really excellent plays, but they are one-note plays. He's not a philosophic writer, but he wrote at least two plays which have been made into utterly superlative movies. One is *The Winslow Boy* and the other is *The Browning Version*. Two five-star movies that you just can't beat as film experiences.

Don't forget Noel Coward. He writes on a more popular and comedic level, but his plays are always enjoyable and witty. *Private Lives* is a charming drawing-room comedy.

Include some of Shaw's other plays. Besides *Saint Joan*, I seriously debated including *Pygmalion*. An excellent movie has been made of *The Devil's Disciple*. The one I was on the verge of choosing was *Man and Superman*, but I didn't because it's even longer than the Schiller play. It has an interlude in it called "Don Juan in Hell," where Don Juan and the Devil have a fifty- to seventy-five-page debate, which is really fascinating and brilliant. I just didn't have the strength to try to cram that in, but at your leisure that is a terrific play to read.

Rostand, a wonderful playwright. *Cyrano de Bergerac* is one of the top plays of all time, ever. I think it's my personal top favorite play ever written. I only left it out of this course because everybody knows it. Rostand wrote a lot of others, including *Chantecler*.

There are several French playwrights. I'm just going to give you the name and you can browse. Scribe; I think he wrote a hundred and fifty plays, all forgotten today, mostly comedies. Sardou. And, of course, Victor Hugo.

Q: I want to know more about the course you are working on.

A: And that's going to be my swan song for today. Briefly speaking, I believe I completed my intellectual evolution from philosophy through literature. And I have now discovered that the thing that really interests me about literature is the ability to evoke and create the whole historic period. And it suddenly occurred to me just about three or four months ago: wouldn't it be great just to study history? In my entire life, I had never been interested in it. I acquired this tremendous interest because now I have the context of a strong interest in concretes and reality rather than general abstractions.

And basically what I would like to do with the remainder of my creative years is do for the world as a whole what I did for one decade in Germany with my first book, *The Ominous Parallels*. In other words, show philosophy as an integrating explanatory power that moves the world. So basically the idea would be from Adam to Clinton, and where are we now? and what can we expect? All of that integrated from the point of view of philosophy.

Now I realize that's highly specialized. But I am starting to read history voraciously now. And I hope to start teaching pure history; history history—not the history of philosophy or the history of literature. I mean kings and battles—the stuff that everybody hates. I am going to start teaching that next spring in one format or another, which you will hear about. And if all goes as planned, I will be on that subject for years to come, and that will be the subject of my next book. So you know as much about my thinking now as I do.

I hope I have made it clear that the authors do not have to be Objectivists or modern in order to offer you the greatest values possible. All of our plays, in one form or another, offer moral values, human passion, riveting conflict, individualism, self-assertion, the strength of a man or a woman, heroism, free will, the logic of plot, brilliantly eloquent language, exalted aspiration, high drama, philosophic depth, and the exhilaration of the sheer pleasure of great art. I hope I've been able to communicate these values and, above all, their abundant availability to you. I hope that if and when you run out of satisfying art that is easy to get at, you have an idea now of where to look for buried treasure. Paraphrasing John Galt, "it's real, it's possible, it's yours"—if only you dig it up.

I want to say that I've enjoyed this course more than anything I've given so far—it's just pure pleasure to me. I love this subject matter.

Editor's Note

During his 1993 course, "Seven Great Plays as Literature and as Philosophy," Dr. Peikoff named *Cyrano de Bergerac* as his personal favorite play. He cited it as a brilliant example of "the combination of a total philosophy and an esthetic execution of genius." The reason he omitted it from the original course was that he felt it was too well-known by Objectivist audiences, and would not fulfill one of his goals in presenting the course, i.e., exposing the attendees to great plays they might not otherwise experience. In 1994, encouraged by popular and persistent demand he presented the following analysis at an Objectivist conference. Obviously, the play could not be included in the final evaluation of the original seven plays, but readers may find it a stimulating challenge to revisit the Esthetic Evaluation and incorporate *Cyrano de Bergerac* in their considerations.

CHAPTER NINE

CYRANO DE BERGERAC

Edmond Rostand

1. Introduction

Our subject is *Cyrano de Bergerac*. The author is Edmond Rostand, 1868 to 1918. Ayn Rand once observed that his death in the flu epidemic after World War One symbolized the end of the individualist era, of which he was a superlatively qualified representative. He was born in Provence to a wealthy, educated French family, got a law degree in Paris, and then turned to literature for his main creative life. He wrote some early plays and poetry that are not too important, and then seemingly out of the blue came his masterpiece *Cyrano*, which was finished in 1897 when he was only twenty-nine and, at the time, unknown except by a few literati in Paris.

Cyrano is a work of unbelievable genius, Rostand's high point. He only wrote two really significant plays afterwards: *L'Aiglon*, about the son of Napoleon; and *Chantecler*, a play which is set in a barnyard with animal characters. These works, whatever their merit, do not come close to equaling *Cyrano*. Few plays do.

For such a romantic play as this, you may be surprised to learn that it is based on the life of an actual seventeenth-century Frenchman named—guess what?—Cyrano de Bergerac, whom Rostand researched thoroughly. This actual Cyrano was born in 1619 and died in 1655 at the age of thirty-six, and was the basis for many of the details in this play.

Listen to this. The real Cyrano was a playwright, a scholar, a Gascon, a soldier and a duelist. He wrote the first science fiction ever, about a journey to the moon—and that's where Rostand got the idea of Cyrano making up those devices to get to the moon. There was a real Montfleury, and the real Cyrano did order him off the stage. Cyrano died from a hit on the head with a log of wood. He had a friend, Le Bret, and a cousin,

Roxane. There was even another soldier at the time who was a stand-in
for Christian. The real Cyrano had a gargantuan nose. He was generally
described in histories as "headlong, independent, abrasive, assertive, unconventional and confrontational."

So you see how very, very much Rostand got from real life. But
what Rostand supplied is something that real life did not: the plot, the
values, and thus the meaning to all these facts. In actual history there
was no friendship between Cyrano and Christian, no plot between them
to woo Roxane and, above all, in real life Cyrano was not in love with
Roxane. So the actual facts, although they are close in so many particu-
lars, just sit there and affect no one. It is Rostand, whose creative mind
gave them a meaning, gave the characters a passionate purpose and
conflicts, and thus made their story immortal.

The story, as you know, is set in seventeenth-century France of the
real Cyrano. The first four acts take place in 1640 and the fifth, fifteen
years later in 1655. If you know anything about the period, this was the
time of *Le Cid* by Corneille; the time that Descartes was writing his
famous works; the time the French Academy was being founded; and
the era of Cardinal Richelieu. It was the exciting new France of the late
Renaissance, France of the emerging modern world.

Cyrano de Bergerac opened in Paris on December 28, 1897, and
was a tremendous success. It will do your heart good to know that
here was a historical justice. One commentator describes it as follows:
"On the opening night Rostand was overcome with nervousness and
overwhelmed with surprise." This is actually true. A half hour before
the curtain rose, he apologized to the company for having involved
them in what was sure to be a disastrous failure. Two hours after the
curtain had been rung down, the audience was still in the theater, still
applauding—and still calling for the author.

The great French actor Coquelin, who created the title role, described
the scene as follows: "There is but one phrase to express the enthusiasm
at our first performance: a house in delirium. After each act the audience
would rise to its feet, shouting and cheering for ten minutes at a time.
The dressing rooms were packed with critics and the author's friends,
who were beside themselves with delight." You get the idea. The play
went on immediately to become a smashing international success, and
one commentator writes: "No other play in history, before or since, has
ever attained a popular success so instantaneous and so enormous."

One reason for this success is that it is a truly great Romantic
play; one of the last great Romantic plays in Western cultural history.

That alone makes it timeless, invaluable, and desperately needed. It's Romantic in all the key attributes: figures who are larger than life, driven by long-range goals; purposeful plot; lyrical style; exalted, uplifted sense of life. It is a unique work of greatness. It would have been just too cosmic an injustice if a play this magnificent—the last fading embers of Western greatness condensed into a brilliant play—had not been received as it should have been. Happily, it was.

2. Plot-theme

Let us build the plot-theme up a step at a time. What is this play about? The first obvious answer is: a great Romantic hero. What is he after in action terms? What is his ruling continuous passion in terms of the play's action? What is his top value? Obviously, his love for Roxane. That dominates from start to finish. And what is his action in regard to her? To make a very simple statement; he works to win her favor, to woo her, to win her love. So we have a story of a great man working to win his love.

If we stop there, we have what you call a nothing situation—a man loves a woman and tries to get her. There is no drama, no conflict, no excitement. We are trying to enter Rostand's mind and see what kind of twist, what kind of gimmick, what kind of ploy would turn it into an immortal situation. I am not saying that historically this is the pattern Rostand went through, but I am just trying to recreate his imagination. Suppose he thinks: what if he tries to win her, not for himself, but for somebody else? Well, for whom? Because it wouldn't be the same play depending on whom he tries to win her for.

For example, suppose Cyrano studied philosophy under a sixty-year-old philosophic mentor, whom he deeply respects. And he thinks that Roxane would benefit a great deal from a relationship with this mentor, who is more philosophically advanced than he. Although the mentor isn't really interested, Cyrano tries to matchmake between the two of them. He is still trying to win her, but obviously this would be an entirely different play; not very much drama, and pure self-abnegation on Cyrano's part. The question is: why is he doing this? (I put this in to show you what a *bad* idea that would be; to show the contrast with Rostand.)

Rostand's idea is that he tries to woo her for his hated rival who loves her but whom he feels is beneath her. That is the key. He tries to win his beloved for his own rival, and so there's a conflict at the very inception. He is trying to win her for Christian, he wants Christian to win. But she is *his* beloved, and Christian is a fool, so he wants Christian to lose. So he wants him to win, and he wants him to lose. He is torn down the middle. Now that is what you call a conflict, and without conflict there is no drama.

Now let's develop the situation. We still haven't reached the plot-theme, but we have a leg up on it. What might Rostand have thought to further develop this? This is the hard part of creative writing, to get your plot-theme. Maybe his next question might have been: why? If Cyrano is in love with this woman, why wouldn't he pursue her on his own? For some reason he is not suitable as a lover—we don't even know what the reason is. Would it be, for instance, that he is already married? That would be very conventional, and if that were the reason you would doubt his real love for Roxane. If he was really passionately in love with her, he would leave his wife in an instant.

So we can infer from that (projecting Rostand's mental processes) that there must be something intrinsic or internal to Cyrano, something about him that disqualifies him from romance; something bad or wrong or flawed or unattractive, which he can't change. Now this is far before plastic surgery, so you have to forget about that. It is not something spiritual; it is something unalterable, given as a physical flaw of some kind that would make him odious to a heroine. And he has to accept this flaw as a one hundred percent barrier: it simply eliminates him from the romantic context.

There is nothing in this situation or in this play that says it has to be a long nose. It could be any version of deformity: he could be a hunchback, he could be a leper—you could exhaust your imagination by going to medical books. Rostand made it simple, basing it on history, on the gargantuan nose. But that is merely a concrete, and if you were writing a paper on this and you said this was a story about a man with a long nose, you would fail automatically. The long nose is an incidental—it has a crucial purpose, but it is not a story about a nose.

Let's put it like this: we have an ugly man—that's the way he is usually described. He is physically deformed; an ugly hero in love with a beautiful woman. Now why do we want her to be beautiful? Well, if she too has a big nose, maybe they would get along okay. He is an ugly man in love with a beautiful woman, who works to win her, not for himself—because that's impossible to him—but for his rival. The rival then must also be beautiful or handsome. He must be perfect on the very count that Cyrano is deformed.

But Rostand would have to think, as he is developing his plot situation: why would this beautiful rival need Cyrano's help? If he has a perfect body, a beautiful face, why would he need Cyrano's help? Obviously, the body is not enough to woo Roxane; something spiritual is needed as well, which Cyrano has and Christian does not. What is it? Well, it is not bravery, because Christian is every whit as brave as Cyrano. You know in essence from the play what the trait was that Rostand gave to Cyrano, one that Roxane wanted and that Christian was miserable at delivering. It can be described in many ways: poetic sensitivity or, put more broadly, intellectual, esthetic, and literary mastery. Or put still another way: the quality of literate, brilliant soulfulness. He has a heroic soul with a tremendous ability to express himself in beautiful, dramatic and eloquent language. On the other hand, Christian, as handsome as he is, is simple. He is called a fool at one point—not that he's retarded—but just a completely ordinary, nice guy. But whatever you say about him, he is inarticulate and he does not have a poetic soul.

This much is necessary to make the plot-theme ring with a real dramatic situation. Here is a plot-theme about sending letters. Letters are just like the nose: there are a hundred different ways in which it could have been done. It doesn't make any difference. The idea is not the *means* by which he woos or the nature of his flaw. The idea is this—and this is the plot-theme as I finally reach it: *A brilliant but ugly man, in love with a beautiful woman, works to win her—not for himself but for his handsome and "stupid" rival.* (In this context, "stupid" means unaccomplished, perfectly ordinary, simple.) You know that if the rival were also brilliant and poetic, that would finish the play completely. Cyrano would have no asset in the struggle, he wouldn't be needed, and the character would just be brushed aside.

Here we have—and see if this suggests something to you on a deeper level—a brilliant intellect in a deformed body, and a beautiful body with a mind of a simple peasant. Does this suggest something as a possible overarching, philosophical, thematic idea that might be a key to open the play? Yes, this play is definitely the mind-body dichotomy—I'll tell you that right now—but not in the way you think, unless you are one step ahead of me. Rostand has a lot of tricks up his sleeve.

From the statement of the plot-theme, we can figure out which are the essential, indispensable characters and what the main conflicts are. And of course from this plot-theme we know right away that the Comte de Guiche is not a main character. The main characters are Christian,

Cyrano and Roxane. Those are the three main characters and that's all; it is a classic triangle. What is the main conflict? Obviously it is Cyrano versus Christian for Roxane. Each wants her desperately. You know Cyrano wants her desperately, despite his actions. But that is just conventional so far: two men, both of whom want the same woman.

What makes this a unique situation is that each character is in a profound inner conflict. Cyrano wants Roxane—but he doesn't want her; he feels that he cannot make her happy, that he must be loathsome to her. He wants her but he renounces her, and yet he still hopes. He wants to use Christian to gain her love but he *doesn't* want to, because he wants her to love him for himself. So he is in conflict. Christian wants to use Cyrano but he doesn't want to, because he also wants to be loved for himself, and not for the letters that he didn't write. They are both in conflict for the same woman, and they are both in conflict about the way they are winning her.

And, of course, they are both in conflict with Roxane: neither of them wants her to know about their plan. And she would want to know about it. This is an implicit conflict that is crucial to the situation, because the moment that Roxane finds out, the play is over. If and when the ruse is exposed, Cyrano would not be able to win her for Christian. And if his premise is right about his own deformity being loathsome, he can't win her for himself—so the play would have no place to go and just peter out.

3. Plot Development

Now let's look to the plot development. I always analyze plot development into three parts. When you are studying plays, it is much more illuminating to try to break them up—if they are classic plays with a structure. The first is the establishment of the situation. In the case of this play, it occupies Acts One and Two. You are given the information to create the basic situation. Then there is the rise to the climax, followed by the denouement and the final resolution, i.e., how it ends. Acts One and Two are the establishment, Acts Three and Four are the rise, and Act Five is the denouement. That is a perfect classic structure.

So let's just look at these three parts that together are the way of carrying out this basic plot-theme. You know the purposefulness of Rostand. Right off the bat, we learn of both men's undying love for Roxane. I like plays that put their cards on the table right away. The duel hasn't even started and already Christian tells us: *I am dying of love. I have to meet her.* He also announces right away, before it even comes up: "I have no wit." *I can't talk to a woman in the style that's necessary; I'm just a simple soldier.* So everything you have to know about Christian, you're hit with immediately.

Cyrano is introduced—brilliant, super-artistic and poetic—but hideous with his long, dangling appendage, although respected because of his courage and prowess with a sword. He, too, tells us that he loves Roxane but has no hope. And, in fact, we learn that one of the reasons he orders Montfleury off the stage is: *that fat pig had the presumption to love Roxane.*

I want you to note here how tricky a situation this is to establish. Once a genius has done it, you read it and say, "Of course." But there was a real problem, which Rostand handled brilliantly, and that was, let us call it, the problem of the nose. The problem is, how does Cyrano view his own nose? If he viewed it with pure despair or disdain or disgust, and went around as a humble, handicapped wretch thinking, "Oh, God, I'm grotesque, I just don't dare look in the mirror, I'm deformed," he would become pathetic. He wouldn't be a hero and the whole play would be lost. He'd end up in some government office applying for an equal opportunity grant.

That is one pitfall that Rostand had to be careful of. But on the other side, if Cyrano took the attitude that appearance is irrelevant, it's only the soul that counts, he'd simply go after Roxane himself and again there would be no play. So he has to remain proud, arrogant, assertive, and heroic despite the nose—while at the very same time being conscious of the tremendous liability of the nose. Now that *is* a problem. He has to be acutely aware of his flaw, while having a proud, righteous, arrogant self-confidence.

Rostand's solution is, in essence, Cyrano's exaggerated playfulness and inventiveness about the nose. He can beat anyone to insulting it, and then defend it against the attack. And so the very nose that is his problem becomes a testament to his brilliance, his inventiveness, his sense of humor, his swordsmanship, his heroism. At the very same time, all those qualities come across as infused with the fact that he *is* sensitive about his nose. He says that openly. He won't let anyone else talk about it, he regards it as an insult and he will fight them to the death for such an insult.

When you see it on stage, it is enchanting and brilliant. But it had to be worked out as a combination; with the result that he is proud, heroic, extravagantly courageous and acutely sensitive about his deformity, all at once. That is what the famous Nose Ballade brings off: this genius brilliantly denouncing his own nose. Jose Ferrer does it well in the movie version. But I have seen quite a number of performances of *Cyrano* and the greatest by far was with Derek Jacobi, which I saw on Broadway in the eighties. It was absolutely breathtaking; a performance like none I could ever have imagined. It was completely romantic and swashbuckling but at the same time so real that you believe that he is actually making up the couplets of the ballad right in front of you. You feel his sensitivity and bravado at the same time.

Continuing with the structure, Act One closes with Roxane's need to see Cyrano and, of course, then the hope: what could it mean? Does she love me? The establishment of the situation finishes in Act Two at Ragueneau's pastry shop. Roxane confesses that she is in love. There are two heartbreaking pages here where we think (and he thinks) that it might be Cyrano. She pours compliments on this unnamed man, compliments that might be applicable to Cyrano, too, until she says: *and the best thing of all, he's beautiful.* At which Cyrano turns pale, because he knows that lets him out. She tells him that it's Christian.

Notice that Rostand is still eager to drive the situation home. Remember that Christian had said at the beginning that he did not know words. Now we need to know that words really matter to Roxane. Cyrano says, "But . . . you who love only words, wit, the grand manner."*What if he's a fool?* And she says with great sincerity, "Then I shall die." So what can Cyrano do? He can't have her, he pauses, he accepts the situation. She begs Cyrano to protect Christian from the fiery Gascons in his company, and he agrees. And then her parting words to him, "Have him write."

You see how it's all being set up. We haven't yet established the situation, but it is being skillfully put together. And then we have another nose scene, which is the meeting of Christian and Cyrano, at which Christian baits him—he wants simply to show the Gascons his courage. And now we see the other side of Cyrano. He can't respond because of his promise to Roxane, but he is impressed by Christian's courage and they get together. Cyrano had already written a letter to Roxane on his own behalf, if there was a chance. When he realized that she loved Christian, he didn't give it to her.

Cyrano says to Christian: *You must write her a letter,* because he had promised that to Roxane. And Christian says: *But I can't.* This would fall flat if it were just out of the blue, but by now we have been led to expect it. Then there is this wonderful exchange where Christian says, "I wish I had your wit." And Cyrano replies: *I wish I had your beauty.*

Then the light bulb goes on, and the idea comes. Let's get together. We each have one crucial ingredient; together we'll make "one hero of romance." We'll win her together. Cyrano does not tell Christian about his own love for Roxane; he says it's just a poetic challenge for him. The situation is now perfectly established. It took two long acts to make it completely convincing. The big problem was to get Cyrano's character right. Once that's accomplished, Rostand feeds in the points that culminate in the establishment of the situation.

Now we go to the rise to the climax, Acts Three and Four. Act Three is Roxane's kiss. Why do we have the balcony scene here? Why not have Roxane read the letters silently and say, "Oh, how wonderful he is!"? It is because this is theater and the first thing you have to see is action. We have to actually watch Cyrano's wooing of Roxane and see how it succeeds and why it succeeds. This is the first rise in a series of rises in these two acts. The first rise of the suspense line: is he going to be able to win Roxane or not?

We learn that a number of letters have been sent and that Roxane is duly impressed, but the pursuit must be dramatized before our eyes. Consequently we have the famous, brilliant balcony scene. Cyrano is hidden at first, providing the lines in stage whispers. Finally he pushes Christian aside—it's just too clumsy a setup—and delivers them himself, with Roxane responding.

This is what you call a really well-made play. Notice again how Rostand carries this out. After a certain point you start to think to yourself, "This is ridiculous. Why can't he just come out and speak for himself?" So Rostand has Christian protest and say: *I'm going to do it on my own. I don't need you anymore. The ice has been broken.* I think Rostand does it very convincingly. These aren't the exact words, but basically Christian comes out and says, "I love you a lot, kiddo." And that exhausts his repertoire. So again Cyrano has to take over for him and you completely accept the situation. From the beginning, this has all been very calculated to get you to this point.

Now we have the scene where Cyrano, speaking in his own voice but hidden in the darkness, declares his own love eloquently, beautifully, soulfully, passionately. He is delivering lines for Christian, but the impact comes from the fact that he is delivering them for himself, first and foremost. She, of course, is profoundly moved. She falls in love: "I am yours, and you have made me thus." So for Cyrano it is the ultimate triumph and yet, at the same time, it is total frustration. He has won for his rival, lost for himself.

Then Christian demands a kiss, and Cyrano is definitely jealous. He does what he can to stop it, because he wants her for himself. But he soon resigns himself. He sees that it is inevitable; it is inherent in the success of the plan. Christian is going to get her one way or the other. So Christian climbs up the balcony, and we hear Cyrano's tragic line: [She is] "kissing *my* words upon his lips." This is a beautiful, eloquent, short, memorable way of illustrating the complexity and the image. You can see the pathos of the situation; his triumph and tragedy together. And it is inherent in the pact. The scheme has worked; Cyrano has made love to Roxane and now Christian cashes in.

I have read accounts that say this is the climax because the purpose was supposed to be that he wooed her. He has wooed her, won her, and it is sealed with a kiss. Remember the climax is the decisive event in the structure, the point when the ending is determined and knowable in principle; when the resolution of the conflict is actually taking place. It may not take place before our eyes (that could be in the denouement) but that which will lead to it has finally been decided. And that has not happened here.

First of all, from the nature of the story itself, if we are intelligent playgoers, we know right away that Christian's triumph must be very short-lived. Why? Can you imagine that the ending is Roxane and Christian get married and live happily ever after, raising little kids? No, because Christian has to talk at some point. By the nature of Rostand's setup, Roxane needs a brilliant, poetic man and Christian is the opposite. So if they got married and spent day after day together, she would be bitterly disappointed. She would realize that it was not this man who wooed her. That would destroy their relationship, reveal the whole scheme and the play would just peter out. The only way to avoid it is to keep her in ignorance of Christian's true nature, once he gets her. Therefore, Rostand does the inevitable. You see, a great playwright does the inevitable—in retrospect. When you are reading it for the first time, it is completely unexpected, but when you look back you see that the logic of the plot-theme required this development. That is the test of a great structure.

Rostand does the logical thing: Christian and Roxane get married, and then he sends Christian off to battle and has him die. That way Roxane goes on thinking he is a noble poet, and the play continues. When Cyrano and Christian are sent off to war away from Roxane, she begs Cyrano to be sure that Christian writes her every day. And then in Act Four Christian is killed.

This development frees us at last to focus on the really climactic question, the real suspense of this play. The climactic turning point is not: does Christian get her? It is: does Cyrano get her? He is the one everybody is rooting for, in spite of the plan that he had cooked up. Cyrano is the hero, he is in love with her, and we gradually come to feel that she is really in love with him. So the rising action and suspense to the climax continue well into the fourth act. That is already a great feat: to have an establishment which catches you up and then rises, and keeps rising into the fourth act, where you don't know what is going to happen—until we reach an event that tells us once and for all what the outcome will be. And that event is the climax, right near the end of Act Four.

We get to it very logically: the cadets are in a desperate situation because de Guiche, the main villain, has in effect sentenced them to death through a hopeless battle. We also know that, despite the danger to his life, Cyrano has been sending letters every day to Roxane, which have inflamed her passion for Christian even further. Finally she can't stand his absence and comes to the camp itself to be with her husband.

(By the way—if Rostand's spirit will forgive me—the standard criticism of this play is that it is completely unrealistic to think that a lover would come to a battlefield to meet her husband. Therefore, many companies around the country simply omit large sections of Act Four for "realism." That gives you an idea of the state of the world, if you had any doubts.)

Anyway, Roxane comes to the camp to be with her husband. She realizes by this time something that we already know: that what she loves about him is not his face but his letters. And we have the scene in which she begs Christian's forgiveness for being so superficial and vain and frivolous as to have loved him only for his body, only for his physical beauty. She tells him: *Even if you were ugly, I'd still love your soul. That's what counts.*

She thinks she is showering upon him the deepest compliment; he gets the message and is devastated because he realizes that she really loves Cyrano. He puts this together with the information he recently acquired that Cyrano risked his life every day to send the love letters to Roxane. He realizes that Cyrano loves Roxane. Cyrano and Roxane are in love with each other—there, he finally gets it—and he, Christian, is the obstacle standing in their path. Simple as he is, he is a man of honor. One of the wonderful things about this play is that the worst people have stature and honor.

There is a wonderful exchange capturing the two antagonists' sense of justice. Christian confronts Cyrano with this information and says, "Shall I ruin your happiness because I have a cursed pretty face? That seems too unfair." And you are to take that as a pure statement of: it is unfair that I get the lady just because I was born with a pretty face, when you have the soul that won her. And Cyrano answers him in kind: "And am I to ruin yours, because I had been born with the power to say what you perhaps feel?" It is a little more dubious as to whether that is an inborn skill. But nevertheless he is trying to see both sides and to be fair. Let's say it is in his professional specialization: I specialize in language; you don't, but that shouldn't be the factor. . . . You see, they are both trying to be completely French heroes.

And Christian has a solution: *tell her. Tell her the whole truth, let her choose between us. I want her to love me for what I am*—I think he says here "for the poor fool that I am"—*or not at all.* Cyrano agrees and goes to tell her.

And now your heart is in your throat, because you think: this could be it, he is going to tell the truth, she will pick him, maybe it will have a happy ending. You don't really think that, if you know Rostand, but you hope despite hope. Cyrano says: *Was it true what you said to Christian, that you would love him even . . .* She starts to say: *Yes, even if he were . . .* —and she can't get the word "ugly" out, looking at him. He says, "The word comes hard—before me," *doesn't it?* She says: *No*—and gets her courage up—*even if he were ugly, grotesque, deformed!* She is carried away by the love of the soul in those letters. And for one moment Cyrano thinks, "It is true!"

But notice his first word after "it is true." "Perhaps." And then the next sentence: "This is too much happiness." This is very instructive—we are going to analyze it later. For a moment he allows a possibility, even though it seems to him inconceivable, that she loves him. He is on the very verge of telling her. And at that instant we learn that Christian is mortally wounded and dying. And what are Cyrano's first two words when he hears that Christian is dying? "All gone."

He goes to the dying Christian and says: *I told her. She made her choice and it was you. You're the one she loves.* He goes off to the final battle, thinking that he is going to die in it. He says, "I have two deaths to avenge now, Christian's and my own."

Anyway, the climax here is clearly "All gone." The climax is the decision not to speak, the instantaneous conviction: *now I can never tell. I've lost her forever.* At that point we have reached the end of the suspense. We know how it must turn out. He is going to lose Roxane, too, and it will be a tragic ending.

The whole question of understanding Cyrano and understanding the play is: why does Cyrano make this decision at the climax? Once Christian is dead, he is out of the way. Why does Cyrano not speak up, especially if he believes that Roxane really loves him? That is the question on which the meaning of this play depends. It is not actually answered until Act Five. But I am postponing it for the discussion of Cyrano's character and the theme. What you have to keep in mind and think about is: why does he behave this way at the climax? Is it inherent in the play as, if it is a great play, it must be?—or is it just accidental? Of course, if it was accidental, that would mean a horrendous flaw at the heart of the play. It wouldn't stand; it wouldn't be believed. But, in fact, it has been thoroughly prepared for and is the only thing possible, given this play.

How many either feel or know that no other action by Cyrano would have been possible in this play? Well, then, the play comes to you to that extent. It's hard to articulate entirely why, but not really when you finally get to it.

As far as structure, we are left only with the denouement and the final resolution, which is Act Five at the convent. Even though we have seen the climax and know how the action will end, we still have some questions that keep our suspense. Roxane must learn the truth. How will she learn it? And how will Cyrano end up? Will he end up crushed or will his spirit somehow triumph even over his defeat?

Notice that it is fifteen years later, which is significant. Roxane has been in a convent, she has given up the world. And Cyrano, too, we learn, has in effect lost the world. He is poor, he is aging, he is alone. But he is still Cyrano. He is still true to his spirit and values, and he comes each Sunday to visit Roxane and bring her the news. In Act Five, on his way to the convent he is struck with a log of wood by some villain, which is exactly how the real Cyrano died. He is dying, yet he remains the same man, the same hero, the same spirit. We know at once that he will die, and we are left with just the famous death scene.

Roxane has Christian's last letter always at her breast and Cyrano says: *I want to read it today.* (Because I am dying, too.) Roxane doesn't know yet. He starts reading, "Farewell, Roxane, because today I die." And it has a tragic double meaning because it was written for Christian; she thinks they are Christian's last words, but it is also true of Cyrano today. It is the same sentiment that he voiced then, with a double meaning.

And, as he reads the letter, it is the same voice—the voice that she heard once before in the balcony scene. It starts to come back to her. He continues. It is too dark to read but, of course, he has it completely memorized. He goes on, and at last she gets it. It is an extremely brilliant, dramatic, heart-rending way for her to find out. She says, "It was you . . ." *It was your tears on the letter.* And again his gallant, heroic comeback, "The blood was his."

She asks: *why tell me now?* He says: *I didn't finish telling you the news: today Cyrano de Bergerac dies foully murdered.* And she says— better than my synopsis—"You shall not die! I love you." And he says, "That is not in the story. You remember when Beauty said 'I love you' to the Beast that was a fairy prince, his ugliness changed and dissolved like magic; but you see I am still the same." So Rostand is consciously saying that he drew the idea from *Beauty and the Beast*, which was a familiar theme in Western literature. But here the Beast (the nose) remains such to the end. So you are told: love cannot prevent it; the flaw—whatever it is—is unavoidable, unconquerable and unsurpassable. This is reality, not the fairy tale. And we are going to feed that into the meaning.

Then we have what I think is the single most haunting and brilliant line in the play; "I never loved but one man in my life, and I have lost him—twice." If you can write a play that gets one line like that across, you have earned your claim to immortality. You don't need more than that. I would read two or three hundred pages to get to one line like that.

Next, we have Cyrano's final death throes in delirium from his injury. He is lunging with his sword at the empty air. "Falsehood! . . . There! There! Prejudice—Compromise—Cowardice," and so on. He is killing all his enemies that he imagines are attacking him, and he says, "There is one crown that I bear away with me. And tonight when I enter before God, my salute shall sweep all the stars away from the blue threshold. One thing without stain, unspotted from the world, in spite of doom, my own. And that is . . ." And she leans over and says, " That is . . . ?" He opens his eyes and smiles at her, "My white plume." And that's curtain.

The white plume was the symbol in the French army of courage, what we would call greatness of soul. It is self-esteem expressed exuberantly and heroically. And that is what he took away from this world, that is the one thing he had left.

It is utterly beautiful and utterly tragic. It is uplifting and admirable and, at the same time, if you followed and were immersed in the story, a very painful ending to watch as this truly great man dies tragically without fulfilling his love. You just sit there and cry, and the curtain comes down. You go home and ponder: what was he telling her? Why does Cyrano have to die? Why does he have to die like this, losing everything? That takes us to his characterization and his motivation, and then we will finally emerge with the theme.

4. Characterization

So let's say a few words about Cyrano's characterization. He is really the only developed figure to study. Roxane and Christian get less attention from Rostand; they are much less complex, basically well-known types. But Cyrano is complex and extraordinary; he's a towering figure, he's one of the great historic figures of drama with one of the worst defects, that is, his deformity. So, of course, the first thing that strikes you about him is the contrast between great mind and deformed face.

In some sense you could say that Cyrano represents the soul-body dichotomy, with Christian being the other side—the beautiful body and the ordinary mind. And together, as Rostand says, they make "one perfect hero of romance."

However, the mind-body dichotomy in this play is hard to explain. Although it is definitely there (it's essential to the play), the character of Cyrano does not manifest that dichotomy in any obvious way. The paradox is this: Cyrano as presented in the play is the perfect union of the spiritual and the physical. He is the perfect example of the integration of the two, not the dichotomy.

If you're an ordinary guy and you want to present the mind-body dichotomy, you'd be like ten thousand other playwrights. You would have a spiritual, artistic, mystic type who shrinks from the physical. Or you would have some kind of brute materialist—or, if you're a leftist, some money-grubbing capitalist—who's empty and scornful of art and contemptuous of the spiritual. So you show someone allegedly specializing in one side and disdaining or fearing the other.

But Cyrano—although in some sense he's trapped by the mind-body dichotomy—represents both sides at their best. He's introduced from word one as, at the same time, a philosopher, a musician, a poet—and a swordsman. He's an artist and a soldier. He has great inner sensitivity and great physical strength and courage. In short, he is terrific in things of the spirit *and* in things physical. Both aspects of him are given equal stress by Rostand. That's what makes him so charming. He's a great soul with a great power to act, a great control over his body. And this is evident from the beginning of Act One when he takes on the whole company to get Montfleury off the stage. It's an act of extreme physical courage. And then he throws a month's pay down to the owner, with the statement: *that's the kind of gesture I like*. So he's in love with drama; it's a thoroughly romantic gesture. I think the purpose of the swordfight in the Ballade is to show his dual mastery of the physical and the spiritual. He's a superlative duelist and a superlative poet, and you see the two of them in action on both fronts at once. He describes himself at one point as a soul clothed in shining armor. And that is how he is actually portrayed. So the Ballade shows a perfect mind-body integration and it's a complete introduction. And, as he ends the refrain, "Thrust home!" his spiritual poem and his physical action come to their climax together.

You will have to reread that speech for the tremendous wit and intelligence it brings about his own nose in the process. You know, "Was this the nose that launched a thousand ships?" He has all these great lines. Valvert the villain says: *well, you don't even have gloves.* And he says: *yeah, I'm sorry, I had a pair and I lost one.* "Some gentleman offered me an impertinence. I left it—in his face." So he is a wonderful character. Watching this on the stage is not an oppressive experience of tragedy. It's fun, it's enjoyable.

If you wanted to go through Cyrano's character consistently, from the point of view of the Objectivist virtues, he has them all. He has every basic Objectivist virtue. I am not going to go painstakingly into them. You obviously recognize his independence and his integrity—specifically his creative integrity; it's the integrity of Roark for his own work. That is stressed by the scene in which de Guiche, Cardinal Richelieu's nephew, who represents the highest level of the establishment says to him: *Let my uncle rewrite a few lines of your play here and there, and he'll approve the rest, and you can finally get it produced.* Cyrano desperately wants to have it produced. Yet he gives a marvelous speech, which, in essence, is: *No thank you.* It is sheer literary pleasure every time you read it. Cyrano wants to see his play produced but he wants to see it produced as he wrote it. His blood curdles at the thought of changing a comma. This could have been written by Ayn Rand. It is exactly the same creative passion and integrity with the same defiance: he will fight everybody—the lords, the establishment, the aristocracy, everybody—for his truth his way, his words his way.

They tell him: you are an extremist. (Now remember, this was written before the Goldwater Convention.) He says, "There are things in this world a man does well to carry to extremes." I mean, you can fall in love with this man.

He is just—that is what motivates his various battles. He is honest in everything except the scheme with Christian, where they are deceiving Roxane. He is productive: he is a soldier plus a playwright and poet. And there is no question whether he has pride. He even has pride in the technical Objectivist definition which is moral ambitiousness: the man who seeks his own moral perfection across the board. This is in contrast to just trying to get some aspects right and saying about flaws, "Well, there's nothing I can do about that; that's just me." Cyrano states openly that his goal is "to make myself in all things admirable." That is the very same idea as moral ambitiousness: to shape myself in all things as admirable, good, right, perfect. This is true pride and he has it. As a result of this unblemished character, he is a true friend; loyal and honorable, the opposite of any kind of devious manipulator.

You can say that his nose is his one area of personal doubt, which he does regard as a major liability, at least in regard to romance. Remember, he says: *I dream and then I see the profile of my shadow on the wall—and then I have my bitter days and I see how ugly I am.* So that is the one problem that he has, but it does not seem to dilute the rest of his character.

Is Cyrano basically selfish or unselfish in entering the scheme with Christian? The standard line of commentators is that Cyrano is the epitome of unselfishness. I quote from one: "We admire his self-abnegation; he is the exemplar of almost superhuman self-sacrifice." Now you get an idea of the abyss to which critical comment can lead you. I grant this much: there are mixed aspects to the play on this issue, which I will discuss.

My first instinct when I hear an analysis like that is: nonsense, he is not unselfish. At least through Act Four, in my judgment, his motivation is completely selfish. First of all, he loves Roxane passionately, and love, as you know, is thoroughly selfish. Also he believes it is metaphysically impossible ever to fulfill his love; he truly believes that the ugliness disqualifies him and that she is in love with Christian. Therefore, the best thing possible to him—possible selfishly—is vicarious lovemaking through Christian. His actual operative goal in the scheme is not to win her for Christian. Observe that he tries to stop Christian from kissing her, and later he is relieved when he hears that their marital consummation has been delayed. That is just the pretext. What he really wants is the chance to be himself with Roxane, to pour out his soul, his feelings, and win her thereby, even if he has to remain hidden physically—even if it is only vicariously.

At the start of the scheme—and I think this is very conscious on Rostand's part—Cyrano says to Christian, "When my words are on your lips that will turn to facts my fantasies." In other words, if I can tell her about my love and get her to respond, this is as close as I can get (given the situation) to turning my selfish, personal dream into a reality. This is the goal that motivates the letters and comes out clearest in the balcony scene. When he wins her, he is overcome by emotion and he asks her: *how can you know what this moment means to me? It's like a dream.* And it is like a dream, because it is his dream as close as possible coming true. His love comes tearing out of his throat, and she is responding, she is reacting, she has been reached by his voice saying his words. That is the fulfillment he has been seeking. When she tells him, "I am yours and you have made me thus," his answer should now become perfectly clear. His answer is, "What is death like, I wonder?"

What is the meaning of that? He says it himself: "I know everything else now. I have done this to you—I myself." In other words, I am ready for death now, because I have lived, I have achieved my goal, I can die now.

This, as I see it, was Cyrano's selfish, personal passion that he believed could be satisfied in no other way. So in this sense, at this point I think there is no question but that he is thoroughly selfish and that is what makes him admirable.

Now we get to behavior in Act Four. He is about to tell her the truth, after Christian discovers it and demands that he speak. At the last second, Christian is killed, and Cyrano's first words are "All gone!" Thereafter he keeps his silence and never tells Roxane until he himself is dying. Why? This is the key to the meaning of the play.

I think there are some lesser reasons before we get to the major one. Partly, his fear of his own ugliness and of her ridicule is never entirely conquered. Even in his moment of believing that ugliness would not matter to her, i.e., at the highest point of his physical self-confidence, the most he can say is: "It is true! PERHAPS. God, this is too much happiness." In other words, it is too good to be true. Even here he can't be one hundred percent sure. I think you can say legitimately that, in part, the reason he never speaks is that the issue of his ugliness motivates him throughout the play. But this is definitely not the whole answer. After all, he was actually about to tell Roxane and then he stopped decisively when Christian died. So why?

Again, first for some lesser reasons. In part, it is his very heroism; his loyalty to his dead comrade; his magnanimity. He can't see taking advantage of the situation. It would amount to talking badly about Christian behind his back when he has just died a hero's death. However you slice it—if you can imagine the scene taking place—he would have to say, in effect, to Roxane, "You know, this guy was really a fool. All the things you liked were really me." That would be too awful in the face of her grief when the corpse is not even cold.

It would very probably even lack objectivity. If Christian had been alive and Cyrano had told her the truth, she would come to him and ask, "Is this true?" He would say yes and she would have believed it. Now that he is dead, you could make up anything and there is nobody to contest it. Cyrano would probably even fear that she would not believe him.

Up to this point I can ascribe it all to noble qualities, and I don't see any self-sacrifice. In other words, I understand it as reticence or tactfulness due to the immediate situation. It would be impossible on Christian's deathbed—or even within a few months, while the grief is still intense.

But here is what the question comes down to. Roxane and Cyrano go on living for fifteen years. Two lives that are empty, wasted, love-starved. Cyrano knows it throughout and could achieve fulfillment for both of them. Despite his nose and his concern about that, he knows that in some sense she loves him because, as he says right after Christian's death, "I am dead, and my love mourns for me and does not know." So why let her mourn? Why reduce him and her to this kind of arid, frustrated fifteen years? Imagine the number of empty nights in those years.

I don't think you could call it anything other than an act of renunciation, an act of abnegation. Whatever else is operating, he is giving up the chance at personal happiness and fulfillment for no one's benefit, in a context where he has reason to believe it would be possible to him. He is thereby condemning himself to a life of misery and deprivation. This is a decision made, not in the heat of heroism, but in the

coolness of years. I don't see how you can describe that as anything
but a sacrifice: he is throwing away, for no rational reason, what they
both want desperately.

I think this decision is the key to the deeper meaning of the play.
There is a broader, deeper meaning that I think you feel, and that is
why you can expect and sympathize with this decision, even though
rationally it does not make sense. There is a deeper reason why he
stays silent and renounces Roxane, and that would lead us, basically,
into the theme.

There is nothing much to say about the other characters. Christian
and Roxane are very conventional, standard characters. So let us jump
to the theme.

5. Theme

The theme in this play is a bit tricky to define. I loved the play for
many years and had a lot of trouble figuring out what the theme was.
It is not immediately obvious, so I am going to lead you to the theme
the way I was led to it. Once you get to it, it seems perfectly clear but it
takes some effort to get there. I asked myself before trying to state the
theme: what can I say about the theme that I am sure is true? I came up
with three points that I know are indisputably involved in the theme
somewhere. Then I tried to put them together into one idea.

The first thought that occurred to me is that this play is, first and
foremost, about the nobility of one man: the greatness of Cyrano;
the heroism of the great individual. The fundamental conflict of the
play—thinking now on the thematic level, not the action level—is
Cyrano, the exceptional, brilliant individual against the establishment, the conventional daily world of society. In this regard Cyrano's
conflict is not primarily with Christian. Christian symbolizes the ordinary guy. He is not a special nor great individual; he is basically like
everybody else. Christian is the representative of the conventional.
True, he is beautiful but the action of the play shows us that his beauty
is to be regarded as a superficial, meaningless quality. What Roxane
discovers is that it is the character, the inner greatness of the man,
which counts. And so we have a picture of a great individual struggling heroically against the conventional world.

Now what does this remind you of as a theme? So far, it is the same
idea as *The Fountainhead* with Cyrano, in effect, the counterpart of
Roark. But there are some crucial differences.

This is the second point that I thought up and the first difference. Roark is a success in existential terms. He achieves his values in the world. At the end, he is standing on top of his skyscraper with his beloved ascending toward him. Cyrano, by contrast, is a failure: he does not achieve his values. He does not succeed in his work as a dramatist and he never unites with Roxane. The tragic thing about him is he wins all the battles but he loses the war. At the end he is spiritually intact but existentially defeated: impoverished, alone, in failing health. And he himself says, "I have missed everything." That is a big contrast, obviously, with *The Fountainhead*.

Why his defeat? What is the difference here between Cyrano and Roark? Some flaw is blatant in Cyrano that Roark doesn't have. It is not the nose *per se*, but let's call it the nose for a minute. There is some kind of soul-body dichotomy operating in the theme of this play, some kind of idea that the spiritual and the physical point in opposite directions; that you can be great in one realm, but a beast in the other; a success in one, and a total failure in the other. There is a metaphysical conflict between the soul and the body that can lead to your defeat.

In this conflict Rostand obviously takes the side of the spirit. He takes the view of the spirit as superior to the body, or the soul above the physical. And thus Roxane's apology to Christian for loving "the mere costume, the poor casual body you went about in."

Obviously this soul-body dichotomy is related to the tragic ending. Look for a moment just to the love story. We have a situation where neither male is a full man, metaphysically speaking. One is a brilliant spirit in a deformed body; the other is a beautiful body covering an undeveloped spirit. So each is like only half a man and, as such, neither can hope to win Roxane. Each is doomed to lose and end tragically. That is why they both have to die without enjoying the love.

This is what you can call "the nose interpretation"; that this is basically a love story. Cyrano has a flaw because he is only half a man, as is Christian. I do not think that is deep enough at all. I do not think that does justice to the play. It is there, but it is an element of a much broader and deeper theme.

The issue in this play, I believe, is broader than the love story. I do not believe that the nose is the basic tragic factor in the play. Rostand was a great Romantic playwright. I just cannot and do not believe that he would make an accident of birth the downfall of his character. After all, the size of your nose is unrelated to philosophy, your character, life—it is just your genes or whatever Rostand might believe. He knows it is a birth product and not a product of his character or soul. Rostand is not that superficial. As a Romantic, I don't think he would ascribe Cyrano's failure or frustration to the accident of an inborn ugliness. It is just too superficial.

I'm not saying the nose is insignificant. Cyrano with an ordinary nose would not be Cyrano but it is not a primary. We need to find some other way to explain the message. Why does Cyrano fail? What is the real meaning of the nose?

The true explanation is given, actually point by point, in Act Five, if you read it like a detective. It is like Rostand is laying out his thought almost syllogistically. I will give you the highlights and then you read those passages and see how they are all set up, one after the other, to emerge with a total meaning.

On page 292 of the Modern Library edition [page 177, Bantam Classics edition] we read that Cyrano in his satires attacks every-one—"the false nobles, the false saints, the false heroes, the false artists." In other words, he is not simply some literary precious that has a new style or attacks one element of corruption in the religion around him. He attacks the representatives of the establishment of society throughout. On the next page we find out that he does this not out of hostility or nihilism, but as a matter of integrity, of being true to himself. He is described thus: "he lives his own life, his own way—thought, word, and, deed." So he is at odds with the totality of his environment; it is *his* spirit versus that environment.

The question is, is it just an accident of the era that Cyrano lived in? Is Rostand's view that the establishment happened to be corrupt in this period because men misused their free will? If so, you could still have a tragic ending, but metaphysically it would not be a proof of the nature of life. I am afraid that that is *not* Rostand's view, and that he is very explicit in telling you how to interpret the clash between Cyrano and the establishment. He had a much deeper metaphysical meaning. He has a really key speech here, which I'll quote from. It is on page 294, Modern Library [page 179, Bantam Classics], and is a truly mystifying speech if you don't get what he is after. This is by de Guiche, the villain, telling his honest feelings.

It is like he is reflecting on something that he has known all his life: "Do you know when a man wins everything in this world, when he succeeds too much." (Right away my ears pricked up. Too much, why would there be *too much* success? Maybe he's done unscrupulous things?) In the very next line: "he feels, having done nothing wrong especially." (He succeeded too much but has done nothing wrong.) "He feels somehow a thousand small displeasures with himself whose whole sum is not quite remorse, but rather a sort of vague disgust." This is from succeeding too much, while doing nothing wrong. He ends up with a feeling of "dry illusion, vain regrets." And Roxane says, "The sentiment does you honor."

Now, there is a statement that is taking us into another domain: that success inherently demands some kind of demeaning, some kind of compromise, some kind of capitulation to the world; that being true to yourself inherently means foregoing success in the world. At this point we are being told that there is a metaphysical conflict between your moral character and your worldly goals. It is one or the other. The play here is taking the turn that it is not illustrating a corrupt society but life, as such, in the universe. There is substantial further evidence of this and this is where you have to read like a detective. Cyrano has just been ambushed by a lackey—as against a noble death on the battlefield, which is what he had always wanted. And what is his comment? He says, "Too logical—I have missed everything, even my death!"

That speaks volumes to me. On the Objectivist metaphysics, a great hero like Roark who gains everything when he is on the top of the skyscraper might conceivably say, "This is just too logical. I got it all, including Dominique riding up the elevator." And that would be logical to him, because it is life as it is metaphysically: it is the complete fulfillment of benevolence. But from Rostand's and Cyrano's perspectives, a great hero who loses everything—even his death—is what is to be expected. That is the perfect logic of the metaphysical situation. That is the way life is, and it is delivered in spades to him, right down to the manner of his death.

Another piece of evidence for this, which is very crucial but goes by fast, is the reference to Molière. Remember, Molière stole a scene word for word from Cyrano, and the crowd roared; they loved it. Observe what Cyrano says when he learns of Molière having taken his scene. "Yes, that has been my life." He immediately equates in his mind what Molière did to him with Christian, as two examples of the same point. As he explains it, Christian stood under the window and won Roxane's applause and a kiss while he, Cyrano, was relegated to the darkness. And now Molière is doing the same thing in the professional arena, winning all the applause while Cyrano is obscure and unknown.

The juxtaposition of these two is crucial, because Molière has nothing to do with Cyrano's nose. We are given three values in this scene that Cyrano loses and bewails having lost: Roxane, his play, and the style of his death. The last two have nothing to do with his nose. What is common to all three is that Cyrano does not achieve the values his great spirit entitles him to win. Even worse, in all three cases it is his greatness and spirit that does him in, in the world. Christian borrowed them, and so did Molière. They took over his spiritual assets and converted them to their own ends while for his spirit Cyrano gained, not fame or love, but the hatred of everyone and finally died ignobly because of it.

What is common to Christian and Molière that enabled them to win through Cyrano's assets? It is not that they are both beautiful in body, because Molière's appearance doesn't even enter into it. What is common is that they both belong to this world; they fit into the world; they are conventional. One writes farces and the other is a simple soldier. They belong, they are part of the crowd. Cyrano does not belong because of his untamed greatness. He is a true spiritual individualist, an utterly unique personality and soul, who repels the people who fit in—and that destines him to defeat.

In other words, the real liability of Cyrano—judged by this passage and the overall action—is not his body but his soul, his spirit. It is too good, too outstanding, too unique for this world and men as they are by their nature. That, I think, is the meaning of the play. The nose is not a primary but merely a visual symbol of Cyrano's uniqueness. His soul makes him an outcast among men, and his nose is like a visual dramatization of his being an outcast. It is a visual reflection of something that sets him apart and causes others to scorn him. What they really oppose is not his nose, but his independent soul.

I would put my view this way. Cyrano is not an outcast because of his nose. His nose is deformed because he is an outcast on a much deeper level, the level of the soul or the spirit. Thus, on page 318, Modern Library [page 193, Bantam Classics], at his death he mentions his two soul mates out of the whole of history, Socrates and Galileo. What is the bond among the three, as he sees it? All of them were condemned by the world for their greatness. It is not an issue that Socrates and Galileo were ugly—that doesn't have anything to do with it. Socrates was forced to drink the hemlock; Galileo was forced to recant. What stands out in his and our memories of that trinity is they did not fit with their contemporaries and were punished for it. Put metaphysically, as I think Rostand sees it, they were simply too good for this world. They could not achieve success here on earth.

That is why what Cyrano has left at the end, his white plume, is purely spiritual. He leaves behind no achievements. What is intact is the purity of his soul.

The soul-body dichotomy, in my opinion, is crucial but not in the literal form of Cyrano's mind versus Cyrano's body. It is in the much deeper form of the soul versus the material world; the spirit of greatness versus metaphysical existence itself. The nose is merely an example, a concrete, a symbol, of the whole physical universe in which a noble soul is doomed.

And so I would define the theme, which is rather heavy, as follows: The heroic free spirit as an outcast in the physical world. This is the theme that all the events add up to.

Obviously, this is a very profound form of malevolent universe and the deepest explanation of why Cyrano never goes after Roxane, even after Christian dies. He does not believe metaphysically that he is entitled to his values. He does not ultimately believe that success can be his. He will fight—he will fight courageously—but he expects to lose.

I also think this was Rostand's personal conviction, and I think this is what disarmed Rostand and therefore Cyrano. It is like a metaphysical disarmament. Reality is set against a noble soul. That leaves you vulnerable to any corrupt moral code, including somebody demanding self-sacrifice or renunciation. On that metaphysics you feel that renunciation is your destiny anyway, by the nature of life.

As added confirmation you might be interested to know that defeat or tragedy is universal in Rostand's works. *Cyrano de Bergerac*, of course, is the case of a man whose nobility serves only to win his beloved for another man. *L'Aiglon*, which means "little eagle," is about Napoleon's unhappy and consumptive son. One commentator describes him as "the sickly boy who knows he can never achieve the heaven-storming strength of his father, the eagle Napoleon." Chantecler, the strutting protagonist cock, who believes that his crowing causes the sun to rise, is forced in the end to realize that it doesn't and that he is really impotent to alter the sun's course. In short, throughout Rostand you have protagonists who are more or less heroic—certainly none that equal Cyrano—but who are doomed to failure.

6. Philosophy

This play, in my view, is a synthesis of two utterly antithetical views or philosophies. It is as clashing a play philosophically as I have ever seen. It is Christianity plus Romanticism. That combination has been around for a long time, but here you have the extreme of each united in one play. Rostand was not a philosopher, but he was obviously drawn to both perspectives.

Christianity is blatant in the theme. Christian literature is full of stories about saints being outcasts in this world. That is a real spiritual-material dichotomy: the saint being burned at the stake for the greater glory of God; the body doesn't count; this world doesn't count; he has a nobility, etc. But in the traditional Christian literature an entire ascetic way of life went with this kind of piety involving sacrifice, poverty, passivity, obedience, not developing your faculties. Remember, Augustine thought that it was a crime to develop your faculties and go out and observe the world and study. He called that the "lust of the eyes." So Christianity was consistent: renounce the world and (it really said) become mindless, blind, obedient; starve, drink laundry water, burn at the stake, and then you will get your glory in the next life.

Rostand in effect took the defeated sense of life of this Christian approach but threw out the otherworldly saint and put in his place a this-worldly, nineteenth-century, individualistic, Romantic hero. He made the protagonist a man of the post-Renaissance world who holds that this life is good, that man has free will, that he determines his future, that there are crucial values at stake here on earth, that it is important to fight for your values, that you should have a whole code of secular virtues such as independence and integrity and justice. In this respect he is not a person who dismisses life but who relishes it. You can see it in the play, in Cyrano's tremendous efficacy. This man can do anything superlatively: he can write, he can love, he can fight. He enjoys life, he enjoys the worldly things about life. He revels in all the worldly virtues, the virtues of efficacy.

And so we have a tremendous anomaly, a profound ambivalence here: a hero with a Romantic, secular, worldly view of life juxtaposed with a metaphysics demanding Christian renunciation. Therefore, if you press it, I simply do not think that the overall philosophy of this play is coherent.

The clash, I think, is mirrored in the genre. Rostand calls this play a heroic comedy. It is comedy, and it is good, spirited, exuberant comedy. I think that flows from the pro-life element. It is not the comedy of sneering at values or a comedy like Molière's pratfalls. It is a comedy of innocent laughter, the laughter of men who enjoy life. It is full of clever lines, delightful scenes, such as Ragueneau with his cherished poems on paper bags, an intellectual baker. It is funny and it is fun. It is like Cyrano's own wit about his nose. In this sense, the play is filled with high spirits. When you watch it, it is not an emotional drain or disaster; it is a pleasure to watch. So that's the comedy.

Yet, against this setting and style, there is the basic story line, which is the very opposite: the tragic story of Cyrano and his defeat in the world. It is a heroic comedy, said Rostand, and the heroism is, in effect, the tragedy—the greatness of Cyrano with the thematic implications.

I think you can see Rostand's split in the very genre. It is as though he wants to express the pleasure and suffering of life at once. It is as though he himself is ambivalent and the play, therefore, is a union of that which cannot be united.

To me, the deepest tragedy of this play is that a character as noble as Cyrano, with his exalted and efficacious spirit, has to see himself as in opposition to reality and, therefore, as defeated in the end. I think what it means is that Rostand still subscribed to the most lethal tenets of traditional Christianity, even though, like the whole nineteenth century, he was no longer religious in the medieval way. He still preserved the lethal tenets of malevolence; the soul-body dichotomy and the nobility of renunciation. In other words, what Rostand had was only a sense of life for this world. He had the Romantic sense of man and life—which is a legacy from Aristotle—but it was combined with an implicit, entrenched Christian viewpoint. And that left him helpless.

This is a microcosm: modern literature has been tragic in this larger sense. It is what you could call the plight of modern man, or the modern hero. He loves this world, not God; he wants his own happiness, not suffering; he wants greatness here, not in heaven. But he doesn't know how to attain his earthly values. He feels he has free will but he has no guide as to how to remake his soul. Even the Renaissance itself, you probably know, was a skeptical period. They had given up rule by religion, but they had nothing to replace it. They didn't know with certainty what to do, what to aim at, or how to succeed.

I think we have that same tragedy that has repeated itself century after century here in *Cyrano*: a hero of wonderful stature with all the virtues—except that Rostand does not identify deliberately the underlying philosophy he has absorbed, and, therefore, he is overcome by the traditional sense of life as tragedy. And given his intellectual legacy and the fact that he was not an original philosopher, I don't think anyone could have done the job better. In that sense, I think we have to always feel grateful to him for the experience of reading or—if you possibly can—seeing this play, even with its ideological flaws.

Q & A

Q: How much of this analysis of *Cyrano* is yours? How much do you know Ayn Rand agreed with?

A: I never discussed the theme of *Cyrano* with Ayn Rand, believe it or not. I was a monomaniac about philosophy, and I always wanted to know: are the senses valid? how do you form concepts? and so on. The only play I really discussed with her in great detail for hours was *Othello* because I had to teach it and couldn't understand it. We went over it and I have whole notebooks of comments.

I know that she loved *Cyrano* as a play. She thought it was a magnificent creation of a man of integrity. I *believe* she would accept this analysis because it is compatible with many things she had written about art and about Romantics but I didn't get it from her.

Q: Can you expand on the meaning of "panache" in this play?

A: Panache is actually the last word of the play in French. Literally, panache is the tuft or the plume of feathers of an old French military helmet. That is why it is often translated as white plume. More broadly, it is taken symbolically to mean—and this is the typical list of qualities it is taken to mean—pride, gallantry, swagger, courage, conceit, and conscious superiority. Now that's quite a mixture, but that's the list.

Rostand himself wrote a passage in French defining it which I translated word for word. Unfortunately, it is not what you'd call a definition by essentials, but it is the concept that he meant. This is what I got out of the translation and I looked up every blessed word in it. He says, "It is not just greatness, but something added to greatness." And then the adjectives that Rostand himself includes are (in this you're getting a special benefit, because it's never been translated but whether this is a correct translation is another question): something *courageous, articulate, theatrical, dramatic, forceful and strong.*

Obviously, *articulate* is very central to that. *Dramatic* is an issue of substance and style. You could not be a man of panache if you are a silent, repressed hero. To be a man of panache, you have to be a man like Francisco; you know, with romantic gestures and tremendous articulateness, beyond having courage. There has to be something theatrical, with a flair to it, to have panache.

What was really interesting to me was what Rostand said in passing, which no one ever mentions; that the man of panache is never disinterested because, he says, even when the man of panache makes a sacrifice for his values, he has a satisfied attitude about himself. His action is interested or self-concerned. He enjoys taking pride in his courage and showing fierce loyalty to his values, so he's self-oriented even when he's sacrificing. Whereas, says Rostand, when the man without panache sacrifices, it is a pure example of self-abnegation and he obviously doesn't like it.

So it meant for Rostand a kind of soul there is no English for. It has to be a combination of spiritual power and articulate, dramatic style. Francisco would be the closest to having that quality of any Ayn Rand character that I can think of. Not Rearden, you see, because he has more of a repressed exterior.

Q: Cyrano says "All gone!" at the climax. I took that to mean that Cyrano thought true love was possible, a perfect mind in a perfect body died there.

A: Well, you're not on the same wavelength as I am. Because I don't think he thinks true love is possible. Not to be consummated. True love as a passion, yes, but not to be consummated in this world. I think that's the issue again of being an outcast.

Q: Can you discuss your opinion of the two movies?

A: What's the other one? The Jose Ferrer one and the one with Depardieu? Well, I never can give you an honest opinion of the Depardieu movie, because I couldn't watch it. I found it boring. In the part I saw, they did not bring out the essence; they played it all down and flat and it antagonized me. Cyrano has to be played with a huge swashbuckling style. It has to be believable, but it has to be high Romanticism. You cannot make it the Frenchman next door.

So it's really unfair for me to comment. I tried to watch it. But I tell you, the Jose Ferrer movie meant so much to me growing up. I lived in Canada sixty miles north of the border and we didn't get many movies. We would drive down to Minnesota or North Dakota to see this movie as teenagers, because it was so fabulous. I mean, I grew up with this movie as an escape; that was the United States to me, what life had to offer, as opposed to Canada. So the Ferrer movie is certainly extremely well done.

I want to say, if ever you get a chance to see the British company that has Derek Jacobi in it, try and see that. First of all, a play is always better to see on the stage than in the movies. It's written to be a play. And the movies can't entirely capture it. They can compensate to some extent, but they can't get what a play is. I like the play form better than the movies. But I never thought I would see anything that was as utterly perfect as that. If I could get tickets, I would just go to every performance of the run. I did go back to see it twice, and I have a treasured T-shirt which has Derek Jacobi as Cyrano, which I don't even wear, because I don't want it to fade.

Given his genius, Rostand created a magnificent play here. It is my own all-time favorite. I feel safe in predicting that so long as the human spirit survives, it will go on being performed, even someday in Atlantis. Thank you.

Made in the USA
Middletown, DE
23 September 2018